PHILOSOPHICAL PSYCHOLOGY

The John Henry Cardinal Newman Lectures

GENERAL EDITOR: *Craig Steven Titus*

The John Henry Cardinal Newman Lecture Series is held under the sponsorship of the Institute for the Psychological Sciences in order to promote an international conversation among the several disciplines that treat the human person. This Washington-based lecture series is held annually, and forthcoming volumes will be published with an eye toward building a body of learned discussion that is catholic both in its breadth of research and in its dialogue with contemporary Catholic thought. The published versions appear under the patronage of St. Catherine of Alexandria in order to demonstrate the conviction of those responsible for the Newman lecture series that the human person flourishes only when the Creator of heaven and earth is loved above all things.

The John Henry Cardinal Newman Lectures

VOLUME 5

PHILOSOPHICAL PSYCHOLOGY

Psychology, Emotions, and Freedom

EDITED BY *Craig Steven Titus*

The Institute for the Psychological Sciences Press
Arlington, Virginia

Distributed by
The Catholic University of America Press
620 Michigan Ave., N.E. / 240 Leahy Hall
Washington, DC 20064

The paper used in this publication meets the minimum requirements of
American National Standards for Information Science—Permanence of Paper
for Printed Library Materials, ANSI Z39.48-1984.
∞

LIBRARY OF CONGRESS CATALOGING-IN-PUBLICATION DATA
Philosophical psychology : psychology, emotions, and freedom / edited by
Craig Steven Titus.
    p. cm. — (The John Henry Cardinal Newman lectures ; v. 5)
    Includes bibliographical references and index.
    ISBN 978-0-9773103-6-4 (pbk. : alk. paper)   1. Psychology and
philosophy.   2. Emotions.   I. Titus, Craig Steven, 1959–
    BF41.P54 2009
    128—dc22   2009017092

CONTENTS

ACKNOWLEDGMENTS

⤳

In the name of the Institute for the Psychological Sciences (Arlington, Virginia), I would like to acknowledge the many actors who contributed to making possible this collection of essays from the 2005–2006 John Henry Cardinal Newman Lecture Series. First of all, I would like to recognize the faithful generosity of Gene and Charlotte Zurlo, who have funded the Newman lecture series from its inception. Furthermore, because of Dr. John Harvey's benevolent sponsorship, the lectures were held at the Cosmos Club (Washington, D.C.), which has continued to offer a fitting ambiance for genteel discussions. The corporate and personal authorities of the Institute for the Psychological Sciences have warmly encouraged the publication of these lectures. Dr. David McGonagle, director of the Catholic University of America Press, and his staff have contributed their competent and careful aid in bringing this volume to fruition, as have Carol A. Kennedy (copy editor) and Gregory Bottaro, Roman Lokhmotov, and Cristina Melendez (graduate assistants). Finally, I would like to acknowledge the foresight of Prof. Daniel N. Robinson, who inspired this series, and the commitment and energy of Dean Gladys Sweeney, who mobilized a host of prominent scholars and organized the series and this publication.

Craig Steven Titus

PHILOSOPHICAL PSYCHOLOGY

one

⤝

Craig Steven Titus

PICKING UP THE PIECES OF
PHILOSOPHICAL PSYCHOLOGY

An Introduction

The notable contributions of the psychological sciences to human well-being, especially over the last century, have led many people to turn to them, in the clinic and through popular literature, seeking relief for their disquiet and suffering. The match, though, between the relief sought and that offered has not always been a satisfactory one. For at the same time, in the midst of a secularization of culture, as Charles Taylor has argued,[1] psychology has disengaged itself (although more in theory than in practice) from some of the positive resources that are most dear to those seeking its assistance, namely, their communities of

1. Charles Taylor, *The Secular Age* (Cambridge, Mass.: Belknap Press, 2007).

faith and their hope in God. There are, however, positive changes afoot. In particular, the vision of the human person that is practiced, at least in some schools of psychology, is in the process of renewal by integrating further personal, social, and spiritual sources. In this optic, the present volume gives a sample of a non-reductionist and non-exclusivistic Christian vision of philosophical psychology that seeks to do justice to the complexity of the human person and its larger resources.[2]

First a working definition. Philosophical psychology is the comprehensive study of the human psyche and person, which is established neither by empirical studies nor by clinical psychology nor even by a priori conceptual analysis alone. Through a critical and ordered appropriation, however, it involves careful observations and reflections that draw on empirical, clinical, and conceptual endeavors according to their own competency. This bridge-building discipline connects elements not only from the psychological sciences, but also from philosophical anthropology, including the ethical and religious traditions that inevitably underlie those reflections. In turn, it provides a basis for psychological, moral, and social applications that recognize deeper human and spiritual resources.[3]

The positive achievements of science and the advancements that they have facilitated in terms of technology, comfort, and health are noteworthy. However, the specialization of the sciences has left a divided realm, in difficulty of explaining the origins, motivation, and finality of the world and human life as we commonly know them and

---

2. See the two introductory essays by Kenneth Schmitz and Romanus Cessario in *Virtue and Psychology* (under consideration), edited by R. Cessario and C. S. Titus. See also E. Christian Brugger et alia, "Anthropological Foundations for Clinical Psychology: A Proposal," *Journal of Psychology and Theology* 36 (2008): 3–15.

3. José Luis Bermúdez defines the philosophy of psychology as "the systematic study of the interplay between philosophical concerns and psychological concerns in the study of cognition." He specifies that it involves "everything that bears upon the scientific study of cognition and behavior." *Philosophy of Psychology: A Contemporary Introduction* (New York: Routledge, 2005), 1–2. However, the disadvantage of Bermúdez's approach is that it is exempt of epistemological and metaphysical concerns of the mind; it focuses on conceptual and empirical analysis of theory-cluster concepts (13–15).

believe them to be. The modern tendency to subdivide, naturalize, and render autonomous the various bits of knowledge has not lent itself to a cohesive vision of psychology, for even within psychology one finds general (theoretical), empirical, and clinical specialties, which find it difficult to recognize a place for a more overarching philosophical psychology.

Progressively since the late Middle Ages, different philosophers and scientists—in order to establish the autonomy of their respective philosophical and psychological disciplines—have effectively dissected the subject matter of philosophical psychology into: physiological psychology, philosophy of mind, cognitive neurosciences, general psychology, philosophy of psychology, epistemology, psychology of religion, metaphysics, and so on. Psychology, moreover, is practically reduced to one (or a couple) of these areas, as is the case when the neurosciences are seen to effectively replace the others, as is a current trend.[4] This is the place neither to critically engage all these research efforts, nor to praise them for achievements in their own functional specialties.[5] Instead, an historical note on philosophical psychology will set the stage in order to go beyond the present status quo. After an overview of the historical situation, I would like to give a short constructive treatment to the topic; then I will let the essayists make their own detailed contributions.

The history of science in general, and of psychology in particular, is a footnote to the overriding human desire to know and to understand the world and its players. Philosophical psychology, in this same vein, seeks to understand the human person and its dignity, the workings of its unifying principle of life (traditionally called the soul), its embodiment, and its capacities, notably including cognition, emotion, and vo-

4. For clarification of some of the confusions found in the practice of the neurosciences, see M. R. Bennett and P. M. S. Hacker, *Philosophical Foundations of Neuroscience* (Oxford: Blackwell, 2003).

5. For another complementary overview, see William O'Donohue and Richard F. Kitchener, eds., *The Philosophy of Psychology* (London: Sage Publications, 1996).

lition. However, modern thinkers have not always admitted that science and philosophical psychology need recourse (in various ways) not only to scientific tools of observation and measurement, but also to language, concepts, reflections, and a worldview and value-system. The need for the latter, though, has become progressively more evident inasmuch as the effectiveness of scientific study through reductionist methods has been identified as progressive and powerful, but also partial. However, in this regard, methodological or weak "reductionism" needs to be distinguished from strong "reductionism." Weak reductionism involves the method that focuses on smaller parts in order to explain the whole (or some part thereof). Strong (or ontological) reductionism holds that the knowledge of basic units and the rules that govern them will suffice to explain the whole.[6] Unless the study of the basic building blocks of the universe yields a "law of [absolutely] everything" and is decisively deterministic—even of every human choice—humankind must seek to understand the life of the psyche, while taking into consideration its common ground (human nature and spiritual interrelationships) and its contingencies (cognition, emotion, and free agency).

As seen in the Allen Bergin and Albert Ellis debate (1980s), it has become more common to accept that a worldview and value-system—Christian or non-Christian; theist, agnostic, or atheist—are inevitably part of the theoretical, empirical, and practical work of psychology.[7] For there is no pre-theoretical (neutral) fulcrum from which to raise science. It is therefore the time to reestablish a philosophical psychology that is adequate to understand the human person in this complex context.

In this prospect, the history of philosophical psychology and the psychological sciences takes on a different allure, when trying to un-

6. See Paul C. W. Davies, "Preface," in *The Re-Emergence of Emergence: The Emergentist Hypothesis from Science to Religion,* ed. Philip Clayton and Paul Davies (Oxford: Oxford University Press, 2006), xii.

7. Allen E. Bergin, "Psychotherapy and Religious Values," *Journal of Consulting and Clinical Psychology* 48 (1980): 95–105. Albert Ellis, "Psychotherapy and Atheistic Values: A Response to A. E. Bergin," *Journal of Consulting and Clinical Psychology* 48 (1980): 635–45.

derstand practical, theoretical, and transcendent influences and foundational principles. Starting a study with ancient thinkers, such as Plato and Aristotle,[8] instead of simply beginning with Sigmund Freud or Wilhelm Wundt (modern experimental psychology) sets out, at least, questions about happiness and excellence in a way that does not inimically pit them against the drive to contemplate what is best and to believe in divinity. Before reductionist modern efforts, ancient philosophers sought to understand the human psyche through the practices and experience, the myth and theater, and the festivals and rituals of their day. While Plato and Aristotle's construals of humankind differed (e.g., the relation of body and soul), they both sought to understand it through the causes, reasons, and meaning behind ancient society, culture, and religion, which were all interpreted as bound to the universe with its cosmic and divine order.[9] It is remarkable to perceive that the schools of thought that find their lineage in either or both of these great thinkers have continued to influence philosophy and psychology to the present. Arguably Aristotle has particular influence in experimental and behavioral psychology as well as ethics and politics, while Plato's influence is often found especially in spirituality and some ethical matters.

Let us focus on Aristotle for a moment (while setting aside his astronomy). Aristotle continues to interest us because many of his distinctions, definitions, principles, and convictions about the psyche continue to influence the psychological sciences and philosophy. In his work *On the Soul (De anima)*,[10] he investigates the soul's nature and properties, as well as the diverse opinions on the topic that pre-

8. See the remarkable studies (and further references) in Daniel N. Robinson, *Aristotle's Psychology* (New York: Columbia University Press, 1989); Jonathan Barnes, ed., *The Cambridge Companion to Aristotle* (Cambridge: University of Cambridge Press, 1995); and Michael Pakaluk, *Aristotle's Nicomachean Ethics* (Cambridge: Cambridge University Press, 2005).

9. William A. Wallace, *Causality and Scientific Explanation* (Ann Arbor: University of Michigan Press, 1977).

10. Aristotle, *On the Soul,* in Jonathan Barnes, ed., *The Complete Works of Aristotle,* The Revised Oxford Translation (Princeton, N.J.: Princeton University Press, 1985).

ceded him. This work of psychology, before the term "psychology," involves a surprising method. At least, it is surprising for those who do not know Aristotle, who not only wrote philosophical treaties on ethics and politics, but also did behavioral (psychological) studies of animals and humans.[11] In the last regard, he used a scientific method of observation, hypothesis, and theory building (although admittedly neither statistical nor modern). However, he realized that his behavioral studies did not exhaust the human subject. His method led him beyond human behavior to seek its sources in human nature; and while investigating the natural order, he discovered something that transcends it. According to Aristotle, "something divine" is found in the intellect and the excellences, the happiness, the friendships, and the contemplation that are thereby made possible.[12]

While less empirical and more speculative (and more overtly religious) than Aristotle, Thomas Aquinas, likewise, built his analysis of human nature on the study of human behavior, based on the principle that a thing is as it acts *(agere sequitur esse)* and confident that reason learns from what the senses represent.[13] In so doing, he did not pit the observational and empirical against the philosophical or the religious. Empirical observations give the outline of human nature (and what is presently designated as the mind-body problem) in the midst of human victories and failures. They inform us about its goals and

11. Moreover, in his other psychological works considered the *Parva naturalia (The Short Physical Treatises),* Aristotle writes as a physiological psychologist (or empirical psychologist); he focuses on the bio-physiological processes *(De memoria et reminiscentia—On Memory and Reminiscence)* and even on dreams *(De somniis—On Dreams).* His studies may be understood in the overall purview of the sciences, in general, and in relationship with his construal of physics and metaphysics, in particular. These works are found in Barnes, *Complete Works of Aristotle.*

12. See Book X (for example, 1177b27–31) in Aristotle, *Nicomachean Ethics,* in Barnes, *Works of Aristotle.*

13. Aquinas treats philosophical anthropology in the *Summa theologiae (ST),* the *Prima pars,* questions 75 through 102, see esp. I, q. 77 and q. 86, art. 1. See also *ST* I-II, q. 55, a. 2, ad 1, and *ST* III, q. 19, a. 2, sc, where he cites John Damascene saying, *"operatio sequitur naturam."*

the function of its capacities. Philosophical reflections, for their part, seek to understand the empirical findings and the normativeness of human nature. Religious sources offer further input concerning the origins, motivations, and finality of human life.

The Aristotelian Thomist tradition of thought has offered a philosophical psychology that appropriates scientific findings about the human person's embodiment (bodily aspects) and critical reflections on human spirituality (which is the domain of psychology, metascience, and religion), within the limits of each one's competency and according to an ordering of the sciences. In between a staunch materialism (that rejects all spiritual and religious sources) and a recalcitrant spiritual worldview (that credits science with merely technological utility), this tradition has sought a properly interdisciplinary dialogue that is supported by a "metascience" (which it has traditionally called "first philosophy" or "metaphysics"). Metascience seeks to coordinate the data of the sciences and spiritual sources without damaging the autonomy of either the special sciences or religion. According to Benedict Ashley, a Christianized form of the Aristotelian tradition (exemplified in Aquinas's works) contends that

> natural science, when built on critically sound foundations, remains limited to the study of material things and their processes, yet objectively establishes the validity of other disciplines and eminently of a distinct Metascience. By the comparison of the results of the special sciences, this Metascience gives a sufficient rational account of the existence and nature of spiritual reality to permit a dialogue between natural science and all the sciences with spiritual worldviews, even those that claim access to mystical knowledge or revelation.[14]

Standing on common ground can facilitate a dialogue between these disciplines and the worldview(s) that underlie(s) them. A philosophical psychology that relies on such a metascience facilitates a rich no-

---

14. Benedict Ashley, *The Way of Wisdom: An Interdisciplinary and Intercultural Introduction to Metaphysics* (Notre Dame, Ind.: University of Notre Dame Press, 2006), 448.

tion and practice of the psychological sciences. Nonetheless, the Aristotelian Thomist perspective on metascience has seen different manifestations, including extremes (such as exclusiveness or historical naïveté). It has also seen a revival in dialogue with the sciences.[15] However, historically speaking, this perspective has run on a different track, influenced by the advances of modern thought and science, but distinct from the various tides of secularization found in the mainstream of modernity.

Charles Taylor has recently brought further nuance to the ways that the history of modern science has become a history of attempts to disengage the study of the sciences from the control of state and religious institutions,[16] but also from integrative traditions of philosophy and religious belief (as is represented in the work of Aquinas). Since at least the advent of the Enlightenment, there are two players in the game of understanding the person and psyche that tend to be excluded in discussions of science and culture, namely philosophy writ large (as a love of and a search for wisdom) and religion (as a worldview and value-system that involves being tied to God through belief and practice). We will first focus on the relationship between the psychological sciences and philosophy, before adding a note on religion.

Some of the most celebrated philosophers and scientists from the fourteenth century on—such as William of Ockham (1287–1347) in his *Summa of Logic,* Francis Bacon (1561–1626) in his *Novum organon scientiarum,* and René Descartes (1596–1650) in his *Meditationes de prima philosophia*—have tried to disengage their scientific claims from larger philosophical issues. They have sought a type of knowl-

15. In addition to Ashley's *The Way toward Wisdom,* notable contributions include William A. Wallace's *The Modeling of Nature: Philosophy of Science and Philosophy of Nature in Synthesis* (Toronto: Pontifical Institute of Mediaeval Studies, 1996). See also Romanus Cessario, *A Short History of Thomism* (Washington, D.C.: The Catholic University of America Press, 2005).

16. The secularization of the sciences is a complex process (and history) that Charles Taylor *(A Secular Age)* has recently brought to light with great nuance. For a focus more on the natural sciences, see also Don O'Leary, *Roman Catholicism and Modern Science: A History* (New York: Continuum, 2007).

edge that is both clear and certain and that is unfettered by philosophical presuppositions or religion. Other roots for the modern separation of psychology from philosophical underpinnings are found in eighteenth and nineteen century thinkers, such as Immanuel Kant (1724–1804), whose distinctions between analytic and synthetic propositions and between a priori and a posteriori propositions laid a conceptual foundation to separate neatly science from philosophy.[17] Auguste Comte (1798–1857), for his part, argued that the history of the sciences involves passing through three phases that progress from theological, through metaphysical, and finally to scientific (positivist) methods as the apotheosis of clarity.[18]

In this context, Wilhelm Dilthey's work (starting with his *Introduction to the Human Sciences*, 1883) seeks to gain a scientific credibility for the human sciences (including philosophy and religion as well as psychology) on a different basis than that of the natural sciences, and completely separated from them. His hermeneutic distinguishes the vision of the human person possible through the natural sciences *(Naturwissenschaften)* from that of the human sciences *(Geisteswissenschaften)*. The natural sciences uncover the causes behind the study of an object. The human sciences, on the contrary, indicate the meaning that the human subject brings forth. The human science perspective accounts for the specifically human "meaning" of acts through the subject's understanding *(Verstehen)*.[19]

In the late nineteenth century, as O'Donohue and Kitchener (1996) describe it, psychologists applied the burgeoning empirical methods and a positivist approach to their subject matter (mind), which was only part of what they had previously considered their subject matter (the human soul, its capacities, and its behavior). They thought that the new scientific (experimental) method was exclusive of philosophy,

---

17. Immanuel Kant, *Critique of Pure Reason* (New York: Anchor, 1966; orig. 1781).

18. August Comte, *System of Positive Polity*, 2 vols. (London: Longmans Green, 1875).

19. See Rudolf Makkreel, "Wilhelm Dilthey," in *Stanford Encyclopedia of Philosophy* (Stanford, Calif.: Stanford University, January 16, 2008), and by the same author *Dilthey: Philosopher of the Human Studies* (Princeton, N.J.: Princeton University Press, 1975).

making the later redundant. The behaviorism of the 1920s (Watson) evidenced a more radical separation of psychology from philosophy in its subject matter (behavior alone) and in its method (pure experimental observation). In the 1930s and 1940s, classical neo-behaviorism (Hull, Skinner) adopted a cooperative relationship with logical positivism, thus making logical empiricism. Between the 1930s and 1960s, moreover, a type of collaboration between psychology and philosophy was reached, based on the idea that the two disciplines were dichotomous (Frege 1953). In this conception, psychology is empirical, synthetic, naturalistic, factual, and a posteriori, while philosophy is nonempirical, analytic, normative, conceptual, and a priori.[20]

In the 1960s (at least in America), several influences—W. V. O. Quine and the cognitive sciences—came to revise this neat, yet uneasy, separation between psychology and philosophy. First in his "Two Dogmas of Empiricism," Quine (1961) rebutted the analytic-synthetic distinction, which in turn put the supposed separation of psychology and philosophy into doubt. He also leveled a critique of the empirical dogma that "all meaningful statements are reducible to empirical observations."[21] He argued, rather, that every statement is interdependent upon others; neither is any statement single nor can a statement be reduced to a single observation. Every statement is embedded in a web of belief.[22] This affirmation overrode the logical positivists' tendency to reduce theoretical terms and paradigms to particular concepts. Thus, concepts are not sufficient to themselves, but need theory. This humility opened the way for a growing appreciation of not only the need for presuppositions and theory per se, but also of the deeper theories that underlie each discipline, including the deepest theories (worldviews or value-systems) that inevitably underlie them all.

---

20. See O'Donohue and Kitchener, *Philosophy of Psychology,* xiv.

21. W. V. O. Quine, "Two Dogmas of Empiricism," *Philosophical Review* 60 (1951): 20–43. The quote is cited in O'Donohue and Kitchener, *Philosophy of Psychology,* xvi.

22. See W. V. Quine and J. S. Ullian, *The Web of Belief* (New York: Random House, 1970).

Quine (1969) later drew a further conclusion that traditional-modern philosophy as normative epistemology must, however, be replaced by a naturalistic epistemology. It is quite telling that Quine stated that this naturalistic epistemology "simply falls into place as a chapter of psychology and hence of natural science."[23] As surprising as it may seem, Aristotle would agree with this string of conclusions, especially the last one. Psychology is a natural science, at least in part. There is a similarity to Aristotle and Aquinas's approach to psychology and to philosophical knowledge, at least, inasmuch as they are empirical and naturalist without becoming empiricism or naturalism. In many cases, however, the contemporary move toward naturalism has favored descriptive observations and the neurobiological studies of mental states, while flattening psychology and philosophy's relationship with any normative order found through both descriptive observation of and prescriptive reflection on human behavior, rational thought, and transcendent aspirations.

The move in many psychological and philosophical theories toward naturalism has taken different forms that, in one way or another, tend to separate them from religion as well as from normative philosophy. On the one hand, this is evident in the progressively exclusive interest in the neurosciences and in the naturalistic reductionist approach to quantifying psychological phenomena,[24] although there are recent nuanced studies on the psychological benefit operative in religious practice.[25] On the other hand, the tendency to ignore philosophical psychology and religion is found also in a clinical ap-

23. W. V. O. Quine, "Epistemology Naturalized," in *Ontological Relativity* (New York: Columbia University Press, 1969), 82. From this cue, O'Donohue and Kitchener *(Philosophy of Psychology)* recognize that psychology and philosophy (epistemology) must establish a new relationship between themselves (at least in the history of analytical philosophy). The operative mode becomes the naturalization of philosophy, logic, epistemology, and philosophy of mind.

24. Bennett and Hacker, *Neurosciences*, 355–66.

25. See H. G. Koenig, M. E. McCullough, and D. B. Larson, *Handbook of Religion and Health* (Oxford: Oxford University Press, 2001).

proach that relies on therapeutic techniques, with little attention being paid to the worldview and value-system of either practitioner or
client (Ashley 2000). In effect, Philip Rieff foretold that such an exclusive and flat therapeutic approach would take hold of society and
undercut recourse to deeper values.[26] In so doing, as Paul Vitz has remarked, psychology has started to act as a religion.[27] An opposite tendency has, however, also been afoot in the notable tendencies (from
within psychology, as well as without) that have called for an awareness of the values that are operative in any therapy, that is, operative
in the client, in the therapist, and in the underlying therapeutic tools
and theories.[28] Current discussions and studies have added distinctions in understanding the human person through attention to values and hermeneutical methods. However, because of constructivist
and relativist presuppositions, as in the case of Cushman's work, they
have often lost sight of the common ground of human nature that underlies the diversity found in human history and culture. Admittedly
an adequate philosophical psychology will need to address with equal
hermeneutical nuance human history and culture, when considering

26. Philip Rieff, *The Triumph of the Therapeutic* (Harmondsworth, UK: Penguin
Books, 1966).

27. Paul C. Vitz, *Psychology as Religion: The Cult of Self-Worship* (Grand Rapids,
Mich.: Eerdmans, 1977).

28. In this regard, we have already mentioned the Bergin-Ellis exchange (1980).
Other contributions include William O'Donohue, "The (Even) Bolder Model: The
Clinical Psychologist as Metaphysician-Scientist-Practitioner," *American Psychology* 44
(1989): 1460–68; Philip Cushman, "Psychotherapy as Moral Discourse," *Journal of The-
oretical and Philosophical Psychology* 13 (1993): 103–13; Stanton L. Jones, "A Constructive
Relationship for Religion with the Science and Profession of Psychology: Perhaps the
Boldest Model Yet," in *Religion and the Clinical Practice of Psychology*, ed. E. Shafran-
ske (Washington, D.C.: American Psychological Association, 1996), 113–47: Edward P.
Shafranske, "Psychotherapy with Roman Catholics," in *Handbook of Psychotherapy and
Religious Diversity*, ed. P. S. Richards and A. E. Bergin (Washington, D.C.: American
Psychological Association, 2000), 59–88; Benedict M. Ashley, *Choosing a World-View
and a Value-System: An Ecumenical Apologetics* (New York: Alba House, 2000); Edwin
L. Hersch, *From Philosophy to Psychotherapy: A Phenomenological Model for Psycholo-
gy, Psychiatry, and Psychoanalysis* (Toronto: University of Toronto Press, 2003).

the normativeness of human nature that underlies cultural changes and personal development.

In the context of the evolutionism-creationism debate, moreover, Richard Dawkins has sought to defend the sciences from fundamentalist god-talk and from all those who believe in God.[29] His approach represents a particular type of biological reductionism that has been critically rejected, as Nicholas Lash says, for its "lack of extended argument, historical ignorance, and unfamiliarity with the literature."[30] It is worth repeating here that neither are religious-based reflections so foreign to science as Dawkins would like us to believe nor can one associate hatred, violence, or bigotry with religion as religion or, at least, with Christianity per se. While starkly reductionist accounts of biology exclude themselves from a dialogue with other disciplines, there are scientific accounts that remain explicitly open to deeper reasons, that is, to some deeper level of explanation; here we can mention the work of Pierre Teilhard de Chardin, Michael Heller, and Stanley Yaki.[31]

In order to overcome the crisis of modernity, which can be seen in the isolationism of the sciences and the narrowing of philosophical psychology, there is need for dialogue, but also for a wider notion of rationality, so that the dialogue partners can recognize common ground. In this regard, Benedict XVI's appeal to exit from the supposed "self-sufficiency of philosophical reflection" applies to scientists and theologians as well as philosophers. The key to better understand

29. Richard Dawkins, *The God Delusion* (New York: Houghton Mifflin, 2006). See also his *The Selfish Gene* (New York: Oxford University Press, 1976; 2nd ed. 1989).

30. On the unscientific nature of Dawkins's discussion of religion, see Nicholas Lash, "Where Does *The God Delusion* Come from?" *New Blackfriars* 88 (September 2007): 507–21.

31. Among their many works, we can mention Michael Heller, *Creative Tension—Essays on Science and Religion* (Philadelphia: Templeton Foundation Press, 2003) and *The New Physics and a New Theology* (Vatican City: Vatican Observatory Publications, 1996); and Stanley Jaki, *The Road of Science and the Ways to God* (Chicago: University of Chicago Press, 1978).

the human person and to widen the horizon of rationality is found in a genuine realism. Benedict XVI says that "the new dialogue between faith and reason, required today, cannot happen in the terms and in the ways in which it happened in the past. If it does not want to be reduced to a sterile intellectual exercise, it must begin from the recent concrete situation of humanity and upon this develop a reflection that draws from the ontological-metaphysical truth."[32] Such philosophical and interdisciplinary approaches seek ways to recognize the validity and fruitfulness of larger conversations about the person that employ clearly identified sources. This is necessary not only in ethics, moral theology, and theological anthropology, but also in philosophical psychology.

As we have intimated, much ado has been made to assure the autonomy of the sciences (including the human sciences) from religion. We would suggest that the time has come, if the human sciences wish to reach maturity, to clarify explicitly the relationship with their intellectual heritage and value-systems, which are found not only in the achievements of law, culture, and art, but also in their sources in religious worldviews. In Western civilization, this source is Judeo-Christian, without forgetting that other religious influences and value-systems have been present since the beginning of recorded history. Far from destroying the integrity of the human sciences, an open recognition of their debt to a common source found in reality (ontology or existence) and ultimately in the transcendent first source and final cause of being will strengthen the relevance of their import. Put another way,

---

32. Benedict XVI, "Widening the Horizons of Rationality," speech delivered in Rome on 7 June 2008. The question remains, though: How can a philosophical psychology be considered serious among the human science disciplines, when open to (or admitting) input from spiritual-religious sources? In two phrases, I can say that the methods of argument that distinguish scientific and human sciences do *not* have to be put at odds, even if they are mutually exclusive when each discipline speaks *ad intra* (within itself), nor does the role of an overarching reflection need to be effectively denied. This point, however, may perhaps only be understood from within a wider notion of rationality and reason.

various forms of pragmatic separation of state and institutional religion throughout history do not foreclose collaboration between science and faith. Religious worldviews and values have contributed to the key ideas and practices of Western civilization—such as kindness, caring, hope, pardon, and justice—that inevitably figure in the research of the human sciences. Admittedly, this is consistent with a Catholic notion that religious faith and practice give guided access to this patrimony, while interdisciplinary conversations, established with methodological clarity, can offer comprehensive breadth and even a proper widening of the modern notion of intelligence and rationality. Rationalist, idealist, nominalist, and naturalist methodologies often are attempts at a type of autonomy that focuses on a distinct piece of the epistemological puzzle. Complementary attempts at rapprochement between faith and science are needed in order to pick up the pieces.[33]

On a constructive note, I would like to return to the notion of a renewed Aristotelian-Thomist perspective, as a methodological starting point that sets out common ground for dialogue and a way to widen the horizon of rationality in philosophical psychology. From this perspective, philosophical psychology employs the observation of change, human experience, and reflections to establish an anthropological framework constituted of human embodiment, cognition, affection, and interpersonal relationships (or community), as well as personal unity (assured by the soul). This four-partite structure of human nature, though, is not simply grasped in observing the inclinations, dispositions, reflections, choices, and actions of a virtuous person in a just and flourishing community, for it is also illuminated by the contrasting weaknesses and failures of mankind. However, in em-

33. For an example of the science-faith dialogue and a more careful discussion of the possible types of interplay between psychosocial findings, philosophical reflections on normativeness, and theological anthropology, see C. S. Titus, *Resilience and the Virtue of Fortitude: Aquinas in Dialogue with the Psychosocial Sciences* (Washington, D.C.: The Catholic University of America Press, 2006), 85–98.

pirical studies, virtue strengths must be distinguished from errors and weaknesses. The approach employs empirical and phenomenological input (which so enlightens human development, success, and failure) in metascience analysis and moral reflections and judgments. In the doing, it makes clear the common ground and the normativeness due to human nature as well as the diversity due to personal development, human error, and cultural settings. Nonetheless, study of these basic capacities permits a more detailed understanding not only of the working of normative human nature, but also of divine grace at each level and overall. This perspective identifies the false dichotomy that pits autonomy and free human action against heteronomy or the influence of divine law and grace. John Paul II recognizes a middle ground (a "participated theonomy") between the two, where mankind participates in God's wisdom and providence in good human action, while at the same time being free.[34] Therein divine grace (and law) acts as a non-conflicting first principal cause of human agency, while the human person exercises his own proper reasoning and exercises free agency (a first instrumental cause).[35]

Such an Aristotelian-Thomist treatment seeks to guard the unity of the person, a unity of knowledge and agency, within an ordering of the sciences. The human person is more than his own experience (experiential knowledge) as subject of action and more than his empirical knowledge as object of study. The different treatments of the sciences do not undermine a primary affirmation of the unity of truth—although each involves a distinctive field and method of study. From this perspective, it is the proper role of philosophical psychol-

34. John Paul II says this is rightly called a "*participated theonomy,* since man's free obedience to God's law effectively implies that human reason and human will participate in God's wisdom and providence." Encyclical letter *The Splendor of Truth (Veritatis Splendor)* (Vatican City: Libreria Editrice Vaticana, 1993), n. 41.

35. Grace thus builds up human nature, while requiring the willed collaboration of the human person. See Servais Pinckaers, "Aquinas and Agency: Beyond Autonomy and Heteronomy," in *The Pinckaers Reader* (Washington, D.C.: The Catholic University of America Press, 2005).

ogy and theological anthropology to be bridge makers that can recognize the significance of natural sciences (biology) and human sciences (psychology) in understanding the unity of the embodied person and the typical developmental trajectories. The cognitive, emotional, and volitional levels are not void of meaning, for they develop as human beings learn to know, to love, and to commit themselves. This means more than the subject's interpretation of nature, of the human body, or of the human soul. For the human bodily and spiritual structure give large guidelines for a life of excellence (such as self-giving, pardon, and courage), in the pursuit of good and truth, for the benefit of the common good and the person alike. In *Veritatis Splendor* (*VS*, n. 48) for example, John Paul II says that

> The person, by the light of reason and the support of virtue, discovers in the body the anticipatory signs, the expression and the promise of the gift of self, in conformity with the wise plan of the Creator. It is in the light of the dignity of the human person—a dignity which must be affirmed for its own sake—that reason grasps the specific moral value of certain goods towards which the person is naturally inclined. And since the human person cannot be reduced to a freedom which is self-designing, but entails a particular spiritual and bodily structure, the primordial moral requirement of loving and respecting the person as an end and never as a mere means also implies, by its very nature, respect for certain fundamental goods, without which one would fall into relativism and arbitrariness.

This passage intimates that a fuller consideration of the human person should not confuse biology with the physical nature of human acts. To deny biologism (biology "as the full science of man" and a strong version of reductionism) doesn't mean denying the significance of distinctive, embodied human inclinations, emotions, reasoning, willing, and acts.[36] John Paul II resists the idea that biology

36. In a different sense, a charge of biologism or physicalism has been laid against (Catholic) natural-law treatments of moral acts that concern the body (notably sexual acts). For this reason, while critiquing objectionable moral theories, John Paul II has

or physical acts can be morally construed without reference to human reason, the moral subject, and the community. Starting from the stance of personal unity (body-soul unity) that assures that the "person is subject of his own moral agency" (*VS*, n. 48), he affirms that the person cannot be fully understood without reference to its capacities, such as cognition and affectivity, intelligence and corporality, reason and will, perception and emotion. But at the same time, being a person is not dependent upon these capacities either; a living human being, before he can exercise these capacities, for example, is still considered a human person.[37] He thus avoids a dualism that is hard to escape when starting from Cartesian or derivative modern perspectives.[38]

As a legacy of the Enlightenment separation of the sciences and of Descartes's dualist understanding of the person and psychology, contemporary sciences continue to struggle in seeking a satisfactory way to explain the relationship of higher-order functions (such as consciousness, free intentional acts, and aesthetic interpretation) and of human embodiment and the diverse studies thereof. For example, a hard interpretation of the Diltheyian distinction between natural and human sciences traps conversation in dualistic dichotomies between material and efficient causes, on the one hand, and human subjec-

---

treated the issue of biologism in the encyclical *Veritatis Splendor* (see especially, paragraph number 48). He seeks to set out a robust understanding of the person and the natural law that resists these charges. In so doing, he employs a strong notion of the unity of the person (soul and body) to argue that moral actions cannot be properly understood apart from a unified conception of the person. He defines the rational soul as the principle of unity of the human person, thus linking reason and free will "with all the bodily and sense faculties. The person, including the body, is completely entrusted to himself, and it is in the unity of body and soul that the person is the subject of his own moral acts" (*VS*, n. 48).

37. For more on the nature of personhood, see John Paul II, Encyclical letter on *The Gospel of Life (Evangelium vitae)* (Vatican City: Libreria Editrice Vaticana, 1995).

38. A late Wittgensteinian critique, as a kindred spirit, goes a long way in breaking the dualist stranglehold. See Fergus Kerr, *"Work on Oneself": Wittgenstein's Philosophical Psychology* (Arlington, Va.: The Institute for the Psychological Sciences Press, 2008).

tive meaning, on the other. Moreover, when set in a dualistic stance, the Diltheyian approach seems to foreclose on the subject, as subject, gaining a level of self-understanding from the descriptive observations about human objective reality (hormonal influences on emotion; effects of cognitive development on judgment; influences of past acts on memory). Admittedly, the simple distinction between the natural and the human sciences does not necessarily sink into a rash reductionism or an entrenched skepticism. It posits two different types of knowledge and diverse foci for the two types of science, however, the bridge between these two must come from elsewhere.

Recent attempts to overcome these dichotomies have turned to the "emergence" metaphor to explain how complex properties or characteristics emerge from less complex ones.[39] In particular, it is called upon when the properties of the whole exceed the sum of the individual parts of an organism or system: for example, when consciousness or intelligent speech seems to arise from neuro-biological activities that in themselves do not explain such "emergent" properties or capacities. However, there are two types of emergence theory.

On the one hand, weak versions of emergence involve a "causal closure of the world" that accounts for the higher-order characteristics and causal relationships as emerging from lower levels. It, for example, correlates the mind to the brain, that is, the law-like mental phenomena to states of the central nervous system. Weak emergence, which is current fare for physicalists and determinists—but also as an uncritical default mode—is the pragmatic starting point for most natural scientists in their practical work of searching law-based explanations for events in the natural world. On the other hand, strong versions of emergence recognize that the micro-level principles cannot explain a complex system's overall behavior, in particular the novel properties that emerge in the system. Rather, higher-order entities, or "laws of

---

39. For an analysis of the history and diverse trends of the notion of "emergence," see Clayton and Davies, *Re-Emergence of Emergence*. See also Philip Clayton, *Mind and Emergence: From Quantum to Consciousness* (Oxford: Oxford University Press, 2004).

complexity" (Paul Davies in the preface to *The Re-Emergence of Emergence,* xiii), exercise a downward causation on their lower-level constituents. A strong version of emergence theory recognizes, for example, that the mind can influence the brain and the body and that ethical laws enhance, rather than contradict, the laws of physics. One advantage of the strong version is that it preserves common-sense insights about human freedom and agency. Another is that it provides a way to explain God's causal influence in the natural world.

In addition to these two advantages of the strong version of the emergence metaphor in sciences, I would like to note one concern in regard to the construal of the human person. The concern arises when contemporary versions of emergence, according to Philip Clayton, resist considering that the complete form of a being is potentially present in its beginning.[40] Without further convictions, some thinkers would, therefore, conclude—in a sort of gradualism—that as properties emerge so does the human person; and before the emergence of distinctive human properties, there is simply a human being. This interpretation of emergence involves an epistemological judgment: when I recognize certain properties—such as signs of intelligence and free self-determination—I know that a person exists. It also involves a presupposition: before there are signs of intelligent and free agency there is no person.

This gradualist presupposition and judgment have significant consequences for the construal of the person and his dignity. They moreover contradict an Aristotelian and Thomist understanding of formal causes. Based on his biological research, Aristotle posited that living beings had an internal principle of growth—a principle of potency—that was responsible for their later qualities or form. He thought, for

---

40. Philip Clayton, "Conceptual Foundations of Emergence Theory," in Clayton and Davis, *Re-Emergence of Emergence,* 4–5. This selective tendency disregards a fuller notion of the potentiality of the soul, concerning which Aristotle says: "[T]he soul is an actuality of the first kind [as knowledge rather than reflecting] of a natural body having life potentially in it" (*De anima* 412ᵃ29–30). A similar selective tendency is found in Bennett and Hacker's *Neuroscience* (14–15), where they admittedly disregard "Aristotle's formulation '[of the form] of a natural body that has life potentially' (*De anima* 412ᵃ20)."

example, that an acorn was an oak tree, albeit in potency. In his moderate realist schema (one that would seek to overcome a subjectivist or idealist or naturalistic approach to epistemology or metaphysics), we can account for additional properties of the person that emerge over time, while also granting them a real causal basis. We can resist considering the human person who emerges (in our knowledge) from its animal embodiment as a chimera. In so doing, we resist the type of emergence theory that would constitute itself willy-nilly as an opponent to the soul and to discussion thereof. Emergence theory, as an epistemological argument, does not replace the conception of a unifying principle such as *soul*, even though it could recognize such a principle, if the theory of emergence would admit the distinction between the proper causes and effects of divine and human agency (divine providence and human, limited autonomy), each according to their own competencies and non-conflicting overall. For example, interpersonal intentionality, as a property of a social rational animal, hearkens to a source that is more than biological processes. It hearkens to a rational soul and even to a source thereof (a first originative cause). The emergence of properties is really a phenomenological or epistemological observation that should not be confused with a metaphysical basis for a judgment about their origin. The appearance of a property does not deny that the groundings of the property pre-exist its being observed.

Elizabeth Anscombe, in her critique of modern moral philosophy, has called for a renewed "philosophy of psychology." She says that modern similitudes of an adequate philosophical psychology have led toward reductionist materialism and dualist misrepresentations of the body and soul.[41] We can add that, more recently, postmodern resemblances tend toward strong versions of naturalist theories of the gradualist emergence of the person, even though they do manifest truths, such as that the whole (the properties of a mature human person) is greater than the parts (the biological elements).

41. G. E. M. Anscombe, "Modern Moral Philosophy," in *Collected Philosophical Papers* (Oxford: Oxford University Press, 1981, orig. 1958), 3:26–41.

In order for contemporary studies to do justice to the human psyche, we need to pick up the pieces left both by the splintering effect of Enlightenment modernity and by the incisive contemporary critiques made thereof. Putting modern reflections in a larger context and correcting overly mechanistic and reductionist infelicities prepares for more fruitful studies. In particular, the methodological barriers, which neatly separate the various academic disciplines, are of relative utility. These divisions need to be respected for valid intradisciplinary work, but they also need to recognize a constructive vision of the ordering of the sciences so as to revitalize the deeper studies of the human person and community that philosophical psychology might allow. The challenge is to manage a comprehensive perspective that both retains the positive progress made in the history of thought and integrates it with recent findings in the functional specialties. An integrative philosophical psychology involves connecting and complementing such studies.

This interdisciplinary collection of essays seeks to make such a contribution. It features scholars of international reputation in philosophy, psychology, political theory, and religion offering philosophical reflections on human embodiment and emotion, commitment and freedom, reason and moral theory. Now I would like to introduce those essays and their unique contributions in finding an order and sense in these pieces of philosophical psychology.

≋

Kevin L. Flannery advances the question of why contemporary moral theory and psychology need a philosophical psychology and of the role that G. E. M. Anscombe (1919–2001) plays therein. By any measure one of the major philosophical figures of the twentieth century, Anscombe stood up courageously to face a self-satisfied philosophical establishment. In her seminal article entitled "Modern Moral Philosophy" (1958), she dared to claim that moral theory as then practiced—without "an adequate philosophy of psychology"—was not only incoherent but dangerous. In this article and her major book *Intention* (1957), she established herself as one of the most careful heirs to Wittgenstein's philosophical legacy. One of the great values of her work is the combat Anscombe waged against philosophical confusions that she understood to lead, among other things, to the legitimization of killing innocents. Moreover, in her critique of modern moral theories, she coined the term "consequentialism" for theories that reduce moral theory to the considerations of foreseen consequences. In her incisive manner, Anscombe insisted that not all that claims to be moral is moral. Her work moreover is of extreme import for establishing the parameters of philosophical psychology. While Aristotle serves a foundational role here, his works nonetheless exhibit a lacuna that Anscombe sets out to fill, namely, the scarcity of an account of intention in human action. Her claim that there was no adequate philosophy of psychology in modern moral philosophy spelled a rejection of a current of secular thought that construed morality apart from human acts. In particular, she rejected the practice of analyzing the concepts of "obligation," "duty," "right," and "wrong" as phenomena or psychological data existing exclusively in the mind. Anscombe expresses her debt to Wittgenstein, whose *Philosophical Investigations* resist the reduction of psychology to thoughts and feelings, on the one hand, and the exclusion of objectively analyzable acts in such considerations, on the other.

In order to establish an adequate philosophy of psychology, she distinguishes between intention and the sentiments or feelings related to thoughts and actions, while both differentiating intention from the force of will needed to act and adjudicating the nature of an overall intention on the species of an act (such as killing the innocent). She discriminates between consequences and the means to achieve them and identifies the psychological and logical aspects of notions such as "belief." The work of constructing an adequate philosophical psychology doesn't simply require originality or comparative study for Anscombe. Rather it must build upon the foundation of great thinkers.

Flannery opens the way for future study of philosophical psychology by posing pertinent questions, including those that touch upon the interpretation of key texts in the tradition of the field, such as Aristotle's *Nicomachean Ethics* (concerning issues such as compulsion and force, voluntary and involuntary action, the effects of threats and emotions, praise- and blame-worthy acts) and Aquinas's *Summa theologiae* (concerning the principle of double effect, for example). Moreover, Flannery notes that although Anscombe is credited with initiating the revival in virtue ethics, she would be singularly unsatisfied with the common tendency to focus on the agent to the detriment of his acts. Rather, her notion of a philosophy of psychology establishes the basis for understanding the close interconnection of psychology, acts, and virtues. How do intentional acts constitute virtues and how do both (acts and virtues) constitute a person's psychology? For Anscombe, it is the role of a philosophical psychology to clarify the conceptual foundation for general psychology and for moral theory, which both need to understand intentional acts and moral virtues in adjudicating what it means to be a good person.

⁓

Taking on the neglected task of constructively correlating the sciences, Benedict Ashley's essay addresses the question of what service philosophy, in general, and metaphysics (or metascience),[42] in particular, render to psychology. In answering the question, he leads the reader through a history of the study of the human psyche that predates the term "psychology" itself and that includes its relationship with the other sciences. While Greek philosophers penned studies on the human psyche, the first use of the term "psychology" itself dates to 1590 in the works of the German philosopher Goclenius (Göeckel). The term, however, did not become popular until 1712, when used in the works of Christian von Wolff (1679–1754). In demonstrating

---

42. Ashley says that the term "metascience" is the logically proper postmodern name for what has been called metaphysics and first philosophy; see *The Way of Wisdom: An Interdisciplinary and Intercultural Introduction to Metaphysics* (Notre Dame, Ind.: University of Notre Dame Press, 2006), 60.

the fortunes of the term and its modern manifestations, Ashley outlines developments in experimental psychology (Wilhelm Wundt and William James), in psychoanalytic (Sigmund Freud), behaviorist (Ivan Pavlov, John Watson, and B. F. Skinner), humanist, and cognitive approaches (Aaron Beck). Ashley reminds us that the content of the term "psychology" was influenced by René Descartes's (1596–1650) revival of the Platonic notion that certitude is found in innate ideas rather than empirical evidence. Curiously enough the resulting and persisting Wolffian distinction between metaphysical philosophy ("rational psychology") and empirical science was also taken up by the neo-scholastic renewal of Thomism encouraged by Leo XIII, even though the distinction confuses Thomas Aquinas's (and Aristotle's) notion and ordering of the sciences.

Ashley takes us behind the Wolffian distinction between philosophy and science in order to identify the more cogent division of the sciences and definition for psychology found in Aristotle's works, which were the first systematic and empirical works on animal and human behavior and in which the previous scholastic tradition identified certain foundations. Unlike Plato, who tried to solve the problem of interdisciplinarity by reducing all truth to a single science, Aristotle defended the different modes of knowing as autonomous sciences or philosophies. He nonetheless also understood that the autonomous sciences in their own ways call for a more synthetic science that integrates their results. This interdisciplinary and integrative science is properly called "philosophy," or the love of wisdom.

Aristotle studied the problems of human conscious behavior—what today we call "psychology"—using a natural science approach (behaviorist method) and under the title of *On the Soul (De anima)*. The nature of this psychology construed as a scientific discipline involves both animal and human levels of behavior, which are respectively studied by natural science and by philosophy. First, the natural sciences explore the nature of animal behavior; for example, study of the human psyche demonstrates the existence of both material and spiritual causes, for the types of changes enacted in human agency (involved in intelligent thought and free agency) demand a spiritual cause. Biology, furthermore, studies animal behavior, which in the case of human persons educes the body-soul problem; for biology can identify that *Homo sapiens sapiens* differs from other animals because of the use of abstract thought and language. Second, another discipline is needed to explain the positive nature of these specific differences. The properly human level (which is never actually separated from the animal level, since even abstract thought instrumentally requires the support of the body) is studied by the synthetic science called either philosophy or metaphysics or metascience. At this level (and in this treatment of the term), philosophy searches to understand the positive nature of ultimate causes of human agency, especially of human self-consciousness, intelligent thought, and free choice. Instead of a dualism, Aristotelian psychology exhibits a thoroughgoing unity of body and soul, matter and form. Its hylomorphic theory is so construed because human intelligence expresses a need for the material body in order to think and choose. While instrumentally in need of its animal base, human intelligence transcends the physical, unlike other animals' (especially great apes') and computers'. The fact that human intelligence differs from artificial intelligence has been demonstrated by Gödel's theorem on formal logical systems. Our brains alone do not explain abstract thought. Self-consciousness, with the role that language behavior plays therein, is the basis for a metaphysical analysis of the difference between matter and spirit. Ashley concludes that the philosophical psychology that comprehends the spiritual tenor of human intelligence and of free agency supports a particular model for mental health. Rather than simply altering behavior and assuaging suffering, psychology rightfully seeks to enable clients to actively transform (at embodied and intellectual levels) their defective evaluations—sidetracked by fantasy or fickle emotions—in order to be capable of free decisions, supported by cooperative emotion, and based on reality.

⇝

Fostering a more complete vision of the human person and society goes in pair with refuting reductionist approaches. In his article, Roger Scruton confronts biological reductionist efforts that seek to discredit the distinctive nature of human freedom, self-consciousness, rationality, responsibility, and interpersonal intentionality. Some thinkers would have us believe that human animality—a biological self—is the all-encompassing reality for the species *Homo sapiens sapiens.* Undeniably, we have biological needs and are influenced by laws of biology that motivate us to reproduce and defend our territory. Nonetheless, by assuming that the functional explanations from biology, sociobiology, evolutionary psychology, and brain science will completely elucidate human behavior, such interpretations reduce human phenomena (such as love, grief, and mourning) to the biological level. Darwin and neo-Darwinians for their part contend that human qualities are continuous with the instincts of other species that promote the survival of the species, organism, or gene; thus the human moral sense is merely a simple step-type development from the social instinct of other species. In the same vein, Richard Dawkins has construed a theory of the "meme" as the means by which culture replicates itself—not unlike the way that genes serve to replicate the human organism. A meme, however, is a mental entity that acts like a virus at the level of the mind, using ideas to propagate themselves (through imitation) while appropriating the energy of the brains that harbor them, as a virus would a cell it has infected. Scruton critiques these hypotheses as subversive and vacuous theories lacking a real basis.

Instead of simply attacking biological reductionism, however, he takes a constructive approach that demonstrates the truths of the human person, of self-conscious "creatures like us" that cannot be adequately accounted for by scientific explanations alone, such as human laughter (which refers to ideals and intentionality), responsibility (which refers to rights, obligations, freedom, and moral sentiments), and personhood (which refers to activities like law-making, rights, and duties and to the first-person perspective of a self-conscious subject). Scruton defends a moral understanding of the human person against attempts that would reduce it to its objective manifestations that are observable through quantifiable or scientific explanations alone. His arguments turn the tables on the reductionism that leads us to misperceive and mis-describe both people and animals and that is radically dissonant with the observable facts of human behavior. Purely biological explanations of our mental life (including human laughter, responsibility, or personhood), end up interpreting metaphysical and moral notions as fictions and offer antagonistic renderings of religion and ethics.

While affirming that we are animals, he affirms as well that we are incarnate persons, with unique rational capacities that underlie our intentional stances and our moral disposition. Scruton distinguishes the competencies of the three disciplines in their descriptions and visions of the human being. Religion on the one hand offers theological grounds for belief (faith-informed reasons) in such truths about the human person. Philosophy on the other offers rational grounds for these truths. Science, furthermore, need not be antagonistic to these disciplines, but when it is, it offers an incomplete account of the human being. The non-reductionist vision of the work of these three disciplines can be seen through the problem of understanding the relationship between the body and the soul. The unity of the body and the soul is a tenet of faith that cannot be fully explained by scientific accounts; rather it is a problem for which we must turn to philosophy for a developed and systematic rational treatment that is advanced in discussions on intentionality. For Scruton, the philosophical perspective on body and soul explains the emergence of qualities of the person in the world of intersubjective attitudes and thus completes scientific observations.

Biological accounts alone are ill-suited to describe the human person in its greatness and its unity. When isolated they promote misperceptions about human beings. However, we should not confuse an attack on biological reductionism (and scientific objectivism) with angelism that would disregard the body and human nature in the moral consideration of human acts. To deny biology—"as the full science of man"—doesn't mean that we deny the significance of embodied human inclinations, emotions, reasoning, willing, and acts. A coherent understanding of the person demands reference to the human body as an integral (essential) aspect of its unity, including the personal nature of desire that needs to be distinguished from dehumanized acts that are based on sensual pleasure detached from interpersonal relationships, responsibilities, and commitments. Against charges of "speciesism" (leveled by Richard Ryder and Peter Singer), Scruton would have us respect nature and other species, without confusing the moral qualities and goals that help to discriminate human persons from other forms of animal life. Lastly, he upholds the role of philosophy in finding truth and of religious faith and practice in communicating what is essential to human persons.

The study of philosophical psychology would be incomplete without an account of human and religious freedom, which takes on new light when put in historical context. In his contribution, Ceslas Bernard Bourdin demonstrates that diverse conceptions of religious freedom issue from the modern histories of Great Britain, the United States of America, and France. In particular, he focuses on the political, philosophical, and theological grounds for the post-revolutionary French vision of religious freedom and of the separation of Church and State in the context of the opposition voiced by the Holy See. Bourdin first paints the historical backdrop of the modern notion of religious freedom and the interdependent conceptions of human rights, republic, nation, and autonomy. The sixteenth-century European crisis of the legitimacy and sovereignty of modern states is rooted in a crisis of the universal and in the displacement of the unifying role that the Holy See had politically played in medieval Europe. With the failure of the Holy Roman Empire and the political challenges raised by reformers such as Martin Luther and Jean Calvin, the center of unity shifted toward diverse monarchies, and the construal of absolute sovereignty (by divine right) became the new institutional form of unity. The appropriation of the transcendent origin of unity by the monarchy led France to regulate religion and its diverse expressions. The splintering of Christendom and the presence of religious minorities, furthermore, raised challenges to the metaphysical, religious, and moral order centered on the common good and beatitude that Enlightenment Rationalist philosophers (Hobbes, Locke, Spinoza, Montesquieu, and Rousseau) replaced by law and contract in the public sphere and by individual conscience in private. The French revolution established a secular unity and religious autonomy, instituting a national sovereignty of the people and requiring the civil constitution of the clergy. Underlying the modern French conflict with the papacy was a philosophical divergence about human autonomy and heteronomy. The enlightenment and properly Kantian goal of letting man attain his majority (or rather emerge "from his self-imposed immaturity")[43] was intended to liberate not only conscience from the influence of the Roman Catholic Church and reason from revelation, but also the State from any concordant with the Holy See and the school from religious sources. The papacy offered resistance at two levels: first, concerning the correlation of Church, state, and society; second, concerning the correlation of reason, liberty, truth, and revelation. Pope Leo XIII's encyclical *Immortale Dei* (1885) expressed an unabashedly theologico-political conception of the interrelationship between Church, state, and society, identifying philosophical (Aristotle) and scriptural (Romans 13:1–8) arguments for the recognition of the divine origin of political power. Moreover, he resisted a type of religious liberty that would undermine a public profession of God (involving the Church's mediation) as a basis for lasting political order. Leo XIII affirmed that the Christian notion of order construes liberty as having its origin in God. However, this liberty of heteronomy-concord attuned

---

43. Immanuel Kant, *Perpetual Peace and Other Essays,* trans. and ed. by Ted Humphrey (Indianapolis: Hackett Publishing, 1983), 41.

by truth and goodness (by promoting social justice, unity, and obedience as so many remedies to disorder) is starkly contrasted with the liberty of autonomy-separation, without barriers against self-indulgent and social excesses. In line with the future Declaration on Religious Freedom (Vatican II, *Dignitatis Humanae*, 1965), Leo XIII recognized that conscience should be able to abide the truth of the natural order and the findings of science without undermining belief in the teachings of revelation *(Immoratale Dei)*. For his part, Pius X's encyclical *Vehementer Nos* (1906) directly addressed the laicity of the French Republic and its law of separation (December 1905), while treating the issues of public worship and papal jurisdiction of the Catholic Church in France. Unique in Europe, the French Republican-laicist agenda of separation and autonomy resisted religion from structuring the social order and education. It labored to establish two separate spheres for politics and religion, by seeking to construe freedom imbued with secular public rules, while relegating the Church to the private sphere. The resistance of Leo XIII and Pius X to this vision (and their affirmation that society requires public worship of God whose mediator is the Church, united in the person of the Pope) is taken up afresh in the vision of the Second Vatican Council (especially *Gaudium et Spes* and *Dignitatis Humanae*). Bourdin affirms in conclusion that in order to attain a pertinent and universal vision of man, contemporary political and theological conversations need to recognize the diverse histories of the terms and voices in this dialogue without assuming that distinct notions of "separation" spell the definitive dissociation of politics, ethics, and religion, or of reason, truth, and freedom.

Addressing the potential collaboration between modern psychology and orthodox theology, Aidan Nichols, in his essay, graphically describes one of last century's illustrious dialogues of faith and science between the Swiss psychologist Carl Gustav Jung (1875–1961) and English Dominican theologian Victor White (1902–1960). Nichols sets the stage for understanding their common interest in psychology and Christianity by presenting the origins and developments of Jung's own religious views. Jung's intellectual itinerary was mostly eclectic, involving empirical psychology and spiritualism (parapsychology), neo-Kantian subjectivism, and Nietzschean amoralism, as well as studies of world religions and mythologies. A difficult trip to India in 1938, however, jolted him out of his romantic attraction to Eastern religions, but not out of his naturalistic approach to religion or his rejection of orthodox Christianity. Aided by a dream, he came to believe that Europe could not stomach non-Western culturally entrenched religions and that his vocation was to heal Christianity through his own theory of psychology. His messianic call and therapeutic service to Christianity was to be, however, on his own terms. Fr. Victor White entered the picture at a time when Jung was open to finding a collaborator within the Catholic Church. In numerous articles published from the late twenties into the forties, Jung sent positive signals about his perception of Catholicism, while rejecting Freud's depreciation of culture and symbol. The Swiss psychologist preferred aspects of the Catholic tradition over Christian denominations and other religions because of its sensitivity to the feminine (through its veneration of the Blessed Virgin Mary and women saints), its humanity (as opposed to the *fide sola* Christianity that he received in his childhood), and its inclusiveness (of elements from other religions).

A common desire for a dialogue between psychology and theology united Jung and the younger White, although the flawed match would not last. The philosopher-theologian was of the temperament to engage contemporary culture from an orthodox Catholic perspective. In particular, he employed the intellectual resources and methodological dispositions of a Thomism that, in White's own view, needed to break free of reified manuals to return to a type of dialogue with contemporary science and culture that epitomized the style of Aquinas's own work. Optimistic from his selective reading of the Swiss psychologist, White initiated a dialogue with Jung in 1948, sending him several essays that exhibited his capacity to synthesize Jung's psychology with Catholic theology and ethics. Without fully understanding, though, the intellectual foundation on which Jung based his work and ignorant of the theological direction that the Swiss psychologist would later take, White sensed a fertile terrain in Jung's theories.

Jung responded enthusiastically to White's initiative, and the dialogue developed to the point that Jung included White within a close circle of trusted collaborators. Jung even thought that the Dominican could take up his intellectual legacy. However, Jung's views did not stop evolving, to the point that White had to rebel. An explosive development was the publication of Jung's *Answer to Job* (*Antwort auf Hiob*, 1952). Although the manuscript was supposed to be experimental and reserved for the inner circle, its publication and English translation (1954) came at an untimely moment, at least for White. A fascination for appropriating the shadow side lead the psychologist to project upon God the human struggle of light and dark, good and evil, which precipitated a grave anthropomorphic deformation not only of the Book of Job, but also of the Judeo-Christian understanding of God. Jung's psychological program and his utterly naturalistic attitude to religion spelled antipathy to Christianity and to doctrines of divine transcendence. Jung's late-breaking clarification that his discussion of the God-image was intended to reconcile antinomic aspects to the human psyche (rather than make pronouncements about God) was not adequate to calm the crisis. The publication spelled the end of White's project to integrate Thomism and analytic psychology. It also meant his academic downfall. White had not foreseen the danger of a Jungian new-age religion, concerning which the Swiss psychologist was the first to coin the phrase the "age of Aquarius." Although the plan to unite Thomism and Jungian psychology overreached what the former could support without doing it substantial damage, Nichols highlights the anthropological promise that drew White to dialogue with Jung and that remains a point of interest in the dialogue about philosophical and religious anthropology. In particular, White appreciated Jung's conceptions of "individuation" (for a coherent integration of a person's psychological capacities), "collective unconscious" (to situate philosophical anthropology in the context represented by the spiritual archetypes of spiritual traditions), and spiritual agency (to recognize the individual's forward-leaning cultural task as spiritual and not simply a Freudian archeology of sexual impulses). White, in particular, appreciated Jung's attribution of spiritual meaning to human emotions, including sexual ones; the Dominican found it to be akin to St. Thomas's theory of how finite acts and feelings participate in the infinite. The English Thomist was convinced he had found a kindred spirit in Jung. His mistake was to think that a Catholic anthropology could support Jung's position, which proved incompatible inasmuch as it mutated later into an undiscerning naturalism.

Entering into other aspectual and historical particulars of philosophical psychology, Richard Sorabji's article approaches the question of freedom and emotion from the perspective of ancient philosophy, particularly that of the Stoics. With their therapeutic approach to emotion, the Stoics were the first to invent cognitive therapy. They held that all emotions could be understood in terms of four basic emotional demeanors (appetite, fear, pleasure, and distress) and as intellectual judgments of value at two levels. One inevitably adjudicates first the harm or benefit present in any emotional state and second the adequacy of one's reaction to it. Importantly, the Stoics distinguished judgments from mere appearances, which involve an involuntary and uncritical view of what seems bad or good or what matters for us and our friends. By distancing oneself from appearances, the Stoic gains the high ground, taking the opportunity to ask whether each appearance is right and whether he should give assent to it. In order to be freed up from the irrational pull of false appearances, Stoic philosophy exercises the capacity to restrain from the common tendency to unthinkingly consent. Putting distance between appearances and acquiescence demands an acquired self-discipline that produces freedom to withhold assent. The danger with undelayed assent is that appearances then determine action and undercut freedom. Moreover, the Stoics distinguish emotions from the physical or mental shock (such as going pale or feeling expansive) that accompany them. Such codicils to emotion are inevitable, but of no importance. All non-essentials aside, the Stoics define an emotion proper as the cognitive agreement that you give upon inspection of the appearance. Nothing else matters. The Stoic notion of curing unwanted emotion involves withholding assent in the face of an underlying wrong evaluative attitude. This type of cure is not a question of willpower, but rather an intellectual effort to attack the thought that something is really good (or truly bad) for you and that your spontaneous reaction is appropriate. This intellectual effort, though, is not an isolated principle, but comes accompanied with cognitive-narrative techniques and exercises, such as: realizing you are not alone in your situation; relabeling attractive with repulsive qualities in order to detach oneself from an appearance (or vice versa); systematically suspecting first thoughts about whether something is really good or bad; daily self-interrogating about one's acts; putting some reservation in desire (such as by adding "God willing" to our thoughts); and expecting what is conventionally called bad fortune. Sorabji compares the ancient Stoic form of cognitive therapy to modern ones, arguing that they both employ behavior and thought processes and both address value judgments and factual misjudgments. Besides, they hold in common an extensive use of imagination, in revaluing and in relabeling, for example. In addition to the presentation of the curative techniques that help to correct beliefs (and to focus attention on what really counts), Sorabji distances himself from the Stoic notion that character alone matters. He moreover identifies the limitations found in Stoic therapy, which is apt to address neither extraordinary difficulties nor bad moods nor the effects of emotions on other people. It also is helpful neither for child-related and less intellectual issues nor for the education of emotions (as irrational movements) that are outside of cognitive judgment. Lastly, he briefly situates the Stoic contribution in the context of the therapeutic insights found in the other major Greek approaches.

nst the backdrop of the ubiquitous desire to correlate rea-
emotion that has guided psychology and philosophy, as well
ature and science throughout the millennia, Daniel N. Robinson's essay defends the thesis "no emotion without a reason." Too often the more potent contributions to the debate have been forgotten
in the name of science's latest contributions or of a theory's supposed
comprehensiveness. While Plato used the metaphor of the struggle
of the charioteer and the two winged horses *(Phaedrus)* to indicate
that rationality must find a way to rule animality, contemporary sciences often lose the forest for the trees, falling prey to the blinding assumptions that rational-emotive processes can be studied as a sum of
constituent parts or that these human phenomena can survive vivi-
section. Robinson establishes the evocative questions and the guiding
definitions needed for a thoroughgoing treatment, while distinguishing not only emotion from reason, but also the logical canons of reason from its pragmatic criteria and emotions proper from feelings,
passions, and moods. He argues that authentic emotions (as opposed
to non-contextual moods and blind passions) have reasons or causal
conditions associated with them. Of particular interest is his treatment of "interest" as a bridge between emotion and reason. A significant development in the social sciences, dating back to Bernoulli's
(1732) accent on the psychological and running through Kahnemann
and Tversky's (1984) accent on the subjective side of decision making, has led to the finding that abstract statistical considerations of
gains and losses do not underlie a rational decision so much as do
one's personal interests. Decision making involves three intertwining
dimensions: what is personal, what is meaningful, and what is felt. To
analyze a decision apart from any one of them would be not to analyze a human decision. With this correlation in mind, deliberation is
deliberating not simply about rationality and the application of principles but also about the merits of feelings that incline one to act.

In the context of Paul Ekman's cross-cultural research on the correlation of facial expressions with six basic emotions or Jaak Panksepp's

evolutionary and neuroscience model with seven basic emotions, Robinson argues that explanations of non-cognitive adaptive mechanisms or neuro-biological functions do not fully account for emotions. The sciences will continue to advance in their findings that correlate emotional states with brain circuitry and chemistry, but this will not explain what is most important. Displacing the study of emotions from the whole person to his brain or even to survival functions does not yield more convincing explanations. In front of the cultural diversity of law, attitudes, and aesthetics, however, there is the common recognition in literature and philosophy that emotions such as anger and disgust need to be appraised, as do all feelings need to be confronted with the facts and with clear-sighted judgment. Robinson argues that strict scientific generalizations about procedural appearances and systemic functions cannot capture the logic to emotion that concerns moral principle and moral ends at the personal, social, and civic level. A discriminating explanation must integrate the person's circumstances and commitments, perceptions and sentiments, understandings and choices. The first-person narrative in particular ties context, perception, emotion, belief, and judgment together. In such an account, personal interest, affect, and reason congeal into a coherent account of intelligent and felt agency.

two

Kevin L. Flannery

WHY DOES ELIZABETH ANSCOMBE SAY THAT WE NEED TODAY A PHILOSOPHY OF PSYCHOLOGY?

G. E. M. Anscombe's Life and Writings

Some time ago, I discussed with Dr. Gladys Sweeney, the academic dean of the Institute for the Psychological Sciences, possible names for the program she was setting up in Oxford, which would be devoted to the study of philosophy in connection with psychology. She mentioned as a possibility the name "The Centre for Philosophical Psychology"—or something very similar to that. My immediate reaction was to say that this was just what Elizabeth Anscombe had said was required if we were to repair the contemporary shambles which is modern ethical theory. So, when some time afterward Dr. Sweeney and I discussed possible topics for this Newman lecture, she quite reasonably suggested that I might explain what Anscombe meant with this call for a renewed philosophical psychology (or philosophy of psychology). I was—and am—happy to do so, as best as I am able, not being an "Anscombe expert," but (shall we say) a friendly admirer.

But before getting to the main theme of this essay, I think it would be a good idea to say something about Anscombe herself—for, although she was one of the best-known philosophers of the twentieth century, philosophers themselves no longer enjoy the public prominence that they did, for instance, in the days of Socrates and Plato . . . or even in the days of Bertrand Russell and Ludwig Wittgenstein.

Gertrude Elizabeth Margaret Anscombe was born on 18 March 1919, in Limerick, Ireland, where her father, a British army officer at the time, was posted. She was educated at Sydenham High School in London, before going up to St. Hugh's College, Oxford, in 1937. At Oxford, she almost immediately converted to Catholicism and, still an undergraduate, became involved in public controversy regarding moral theory. In 1939, along with her friend Norman Daniel, she wrote a pamphlet bearing the title, "The Justice of the Present War Examined." Because it described itself as presenting a "Catholic view" and because the authors had failed to get an *imprimatur,* the then archbishop of Birmingham, Thomas Leighton Williams, insisted that the authors withdraw the pamphlet—which they did. The pamphlet had to do especially with the intentional killing of civilians in war.

Soon after finishing at Oxford and having married Peter Geach, also a Catholic and a philosopher, she won a research fellowship at Newnham College, Cambridge, where she came in contact with Wittgenstein, whose interlocutor and close friend she became. After his death in 1951, by which time she had moved back to Oxford as a fellow of Somerville College, she did a translation of his masterpiece, the *Philosophical Investigations*—a translation that is almost never challenged for its fidelity to the original, a very unusual thing with translations of philosophical works. In 1959, she also published a book entitled *An Introduction to Wittgenstein's "Tractatus,"* which my own undergraduate tutor in Wittgenstein (Brian McGuinness) warned me was more difficult to understand than the work itself. In any case, it is clear that Anscombe was heavily influenced by Wittgenstein and understood his often very subtle doctrine like few others who have made use of it since.

In 1956, Anscombe publicly opposed Oxford University's bestowing an honorary degree on President Harry S. Truman. She opposed the degree because of Truman's instrumental role in the bombings of Hiroshima and Nagasaki. "Having a couple of massacres to his credit," she argued, ought to disqualify him. Around this same time—that is, in 1957 and 1958, respectively—Anscombe published two works that solidified her reputation as a philosopher in her own right: the book *Intention* and the seminal article "Modern Moral Philosophy."

As to the first, the recently deceased doyen of American analytic philosophy Donald Davidson called it "the most important treatment of action since Aristotle." (Unlike Anscombe, he had not read much Thomas Aquinas.) *Intention* is a difficult book, written in a style that somehow combines colloquialism and great precision of expression. In it Anscombe often cites Wittgenstein, usually favorably,[1] and she devotes a long section to an exposition and discussion of Aristotle's practical syllogism.[2] Her attitude toward Aristotle is especially important for anyone asking himself how to put together a program in the philosophy of psychology. She cites him often; and even when she is not doing so, one has the sense that her arguments and insights are put forward within the intellectual space cleared—although not completely—by his ethical writings. But her main task in *Intention* is to fill a lacuna in his ethical theory: the lack of an account of "the intention with which" someone does something.[3]

1. An exception would be her remark that "Wittgenstein seems to me to have gone wrong in speaking of the 'natural expression of an intention'" (G. E. M. Anscombe, *Intention* [Ithaca, N.Y.: Cornell University Press, 1957], 5).

2. Ibid., 58–67.

3. That this was her task in *Intention* becomes more explicit in an essay first pub-

So, for Anscombe, the philosophy of psychology, although certainly involving the study of authors who have gone before us, was not just a historical discipline. Besides Wittgensteinian and Aristotelian ideas, we find in *Intention* a good deal of Anscombe herself. Still, she would have been the first to deny that her object was to put forward an original theory. As her daughter Mary Geach now tells us in the introduction to the Italian translation of *Intention*, Anscombe was out rather to combat philosophical confusions such as that which led defenders of Truman to excuse his actions on the grounds, for instance, that he "only wrote his name on a piece of paper."[4] She thought that some of the most effective weapons in this struggle against confusion were to be found in the past.

Anscombe's second major piece from this period, the essay "Modern Moral Philosophy," puts forward two general theses: first, that modern philosophy can no longer speak intelligibly of "the moral" (a theme we shall consider shortly); second, that the differences among modern moral philosophers are deceptive. They are all basically trying to do the same thing, she says: undermine the traditional idea that there exist absolute prohibitions against particular types of actions, such as the deliberate killing of innocents. Although in "Modern moral philosophy" Anscombe famously coins the term "consequentialism" to refer to theories that make the moral primarily a function of foreseen consequences, she acknowledges too that consideration of consequences is not the real problem: the estimation of possible consequences has a perfectly legitimate place in practical reasoning. Much more insidious are the confusions generated by consequentialism's manipulation of the concept "intentional." One such manipulation is the denial that there is a significant distinction between in-

---

lished in 1965: G. E. M. Anscombe, "Thought and Action in Aristotle: What Is Practical Truth?" *From Parmenides to Wittgenstein*, vol. 1 of *Collected Philosophical Papers* (Minneapolis/Oxford: University of Minnesota Press/Basil Blackwell, 1981), 66–77. See also Anthony Kenny, *Will, Freedom and Power* (Oxford: Blackwell, 1975), 18.

4. Mary Geach, preface to the Italian translation of *Intention* (G. E. M. Anscombe, *Intenzione* [Rome: Università della Santa Croce, 2004]).

tentionally killing and, in some instances, non-action while knowing that death will occur. "Indeed," says Anscombe, "the interests served by those who argue that such non-action is equivalent to murder are not those of promoting an [at any rate] impossible moral concern but rather those of breaking down the objection to murder as this is commonly understood."[5]

Anscombe remained in Oxford, teaching, writing, and raising her seven children, until 1970, when she was appointed to the chair in Cambridge University previously held by Wittgenstein. In 1981 a number of her "collected papers" were published in three volumes, containing essays on a wide range of topics, including a number on explicitly Catholic topics, such as "You Can Have Sex without Children: Christianity and the New Offer" (1968) and "On Transubstantiation" (1974). She held her chair at Cambridge until retirement in 1986; she died on 5 January 2001. "Her last intentional act," according to one obituary, "was kissing Peter Geach."[6] Fairly recently another volume of Anscombe's essays has been published under the editorship of her daughter and her son-in-law Luke Gormally. The general editor of the series in which this volume appears, John Haldane, tells me that more such volumes are planned.[7]

An "Adequate Philosophy of Psychology": The Negative Side

That brings us (by way of a rather long preface) to our main theme: Anscombe's reason for saying that we need today a philosophy of psy-

---

5. G. E. M. Anscombe, "Murder and the Morality of Euthanasia," in *Human Life, Action and Ethics: Essays by G. E. M. Anscombe*, ed. Mary Geach and Luke Gormally, St. Andrews Studies in Philosophy and Public Affairs (Exeter, UK: Imprint Academic, 2005), 274.

6. John M. Dolan, "G. E. M. Anscombe: Living the truth," *First Things* (May 2001): 13.

7. The first volume is cited in note 5 (above); a second volume has been published since this text was written: *Faith in a Hard Ground: Essays on Religion, Philosophy, and Ethics by G. E. M. Anscombe*, ed. Mary Geach and Luke Gormally, St. Andrews Studies in Philosophy and Public Affairs (Exeter, U.K., and Charlottesville, Va.: Imprint Academic, 2008).

chology. She makes this call in a number of places, but most promi-
nently in the second sentence of "Modern Moral Philosophy": "[I]t is
not profitable," she says there, "for us at present to do moral philosophy; that should be laid aside at any rate until we have an adequate
philosophy of psychology, in which we are conspicuously lacking."[8]
What does she mean in saying this? I propose to answer this question in two phases: the first negative, the second more positive. That
is, I shall attempt first of all to determine what Anscombe is rejecting,
then to speak more generally about what she would regard as an "adequate philosophy of psychology." This latter task will involve running
very quickly through some issues that, I believe, Anscombe would say
the philosophy of psychology needs to address.

It might be thought that when Anscombe calls for a new philosophy of psychology, she is reacting against the type of philosophical
psychology that had been studied in Catholic universities for generations. That Anscombe was aware of this tradition at her back is
apparent, for in one of her essays she refers her readers to "any old
fashioned rational psychology in the scholastic tradition."[9] She is referring here to the admittedly dry and technical manuals in use, especially in the formation of priests, even while she was writing: works
such as the Jesuit Tilmann Pesch's *Institutiones psychologicae*.[10] But
Anscombe has none of the "anti-scholastic" sentiment so present, si-

8. G. E. M. Anscombe, "Modern Moral Philosophy," in *Ethics, Religion and Politics*,
vol. 3 of *Collected Philosophical Papers* (Minneapolis/Oxford: University of Minnesota
Press/Basil Blackwell, 1981), 26.

9. G. E. M. Anscombe, "Analytical Philosophy and the Spirituality of Man," in *Human Life, Action and Ethics*, 4.

10. Tilmannus Pesch, *Institutiones psychologicae secundum principia S. Thomae
Aquinatis ad usum scholasticum* (Friburg: Herder, 1896). Pesch's manual is organized
according to theses, such as, for instance, "Because of the intellectual life which is in
man it is necessary to say that the human soul is not an accident but a substance" (thesis 17) or "The theory of potencies proposed by Aristotle can be defended from every sophistical objection [*cavillatione*]" (thesis 36) or "The specific object or the proper
common object of the human intellect in the present life is the intelligible in the senses"
(thesis 45).

multaneously with her own writing, among Catholic scholars on the European continent, such as Hans Urs von Balthasar and Karl Rahner. This may be because she was a convert to Catholicism—or, more likely, because of her high regard for the methods of analytic philosophy, which are quite consonant with scholastic methods.

No, what Anscombe was rejecting in calling for a new philosophy of psychology was a current of more secular philosophy that had long previously excluded the precise analysis of human acts from its consideration of the moral. At the beginning of "Modern Moral Philosophy"—in fact, immediately after the remark about our lack of an adequate philosophy of psychology—she writes as follows: "[T]he concepts of obligation, and duty—*moral* obligation and *moral* duty, that is to say—and of what is *morally* right and wrong, and of the *moral* sense of 'ought' ought to be jettisoned if this is psychologically possible; because they are survivals, or derivatives from survivals, from an earlier conception of ethics which no longer generally survives, and are only harmful without it."[11] This position—that we ought to jettison the moral—sounds, of course, more than a little strange coming from a moralist, but it makes a great deal of sense once one understands what Anscombe means here by "the moral." It refers, at least indirectly, to an understanding of psychology that sees itself as studying phenomena or data that exist necessarily—and exclusively—"on the inside" (in the mind).

In the *Philosophical Investigations*, Wittgenstein begins his discussion of intentionality [§§428–693] with this remark: "'This queer thing, thought'—but it does not strike us as queer when we are thinking. Thought does not strike us as mysterious while we are thinking, but only when we say, as it were retrospectively: 'How was that possible?' How was it possible for thought to deal with the very object *itself*? We feel as if by means of it we had caught reality in our net."[12]

11. Anscombe, "Modern Moral Philosophy," 26; emphasis is all Anscombe's.

12. Ludwig Wittgenstein, *Philosophical Investigations/Philosophische Untersuchungen*, 3rd ed., trans. G. E. M. Anscombe (Oxford: Basil Blackwell, 1968), §428. P. M. S.

Wittgenstein means here that the tendency of then contemporary psychology—he probably had in mind Wolfgang Köhler's book, *Gestalt Psychology*,[13] but his point is quite general—is to focus exclusively upon what it considers its special subject matter, "the inner." But, once we do that, it becomes a problem how to deal "with the very object *itself*"—that is, how to deal with the object of thought, which (in some sense) is independent of "the inner." The temptation is to ignore the object altogether and reduce psychology to the study of thoughts—plus feelings, "psychological states," and the like. All this applies in an obvious way also to intention: an intention becomes not essentially the intention to do such-and-such—where "such-and-such" is an objectively analyzable act—but rather a feeling we supposedly have when doing something intentionally. As such, intention becomes just another feeling or psychological state, like felt sympathy for others or animosity.

The result of applying such an approach to morality is that morality becomes a sort of layer of sentimentality added *to* human action in such a way that an action itself might be utterly shameful but can be declared morally upright in accordance with an argument that, in the end, has nothing to do with what the person actually does. Think, for instance, of the parish priest who says that the Church's reasoning with respect to contraception or in vitro fertilization is valid and sound—and yet also tells his parishioners that their only moral obligation is to follow their conscience. Or think of the many movies one sees in which marital infidelity is so enveloped in an atmosphere of chirpy banter and romantic song that anyone mentioning harm to children or broken faith would be considered not just a cad but an opponent of all that is good. In all such cases, "the moral" has in effect

---

Hacker identifies §§428–693 as Wittgenstein's treatise on "mind and will." Well worth reading is his essay "Methodology in Philosophical Psychology," in the first part of his commentary on these numbers: P. M. S. Hacker, *Wittgenstein: Mind and Will* (Oxford; Malden, Mass.: Blackwell Publishers, 2000), part 1, 111–55.

13. See Hacker, part 1, 111.

become detached from the only material that could give it coherent meaning. It is, as it were, lopped on top of human action: like sweet sauce, to disguise rancid meat.

To do some summing up, therefore, Anscombe's negative position in "Modern Moral Philosophy" is that, in our present intellectual culture, intention has become confused with the feeling one sometimes has of pushing an act along by force of will. Since we make this confusion of intention with feeling and since feeling (or sentiment) is itself so easily confused with the moral, it becomes very easy to excuse even the most heinous acts by attending to things quite irrelevant to their moral quality. For Anscombe the key example was always the bombing of Hiroshima and Nagasaki. The argument was indeed made at the time that such killing was necessary in order to avoid an even worse outcome; but the action ultimately came to be regarded as moral because people were disinclined to believe that good old, plain-speaking Harry could be guilty of mass murder. Anscombe was never taken in by such dodgings of the moral issue: she knew that morality was about human acts performed . . . and intended.

The Positive Side: The Aristotelian Tradition

What, then, would be the more positive side of Anscombe's call for "an adequate philosophy of psychology"? What was she calling *for*? Although, certainly, she was much immersed in contemporary philosophy—Wittgenstein bestrides the world of analytic philosophy, however narrow, like a Colossus—when Anscombe turned to concrete issues in the philosophy of psychology she turned, as we have already seen, to Aristotle. Unlike philosophers such as John Stuart Mill, Henry Sidgwick, and G. E. Moore, whom she criticizes in "Modern Moral Philosophy," Aristotle—and those who follow his general approach (such as Thomas Aquinas)—do exactly what Anscombe thinks moralists should do: they talk about acts.[14] This is not to say

14. Besides Aquinas, I have in mind the so-called "manualists," such as A. Lehm-kuhl, J.-P. Gury, and H. Noldin.

that she would have been in favor of students of philosophy closing themselves off from contemporary influences; but neither would she have been in favor of—or seen any advantage in—trying to construct a philosophy of psychology from scratch: ignoring the foundational work of others, greater than ourselves. Indeed, the notion that we can ignore this tradition is a consequence of the general approach that caused the crisis of modern moral theory in the first place: that is, the approach that says that the moral is something that *I* impose upon the world.

Anscombe constantly reminds us that the philosophy of psychology is an enormously difficult discipline. "Belief," she says at one point, "is the most difficult topic because it is so hard to hold in view and correctly combine the psychological and the logical aspects."[15] If you believe that *p* and also believe that "if *p* then *q*," do you necessarily believe also that *q*? That would seem logical, but we all know that we often disbelieve the consequences of our own beliefs when they are pointed out to us: that, indeed, is the very basis of Platonic *elenchos* (or dialectic). The same sort of thing can be said about most any other aspect of philosophical psychology—and, in particular, about intention. Suppose that I know that creating an explosion to open a way to free a dozen miners will also kill the thirteenth. In creating the explosion do I *intend* to kill the one? Or, to use one of Anscombe's own examples, does "being done intentionally" necessarily involve an intention *to do* that thing? But what about someone who "applies some extra force to a telephone dial-piece because it is a bit jammed"?[16] It seems correct to say that Master X intends *to* phone Miss Y, but wrong to say that he intends *to* unjam the dial-piece. And yet he does it intentionally.

Because the matter of which moral decisions and intentions are constructed is so hard to work with—just when we think we have finally grasped an object of study we turn it slightly and see it quite

---

15. G. E. M. Anscombe, "Practical Inference," in *Human Life, Action and Ethics*, 138.

16. G. E. M. Anscombe, "The Causation of Action," in *Human Life, Action and Ethics*, 95.

differently—the temptation is strong simply to give up the effort and opt for some more manageable criterion of the moral, such as utility or (for instance) the determinations of "reflective equilibrium," as in John Rawls. But to do this would be to flee down avenues that are well paved at the beginning, but known (in fact) to dissipate into rutty paths leading nowhere: useful perhaps for the advancement of an academic career, but ultimately incapable of breaking through to a fully satisfying understanding of the moral.

So, if we are really serious about understanding morality, we must not be frightened off by the seemingly intangible character of the material to be studied, and we must not refuse to turn to what philosophical help is available in the works of philosophers who have recognized that morality ultimately comes down to acts. This is to say that we must not hesitate to turn to works such as Aristotle's *Nicomachean Ethics* and the second part of Aquinas's *Summa Theologiae*. It is in these two works (and others in the same tradition) that we find the basis of a program corresponding to Anscombe's vision of an adequate philosophy of psychology.

The Aristotelian Analysis of Acts

I would like now simply to run through some issues in Aristotelian action theory (philosophical psychology) that would have to be discussed in any such program. It is generally recognized that Aristotle's ethics contains two general areas of concern: acts and virtues. It is also sometimes pointed out that both Aristotle and Aquinas devote many more pages to the virtues than they do to acts.[17] But this says

17. Aristotle's *Nicomachean Ethics* comprises ten books. The first five chapters of book 3—less than ten pages in the standard English translation—contain Aristotle's action theory. By contrast, the whole of book 2, the rest of book 3, and then the whole of books 4 and 5 are devoted to various virtues. That comes to about fifty English pages. One can verify similar things with respect to Aquinas's *Summa* simply by looking at the volumes on the shelf: the *Secunda secundae*, which is all about virtues, is much fat-

nothing at all about the importance of acts for Aristotle and Thomas Aquinas. The sections in Euclid's *Elements* devoted to definitions and postulates are also extremely brief: most of that work is, of course, taken up with proofs developed from these basic ideas. But if you were to take away the definitions and postulates, you would take away also the proofs. On the other hand, you can take away any number of individual proofs—or even, in a sense, all of them—without harming the integrity of classical geometry itself. In the *Nicomachean ethics*, Aristotle's remarks on acts function much like Euclid's definitions and postulates: the system—such as it is—depends on them.

So, it would be extremely important for anyone attempting to follow Anscombe's program to study the first principles of action theory as set out in the first chapters of the third book of Aristotle's *Nicomachean Ethics*. And, indeed, as surprising as this may seem, there is still work to be done simply to understand what Aristotle says there. One difficult passage is that where he talks about compulsion or force (in Greek, *bia*).[18] In setting out his definitions, he says that "that is compulsory [*biaion*] of which the moving principle is outside, being a principle in which nothing is contributed by the person who acts or is acted upon, e.g. if he were to be carried somewhere by a wind, or by men who had him in their power" [*EN* iii.1, 1110a1–4]. Anything done on account of such force, he says, is involuntary.

But what sort of situations does Aristotle have in mind? Commentators are now pretty much agreed that, when he speaks of being "carried somewhere by the wind," he does not have in mind the brute force that is present when, for instance, a person is picked up bodily by the wind and dropped somewhere else, but rather a situation such as might happen at sea when a captain cannot bring his ship into one port and is forced to bring it into another. But if this is the correct interpretation, what are we to make of the remark, a few lines later, to

---

ter than the *Prima secundae,* about 12 percent of which is devoted to the analysis of human action.

18. See Kevin L. Flannery, "Ethical Force in Aristotle," *Vera Lex* 6 (2005): 147–62.

the effect that someone who throws goods overboard in a storm must be said, in the final analysis, to act voluntarily [*EN* iii.1, 1110a9–19]? Is this case not parallel to the case of the captain who brings his ship into an undesired port? Why, then, is this latter described as involuntary, the act of jettisoning goods as voluntary? What is the difference?

Or take another example that occurs in this same section of the *Ethics:* that of a person ordered by a tyrant to do something base, the tyrant all the while holding the person's family and threatening to do them harm. Aristotle says that a base act performed even in these dire circumstances is voluntary; and yet, in book five of the same work, he suggests that the act of striking another after an unjust provocation is non-culpable—and, therefore, apparently involuntary (see *EN* v.8, 1135b25–27). What is the ethical difference between the external pressure brought to bear by the tyrant and the internal pressure triggered by an unjust attack?

I have no intention of answering such questions here—even though doing so (I am convinced) would show Aristotle's theory to be consistent and compelling. My intention is simply to back up my statement that there is work yet to be done—even to understand a text that has been with us for some 2,400 years. Since Aristotle has such a sound and subtle understanding of human action, figuring out what these texts mean is useful—perhaps even essential—for developing an adequate philosophy of psychology.

And problems of interpretation are present not only in the study of Aristotle but also in the study of Aristotelians, such as Thomas Aquinas. Here one need only mention the *locus classicus* for the traditional doctrine of the principle of double effect (*Summa theologiae* II-II, q. 64, a. 7), where Thomas famously says, "Nothing prohibits one act's having two effects, of which only one is in the intention [*in intentionem*], the other beside the intention [*praeter intentionem*]. But moral acts receive their species according to that which is intended, not from that which is beside the intention." To use an example that not only exercised Anscombe but also is of urgent contemporary relevance, does this mean that a military commander's overall intention fixes the "species" of his act, that is, the sort of thing he does? But what if his overall intention is civil self-defense (or some such thing) but his achieving this involves the targeting and killing of innocents? If the commander's action can be called moral simply on the grounds of his overall intention, one would seem to be able to say the same of nearly all acts of terrorism, such as those performed by Hamas or al-Qaeda in the Middle East. Not to mention Hiroshima and Nagasaki.

The Aristotelian Analysis of Virtues

As I have said, my goal here is not to answer questions but simply to raise them. So let us move on to a final topic, which is Aristotle's analysis of the virtues. As anyone with the slightest acquaintance with the contemporary academic scene knows, "virtue ethics" has in recent years become an identifiable "school of thought," virtually on a par with more established schools such as utilitarianism, Kantianism, and anti-realism. The initial moving cause of virtue ethics is universally recognized to have been Anscombe's essay "Modern Moral Philosophy," although interest in virtue ethics was greatly augmented by Alasdair MacIntyre's book *After Virtue*.[19] But, despite her seminal association with virtue ethics, there is reason to believe that Anscombe would not feel entirely comfortable among its current-day practitioners.

The introduction to the volume entitled *Virtue Ethics* in the standard textbook-collection series, "Oxford Readings in Philosophy," con-

19. Roger Crisp and Michael Slote, while acknowledging Anscombe's original influence, suggest that the "the main lines of Anscombe's critique [of modern moral philosophy] were foreshadowed in Arthur Schopenhauer's *On the Basis of Morality* (1841)," Roger Crisp and Michael Slote, eds., *Virtue Ethics,* Oxford Readings in Philosophy (Oxford: Oxford University Press, 1997), 2.

tains the following sentence: "Another striking feature of virtue ethics is its focus on moral agents and their lives, rather than on discrete actions (telling a lie, having an abortion, giving to a beggar) construed in isolation from the notion of character, and the rules governing these actions."[20] This reticence with respect to the analysis of acts is certainly not "a striking feature" of Anscombe's work, who, as we have seen, says in "Modern Moral Philosophy" that that which united all the moralists she criticizes is precisely their refusal to say that "to kill the innocent as a means to any end whatsoever" is always immoral.[21] Although Anscombe's essay is included in the Oxford Readings volume, she would certainly have included many members of that school among the modern moral philosophers who have rendered talk of "the moral" incoherent.

For Anscombe, the place to start is not with virtues, which we do not understand, but with the philosophy of psychology—which we also do not understand but which is our only way to a sound understanding of the virtues. Here, doubtless, we also see the connection between the philosophy of psychology and psychology itself. If there is such a close connection between particular acts and the virtues, there must be close connection between acts and a person's psychology: his behavior and characteristic reactions.

Of course, it is very difficult to trace the beginnings of a person's psychology to particular actions—and it would certainly be wrong to presume that one could understand a person's psyche with anything near the precision with which one can understand a system of geometry, that is, by tracing theorems back to their principles. But neither can the psychologist ignore the fact that virtues (and vices) are born of concrete acts. It is not illegitimate to ask, for instance, how involvement in killing the innocent—even on the part of, by all appearances, perfectly nice people—has a bearing on family life or on any other

---

20. Crisp and Slote, 3.
21. Anscombe, "Modern Moral Philosophy," 33–34.

aspect of relational behavior. It is not illegitimate to ask, for instance, how a sexual act with a minor in his past might have a bearing upon the pastoral life of a possible future priest. But in order to understand such connections between virtues and vices and particular acts, we need also to understand which acts are genuinely intentional—and to what degree.

Conclusion

I would like to conclude with a fairly long—and typically complex—passage from "Modern Moral Philosophy" where Anscombe speaks to this very issue. That is to say, she talks in the passage about the relationship between acts and virtues (and also alludes to the study of Aristotle):

> In present-day philosophy an explanation is required how an unjust man is a bad man, or an unjust action a bad one; to give such an explanation belongs to ethics; but it cannot even be begun until we are equipped with a sound philosophy of psychology. For the proof that an unjust man is a bad man would require a positive account of justice as a "virtue." This part of the subject-matter of ethics is, however, completely closed to us until we have an account of what *type of characteristic* a virtue is—a problem, not of ethics, but of conceptual analysis—and how it relates to the actions in which it is instanced: a matter which I think Aristotle did not succeed in really making clear. For this we certainly need an account at least of what a human action is at all, and how its description as "doing such-and-such" is affected by its motive and by the intention or intentions in it; and for this an account of such concepts is required.[22]

Here we find, *in nuce,* the answer to the question posed in the title of this essay: Why does Elizabeth Anscombe say that we need today a philosophy of psychology? We need it, she says, in order to under-

22. Ibid., 29.

stand what it means to be a good and virtuous person. We need it in order to understand how bad acts affect a person "underneath"—that is, how they affect even good old plain-speaking people who may have been involved in mass murder. We need it to understand our culture, so wrapped up as it is in bringing about death. The philosophy of psychology (or philosophical psychology) is not the same thing as psychology. But it is an integral part of the same enterprise.

three

Benedict Ashley

HOW METAPHYSICS SERVES PSYCHOLOGY

What is "psychology" and what is "metaphysics"? Psychology and its practical application, psychotherapy, are very familiar terms today, although their precise meanings are often disputed. The ancient Greek saying "Know thyself" shows that humans have always been interested in themselves and others. Yet "psychology" is a word that first occurs in 1590 in the writings of a rather pedantic German Protestant philosopher, Rudolph Göeckel (Goclenius).[1] It did not become popular before 1719, when another even more pedantic German Protes-

1. Some sources attribute it to Luther's reformer Phillip Melancthon (1497–1560), who Protestantized the German universities, but it is not found in his published works. Others attribute the term to Otto Casmann (1562–1607), but he used it in print four years after Goclenius; see Marko Marulic (pseudonym for K. Krstic), "The Author of the Term 'Psychology,'" 1964 *Acta Instituti Psychologici Universitatis Zagrabiensis*, no. 36, 7–13, at http://psychclassics.yorku.ca/Krstic/marulic.htm.

tant philosopher, Baron Christian von Wolff (1679–1754), professor at the Universities of Marburg and Halle in Prussia, began publishing his immense textbook *Rational Ideas on the Power of Human Understanding.* It was so popular not only in German universities but throughout Europe that it became, as it were, the bible of the Enlightenment. The Enlightenment's greatest thinker was Immanuel Kant (1724–1804), who was educated in Wolff's philosophy and, although he came to criticize its dogmatism, never escaped from its idealistic rationalism.

Two volumes of Wolff's textbook were titled *Psychologia empirica* (1732) and *Psychologia rationalis* (1734). He had been a disciple of the great mathematician, scientist, and philosopher Gottfried Wilhelm Leibniz (1646–1716), who was a follower of René Descartes (1596–1650). Descartes had revived the ancient Platonic notion that the certitude of knowledge rests not on empirical evidence but on innate ideas. Like Descartes and Leibnitz, Wolff was a thorough rationalist and assumed that metaphysics, because it deals with innate first principles, is what is first known to us. Although he gave much more value to sense knowledge than they had done, he accepted Leibniz's view that *general* metaphysics, or *ontology* (again a term invented by Goclenius) is concerned not merely with what is actual but first of all with what is "possible." Hence he considered "rational psychology" as a branch of "special" metaphysics that applies "ontology" or general metaphysics to particular fields of knowledge. Thus he distinguished it from "empirical psychology" based on sense observation. This Wolffian distinction between metaphysical "philosophy" and empirical "science" was taken up by neo-scholastics and became common among Thomists even after Leo XIII's revival of Thomism, although in fact it is quite contrary to St. Thomas Aquinas's views. The danger of this terminology, which Wolff did not foresee, is that in our modern universities "philosophy" has become a marginalized department grouped with the "soft-headed humanities" over against the dominant "hard-headed" empirical sciences.

Little came of Wolff's notion of an empirical psychology for almost a century and half, until in 1879 the physician Wilhelm Wundt (1832–1920) set up the first laboratory of experimental psychology at the University of Leipzig. He had been a student of the noted physicist Hermann L. F. von Helmholtz (1856–1939), who had written a *Handbook of Physiological Optics* that inspired Wundt to study visual perception. Wundt wrote in his *Principles of Physiological Psychology* (1902):[2]

> Psychological inquiries have, up to the most recent times, been undertaken solely in the interest of philosophy; physiology was enabled, by the character of its problems, to advance more quickly towards the application of exact experimental methods. Since, however, the experimental modification of the processes of life, as practiced by physiology, oftentimes effects a concomitant change, direct or indirect, in the processes of consciousness—which, as we have seen, form part of vital processes at large—it is clear that physiology is, in the very nature of the case, qualified to assist psychology on the side of method; thus rendering the same help to psychology that it, itself received from physics. In so far as physiological psychology receives assistance from physiology in the elaboration of experimental methods, it may be termed experimental psychology.

In America Wundt's approach was quickly taken up by William James (1842–1910), who, however, always thought of himself as a philosopher rather than an experimental scientist. Having read Wundt, James in 1875 became the first professor of psychology at Harvard, where he set up the first psychological laboratory in America. Later he admitted, "The first lecture in psychology that I ever heard was the first I ever gave." In 1909 he met and was much impressed by Sigmund Freud, who had begun to use the term "psychoanalysis" in 1896. Wundt had adopted the model of "psychological parallelism" between bodily, physiological processes and conscious introspection. Freud, on the other hand, was a thorough materialist, yet he built and tested

2. Wilhelm Wundt, *Principles of Physiological Psychology,* trans. Edward Bradford Titchener (Sonnenschein, 1904), 2–3.

his theories, as Wundt had done, on the clinically observed subject's introspective experiences.

Influenced by the work of the Russian Ivan Pavlov (1849–1936) on conditioned reflex behavior in animals, the American John Watson (1878–1958) in 1912 reacted vigorously to Wundt's introspectionism as unscientific. He sought in research to replace introspection with *behaviorism*. This approach was then radicalized by B. F. Skinner (1904–90), who claimed that the human subject is a "black box" whose interior conscious experience, if it exists at all, is inaccessible to scientific research. Therefore, psychology must be content to study externally observable human behavior. Today with the development of a more moderate behaviorism by Aaron T. Beck and others, cognitive behaviorist therapy, proven to be the most effective of the many modes of psychotherapy, leads the field. Yet, as the many studies on current "models of personality" show, the scope and method of "psychology" remains very controversial. One author, George Boeree,[3] groups current theories into three "forces":

1. The *Psychoanalytic* that seeks explanation of human behavior in the unconscious.

2. The *Behavioristic* that seek explanations in external behavior in relation to the environment.

3. The *Humanistic* that seeks explanations in conscious experience.

Cognitive therapy combines features of all three views but is primarily behavioristic.

How then are we to define "psychology"? We need to go back behind Wolff's distinction between philosophy and science to the tradition he confused. The previous scholastic tradition was rooted in the thought of Aristotle, who wrote the first systematic, empirical works on animal and human behavior. For him "philosophy" included all critical and logically expressed knowledge. Thus it meant what today

---

3. http://www.ship.edu/cgboer/perscontents.html.

is meant by the term "science": (a) the empirical study of nature; but also (b) mathematics. Furthermore "philosophy" included (c) the ethics of individuals, families, and the state aimed at guiding human life toward happiness; and (d) the many and various arts or technologies that produce the instruments of a good life, such as medicine, agriculture, and architecture. Thus ethics and technology are practical sciences that apply the theoretical sciences, such as natural science and mathematics, whose goal is simply the contemplation of truth, which Aristotle argued was true happiness. Finally Aristotle developed logic as an art that produces consistent and verifiable thinking in both the theoretical and practical sciences.

This careful distinction between different types of autonomous sciences or philosophies impelled Aristotle to face the problem today called "interdisciplinarity," or how first to distinguish these various sciences clearly and then to relate and synthesize their valid results. Plato had tried to do this by reducing all truth to one science, but Aristotle was determined to defend the autonomy of different modes of knowing. Hence he tried to identify which one of the sciences just listed is the "first," not first as first known, but first as highest because it can synthesize the results already achieved by the other lower sciences. If there is such an interdisciplinary science it most properly and eminently can be called philosophy, the love of wisdom.

Aristotle's work, in which he struggled with this question but which he left unedited and untitled, some editor named the *Metaphysics*. Today this problem of interdisciplinarity has grown even more urgent in view of the "information explosion" that fragments our culture. In the *Metaphysics*, as he searches for a solution, Aristotle tests each of the sciences as a candidate for this task and seems to favor natural science, of which he was so fond. But he had to admit that, although natural science is basic to all our knowledge, its point of view and methodology, for reasons I will explain shortly, are too narrow to extend to all valid types of knowledge.

In the interdisciplinary scheme of knowledge that Aristotle finally adopted, the problems about human behavior that we now study in "psychology" were located first of all in natural science. Aristotle introduces this science in the *Physics* with a study of the general forces that produce change in our world and then proceeds in other works to treat the more specific topics we today study in physics, astronomy, chemistry, and biology. As a member of a family of doctors, Aristotle in his works gave most extensive attention to biology. The critical introduction to this biology is called *The Classification of Living Organisms* and is the *De anima* or *Study of the Soul,* which for Aristotle means *On the Behavior of Organisms* and deals primarily with organisms' conscious behavior. Thus before Wolff what we today call "psychology" was called *De anima* or the *Study of the Soul* and followed a behavioristic methodology.

Long before he got to *De anima* in his natural science, however, Aristotle ran into the difficulty that the scope of natural science is necessarily too limited to serve as the synthesizing first philosophy he was seeking. Already in his *Physics* VIII he asked, "What are the prime movers or fundamental forces of nature?" Modern physics since Newton also reduces all causal explanation to the fundamental forces of gravity, electromagnetism (or the electroweak force), and the strong force that glues the nuclei of atoms together. These are nature's prime movers, to which current science limits its explanations, but are they really prime?

Aristotle hypothesized that the fundamental or prime forces moving material bodies are gravity, heat, cold, and dryness, but he was right only as to gravity. Nevertheless he was able to demonstrate simply from the fact that material things change that any material prime mover such as gravity must itself be activated by some unchanging or spiritual cause and ultimately by one supreme spiritual Uncaused Cause. It was this conclusion based empirically on the most general principles of natural science that convinced him that the supreme interdisciplinary science could not be natural science. Instead this first science that treats of spiritual as well as material causes, causes must be a "divine science," a "theology," based not on revelation, however, but on what reason can learn from what the senses can observe about the features analogically common to both material and immaterial substances. Hence the validity of metaphysics depends on the natural scientific proof of the existence of such immaterial first causes. The further exploration of the positive nature of these ultimate causes, once natural science has proved their existence, lies outside the scope of natural science and belongs to metaphysics.

Yet Aristotle also found that at two of the more specific levels of the development of natural science, the existence of spiritual agents, at the general level, again emerges. At the first more specific level, Aristotle met in his astronomy, the *De caelo,* the problem once more prominent in current cosmology: the debates over the Big Bang or the Big Crunch and whether a "Unified Theory of Everything" is possible.

At the second still more specific level, that of biology, Aristotle in the *De anima* encountered what today is called the Mind-Body Problem. St. Thomas Aquinas was to carry out this inquiry much further than Aristotle did, but along the same lines. They first researched an animal psychology because it is apparent from the behavior of animals that they differ from plants in that they can make appropriate behavioral responses to their environment and the condition of their bodies that implies they are conscious of these stimuli. But what animal has written a book, a scientific book on animal psychology? Why then do humans in certain respects act so differently than other animals?

The difference is that human animals can think abstractly. Yet Aristotle, himself, stopped short in natural science of saying anything more specific about human consciousness. It was Aristotle's best pupil, St. Thomas Aquinas, who, taking courage from what Gospel revelation tells us about God's work, took up that difficult task of dealing with the metaphysical or spiritual level of human self-consciousness. Therefore—and this is my essential point here—"psychology" has two levels, animal and human, and thence is really a double discipline.

Wolff was right about that, although wrong about the relation between these two levels.

First, psychology is the department of natural science that deals with animal behavior. Second, psychology as it is a study of specifically human consciousness and free choice has to pertain to metaphysics because intelligent thought and free decision are spiritual behaviors that transcend the forces of material nature. Yet psychology has a genuine unity because our human intelligence to think in a natural way requires the service of the material body that it animates.

Now, to show how this distinction can prove important for research in psychology today, let us consider how St. Thomas Aquinas set up this double discipline. He based his research on Aristotle's findings that were based on an extensive study of human behavior in the intense political life of the Greek city-states. Aquinas also took into account the long Christian tradition of pastoral experience and examination of conscience, such as found in St. Augustine's *Confessions,* historically the first autobiography of interior life. Aquinas's methodology in this psychological research, although not experimental or served by mathematical measurement or modern instruments of observation, is strictly behavioristic. His methodological principle was "a thing is as it acts." Hence our analysis of human nature must be built up by analyzing human behavior.

First of all, it must deal with the bodily functions of nutrition, growth, and reproduction, which are common to all organisms and whose limits condition all of human behavior. Second, it must study the animal functions of sensation and the affective drives by which animals respond to external stimuli and to the conditions of their own bodies. Wundt's work was mainly with this animal psychology. It is odd that although today we have learned much about the sense organs and the brain of which Aquinas was ignorant, yet current psychology remains very vague in its definitions and distinctions of such terms as "consciousness," "feelings," and "fantasy."

Traditionally the "external" senses are distinguished from the "internal" senses, but this is confusing, since the so-called external sense of touch also informs an animal about the state of its body, including that of its internal organs. Therefore, I prefer to use the terms "primary" and "secondary" senses. Aquinas first treats of the five primary senses, of which touch is the most fundamental and existential, while sight and hearing obtain the most information. Then he points out how that animal behavior shows that most animals, including human persons, since they are also animals, together with the five primary senses, have also four secondary senses that provide not only sensations but perceptions. The first of these secondary senses is the *synthetic* sense *(sensus communis)* that puts together in a composite image all the data the five primary senses provide. For example your perception of a rose is not just a red blob but synthesizes its color, texture, and odor, as is evident from your behavior when you see it and promptly try to smell it. Not much research has been done on this synthetic sense, except as regards "synesthesia," a pathology that causes the victim to confuse sounds and colors.

On the other hand, the second interior sense, *memory* and *recall* and its pathology, "amnesia," is much studied in Freudian psychoanalysis. What specifies an image as remembered is that it contains a chronological reference. What I remember is not merely a rose but when and where I saw this particular rose.

The third secondary sense is "imagination," a name too often used today confusedly to apply to all four secondary senses. What specifies it is that it first separates an image or images supplied by the two senses just mentioned from their chronological order and sometimes from their synthetic correlations and thus creates a generalized image. This we can then cut up or combine with other images by "imagining," "fantasizing," or thinking "creatively." Thus I imagine a blue rose with two hundred petals and golden thorns even though I have never seen such a rose, nor probably ever will. All practical thinking depends on the imagination, since before I do or make anything I have to imagine doing or making it as well as imagine the final outcome of my behavior. "Creativity" has been much researched, but the imaginations of geniuses such as Da Vinci or Edison remain mysterious.

Most remarkable of all is the fourth secondary sense, which Aquinas called the *vis cogitativa,* or "thinking power," or in animals the *vis aestimativa,* or "estimative power," also called the "discursive sense," "animal intelligence," or "instinct." I prefer to call it the *evaluative sense.* We know it exists because animals respond to stimuli from the primary senses in a way appropriate to their basic physical functions. For example, we animals scratch our skin when it is irritated. In higher animals, moreover, learning can further specify these set instincts. A dog barks at strangers, but runs to meet its master. Because human instincts are so general we can learn more than other animals; compare a trained dog's tricks with the skills of an athlete or a pianist. Modern psychology and psychotherapy are especially interested in "feelings," "emotions," and we talk much about "values." Besides the cognitive senses that direct behavior, Aquinas also recognizes the *affective* powers of animals that respond to the positive or negative images presented by the evaluative sense. In modern terminology the notion of internal "feelings" is very ambiguous, since "feeling" also means a primary sense, "touch." Aquinas more precisely uses instead the term "passion" and means not a conscious sensation as such but an "affect," that is, a change in the body in reaction to some image in the evaluative sense that stimulates a bodily process. For example, when you are studying, some odor of food may reach your primary sense of smell and then arouse an image in your secondary senses. Although you are not yet conscious, or at least attentively conscious, to this odor-image, it stimulates your hunger drive, and your stomach begins to churn even before you notice it. This affect below the level of consciousness is what Freud rediscovered and called the "Unconscious" or "Id."

Most of the informational images in our secondary senses are neither pleasurable or painful, nor attractive or repulsive. But when the cogitative evaluative sense perceives a stimulus as positive or negative in relation to animal needs, it causes a change in the physiology of our bodies, of which, at least at first, we may be quite unconscious. It is the evaluative sense that determines whether this passion is positive or negative. Thus the evaluative sense is at the center of every animal or human response to its environment or bodily states. Little research, however, has been devoted today to understanding this process.

Human beings for Aquinas are animals. But they are animals that unlike other animals are *persons* because the human vitality or soul is capable of abstract cognition and free affectivity, which involves more than animal consciousness. The behavioral evidence for this is overwhelming. The extensive experiments that have been made in recent years to teach chimpanzees to talk have made clear that they can't. They can, indeed, signal, as birds chirp to their young or sing to attract their mate, and they can express feelings of pain or pleasure, but these signals are not true language. Semioticians have shown that animal signals do not include such signs as "and," "is," and "therefore," which are found in all human languages and quite early in the language of young children.[4] These are syntactic signs that do not signify imaginable realities but purely mental, logical relations. Hence although the higher animals can learn remarkable tricks, sometimes by imitation or by serendipity (by accident), these behaviors are utterly disproportionate to the varieties of cultures, languages, and technologies exhibited by the human species.

Rather than enlarge on this point, let me just mention one example of how Aquinas's view that human intelligence transcends the physical has not been refuted but has been supported by modern research. In the last century the mathematician Kurt Gödel dem-

---

4. See Thomas A. Sebeok and Robert Rosenthal, *The Clever Hans Phenomenon: Communication with Horses, Whales, Apes, and People* (New York: New York Academy of Sciences, 1981). According to John Deely, *Four Ages of Understanding: The First Postmodern Survey of Philosophy from Ancient Times to the Turn of the Twentieth Century* (Toronto: University of Toronto, 2001), 736–37, the human person is "the semiotic animal" since only humans properly use signs.

onstrated that no formal logical system based on a finite number of axioms can prove itself either self-consistent or complete. Computers, so often cited to show that some day we will have artificial intelligence, operate on programs that are analogous to a formal logical system. Yet because, as Gödel proved, this means that no computer can ever have a program able to solve every problem that in the terms of its program human intelligence can invent. We will always be able to propose a new problem in the same terms, but may have to invent a new program to solve it. This means that while our brain is the organic seat of the secondary senses, we do not think abstractly, that is, intelligently merely with our brains, although we have to use our brains to think intelligently, as we have to use instruments to write our thoughts or computers to do elaborate computations.

Aquinas was no dualist like Descartes, who held that we have innate ideas. Aquinas was very aware that human consciousness is first of all basically the same as that of animals, but also maintained that it transcends animal consciousness, which it uses instrumentally. Subhuman animals are conscious, but not self-conscious. A dog can look in a mirror, see something on its skin, and then scratch it off. This behavior looks self-conscious and even borders on it, but can be well enough explained as only a learned reaction based on the evaluative sense. True self-consciousness can be certainly evidenced only by persons who have a true language and can say, "I am thinking and what I am thinking about is the difference between you and a dog." It takes a metaphysical analysis of the difference between matter and spirit and the relations between them, however, to understand adequately the differences between these two ways of behaving.

This brings us finally to psychotherapy, whose principal form is the "talking cure," in which the therapist and the client have long sessions in which the client reveals her or his fantasies and feelings to a therapist, who responds empathetically. What is the goal of psychotherapy? Obviously it is mental health, just as the aim of medicine is physical health. Too often, however, this goal today is defined as "adjustment," that is, enabling the person to stay alive without too much mental pain. Instead I believe, on the basis of Aquinas's behavioristic analysis that I have sketched, the aim of psychotherapy should be to enable clients to transcend their defective evaluation of their life experiences, so that they are able to make free decisions no longer on fantasies and feelings but on reality. The empirically verified superior effectiveness of cognitive therapy compared to other forms of therapy, I believe, confirms this analysis. Yet the psychotherapist is not an ethical or spiritual counselor, because that moves into the metaphysical realm. Of course, sometimes a therapist touches on these spiritual aspects of the client's life, just as the psychotherapist sometimes touches on medical problems, but generally such matters should be referred to specialists.

four

Roger Scruton

CONFRONTING BIOLOGY

We human beings are animals, governed by the laws of biology. Our life and death are biological processes, of a kind that we witness in other animals too. We have biological needs, and are influenced and constrained by genes with their own reproductive imperative. And this genetic imperative manifests itself in our emotional life, in ways that remind us of the body and its power over us.

For centuries poets and philosophers have told stories about erotic love—Plato leading the way. These stories have endowed the object of love with a value, a mystery, and a metaphysical distinction that seem to place it outside the natural order. And in these stories biology seems hardly to figure, even though they are stories that would make

I am very grateful to Dan Dennett, Anthony O'Hear, Craig Titus, Paul Vitz, and David Wiggins for comments on an earlier version.

little sense were it not for our condition as reproductive animals, who have established their niche by sexual selection.

We are territorial creatures, just like chimpanzees, wolves, and tigers. We claim our territory and fight for it, and our genes, which require just such an exclusive claim over habitat if their replication is to be guaranteed, depend upon our success. Yet when we fight it is, as a rule, in the name of some high ideal: justice, liberation, national sovereignty, even God Himself. Once again, it seems that we are in the habit of telling ourselves stories, which make no reference to the biological realities in which they are rooted.

The most noble of human attributes also have their biological underpinning—or so it seems at least. The self-sacrifice that causes a woman to lay everything aside for her children; the courage that enables a human being to endure the greatest hardships and dangers for the sake of something that he values; even those virtues, like temperance, that seem to require us to vanquish our own desires—all these things have seemed to many people to have their counterparts among the lower animals, and to demand a single explanation, generalizable across species. Personal affection has been brought within the fold of biology, first by Freud's highly metaphorical and now largely discredited theory of the libido, more recently by the attachment theory of John Bowlby, for whom love, loss, and mourning are to be explained, at least in part, as phylogenetic products of our need for a "secure base."[1] Bowlby was a psychiatrist, acutely aware that human beings do not merely inherit their emotional capacities but also adapt and refine them. Nevertheless, he described love, grief, and mourning as biological processes, and argued that "the child's tie to his mother is the human version of behaviour seen commonly in many other species of animal."[2] By putting that behavior in its ethological context he was able to give a far more plausible account of our primary attachments

1. John Bowlby, *Attachment and Loss*, vols. 1–3 (New York: Basic Books, 1969–80); *A Secure Base* (New York: Routledge, 1988).

2. Bowlby, *Attachment*, 1:183.

than those given by Freud and his immediate successors. Our personal affections, he argued, are to be explained in terms of the function that they perform in our "environment of evolutionary adaptedness," and the explanation will not be couched in terms that make any radical ontological division between us and the lower animals. The discovery of the hormone oxytocin, and its effect in predisposing animals of many different species toward affectionate relations with their kind, has further encouraged the view that attachment can be understood and explained without reference to the stories with which we humans embellish it.

When Darwin and Wallace first hit on the idea of natural selection the question arose whether our many "higher" characteristics, such as morality, self-consciousness, symbolism, art, and the interpersonal emotions, create such a gap between us and the "lower" animals as to demand explanation of another kind. Wallace at first thought that they did not, but later changed his mind, coming to the conclusion that there is a qualitative leap in the order of things, setting the higher faculties of human kind in a different category from those features that we share with our evolutionary neighbors. As he put it: "we are endowed with intellectual and moral powers superfluous to evolutionary requirements,"[3] and the existence of these powers could therefore not be explained by natural selection for fitness.

Darwin, however, remained attached to the view that *natura non fecit saltus,* and in writing *The Descent of Man* tried to show that the differences between humans and other animals, great though they are, can nevertheless be reconciled with the theory of step-wise development.[4] For Darwin the moral sense is continuous with the social instincts of other species.[5] Through the theory of sexual selection, he gave an enhanced account of the resources on which natural selection

---

3. A. R. Wallace, *Natural Selection and Tropical Nature: Essays on Descriptive and Theoretical Biology* (London: Macmillan, 1891). See also *Darwinism* (1889), ch. 15.

4. Charles Darwin, *The Descent of Man*, vol. 1 (New York: Appleton, 1871).

5. Ibid., 71–72.

can draw, and made the suggestion, taken up in our own time by Steven Pinker and Geoffrey Miller, that many of the "higher" faculties of man, such as art and music, which seem, on the face of it, to be devoid of any evolutionary function, should be seen as resulting from selection at the sexual level.[6] Darwin went on to give an account of human emotions, in which their expression in the face and gestures is compared with the expression of emotion in other animals: and his purpose in all this was to suggest that the perceived gap between us and our evolutionary cousins is no proof of a separate origin.[7]

This controversy has taken on an entirely different character since R. A. Fisher's pioneering work in population genetics.[8] Problems with which Darwin wrestled throughout his life—the sexual selection of dysfunctional features (the problem of the peacock's tail), for example, or the "altruism" of insects (the problem of the ant-heap)—are radically transformed when the locus of evolution is seen as the self-replicating gene, rather than the sexually reproducing animal.[9] And, as John Maynard Smith and G. R. Price showed in an elegant paper,[10] the new way of looking at natural selection, as governed by the replicating "strategies" of genes, permits the application of game theory to genetic competition, which in turn delivers a neat solution to another famous problem—that of aggression, noticed by Darwin and spelled out in detail by Lorenz.[11] The rut among stags can be derived as an "evolutionarily stable strategy": one that enables the genes of rutting

6. Steven Pinker, *How the Mind Works* (London: Allen Lane, 1997), 522–24. Geoffrey Miller, *The Mating Mind: How Sexual Choice Shaped the Evolution of Human Nature* (New York: Doubleday, 2000).

7. *The Expression of Emotion in Man and Animals* (New York: Appleton, 1898).

8. R. A. Fisher, *The Genetical Theory of Natural Selection* (1930), rev. ed. (New York: Dover, 1958).

9. See the lively account by Helen Cronin, *The Ant and the Peacock: Altruism and Sexual Selection, from Darwin to Today* (Cambridge: Cambridge University Press, 1991).

10. J. Maynard Smith and G. R. Price, "The Logic of Animal Conflict," *Nature* 246 (1973): 15–18.

11. Konrad Lorenz, *On Aggression*, trans. Marjorie Kerr Wilson (New York: Harcourt Brace, 1966).

stags to reproduce themselves, while providing the genes of hinds with the best return for their reproductive investment. This approach, generalized by R. Axelrod,[12] has had profound consequences, for example in showing that there might be an evolutionary advantage in reciprocally altruistic cooperation, even when not part of kin selection (as when female bats share their booty of blood with other unsuccessful females in a colony). It has also suggested a general theory of "altruism," alleged by its supporters to explain not only the inflexible self-sacrifice of the soldier ant, but also the fear-filled and heroic self-sacrifice of the human soldier.[13] In short, we seem to have been brought a step nearer the proof of Darwin's contention that the moral sense is continuous with the social instincts of other species.

The genetic approach has not been without its critics. Advocates of "group selection" have argued that selection must occur at higher levels than that of the gene if we are to account for such socially complex behavior as the self-limitation of populations and the dispersal patterns of herds.[14] To this it has been in turn objected that until we can trace apparent selection to the genetic level we have given no real account of how it works.[15] For a long time, indeed, the idea of group selection was dismissed as a hangover from the old theory that it is the species, rather than the gene, that is the unit of biological development.[16] However, the arguments for group selection from female sex-

12. *The Evolution of Cooperation* (New York: Basic Books, 1984).

13. See, for example, Matt Ridley, *The Origins of Virtue: Human Instincts and the Evolution of Cooperation* (London: Viking, 1991). It is important to recognize that the game-theoretic approach to altruism is distinct from the theory of "inclusive fitness," defended by W. D. Hamilton, "The Genetical Theory of Social Behavior," *Journal of Theoretical Biology* 7 (1964): 1–52, according to which altruism extends to kin, and in proportion to the degree of kinship.

14. V. C. Wynne-Edwards, *Animal Dispersion in Relation to Social Behaviour* (Edinburgh: Oliver and Boyd, 1962). The original inspiration here is Konrad Lorenz, *On Aggression.* Wynne-Edwards is somewhat cantankerously criticized by Richard Dawkins in *The Selfish Gene,* 7–10.

15. See Cronin, *The Ant and the Peacock,* 287–90.

16. See, for example, G. C. Williams, *Adaptation and Natural Selection: A Critique of Some Current Evolutionary Thought* (Princeton, N.J.: Princeton University Press, 1966).

ratios and avirulence are now well-established, and Elliott Sober and David Sloan Wilson have effectively reconciled genetics and group selection, by showing that the group can function just as well as the individual organism as a replicative vehicle in the service of a gene.[17]

Others have been skeptical of the assumption that there can be small-scale transitions that lead by a chain of changes from the social behavior of animals to the social behavior of people. In particular, Chomsky has argued that the acquisition of language is an all-or-nothing affair, which involves acquiring a rule-guided and creative capacity that cannot be built up from singular connections between words and things.[18] A Chomskian would be dismissive of those attempts to inflict language on animals—on chimpanzees and dolphins, for example—that were once greeted with such enthusiasm, as the proof that they are like us, or we like them.[19] Whatever the interest of the word-thing/word-experience connections that animals can make, these are connections of a radically different kind from those embedded in a transformational grammar. They are piecemeal associations that, detached from generative rules and semantic organization, remain no more vehicles of thought, dialogue, and interrogation than the warning cries of birds and bonobos, or the wagging tails of dogs. Again, the objection is not widely regarded as conclusive, and geneticists have advanced theories of "proto-language" that attempt to show both that there could be piecemeal advances toward linguistic competence and that these advances would be selected at the genetic level.[20]

17. Elliott Sober and David Sloan Wilson, *Unto Others: The Evolution and Psychology of Unselfish Behaviour* (Cambridge, Mass.: Harvard University Press, 1998).

18. See especially *Language and Mind* (New York: Harcourt, Brace, and World, 1968), 62, in which language is described as "an example of true emergence—the appearance of a qualitatively different phenomenon at a specific stage of complexity of organization."

19. For the attempts see Eugene Linden, *Apes, Men and Language* (New York: Saturday Review Press, 1974); for the enthusiasm, see Mary Midgley, *Beast and Man* (London: Routledge, 1979), 215–51.

20. See, for example, John Maynard Smith and Eörs Szathmáry, *The Major Transitions in Evolution* (Oxford: W. H. Freeman, 1995), 303–8.

Debates in this area have become complicated by the attempt to connect the social sciences—whose theme is culture—with the biological theory of our social instincts—whose theme is genes. That human beings have cultures is an adaptive trait, even if it is one that leads, in certain circumstances, to maladaptation.[21] And cultural traditions exert their own selective pressures on human gene pools.[22] It has even been argued that animals have evolved a capacity for social learning comparable to that which we study under the rubric of culture.[23] But the question how to integrate cultural evolution into the story told by genetics is a subject of extended, and sometimes fierce, controversy among biologists. To a great extent the study of "evolutionary psychology" has emerged in answer to that question. The hope is to give an account of the human brain and its functions that will reconcile what we know about our social and mental capacities with the hypothesis of natural selection among self-replicating genes.

But what exactly do we know about our capacities, and how does that knowledge make contact with the results of modern biology? We know that the human species has adapted to its environment; but we also know that it has adapted its environment to itself. It has passed adaptations to its offspring not only genetically but also culturally. It has shaped its world through information, language, and rational exchange. And while all those features can be acknowledged by biology and given a place in evolutionary theory,[24] that theory will, in the first instance, concern not the replication of genes, but the reproduction of societies. Moreover, human societies are not just groups of coop-

21. See the argument of Peter J. Richerson and Robert Boyd, *Not by Genes Alone: How Culture Transformed Human Evolution* (Chicago: University of Chicago Press, 2005), chs. 4 and 5.

22. Ibid., ch. 6.

23. See Eytan Avital and Eva Jablonka, *Animal Tradition: Behavioural Inheritance in Evolution* (Cambridge: Cambridge University Press, 2000).

24. As exemplified, for instance, by Kim Sterelny, in his theory of cumulative niche construction. See his *Thought in a Hostile World: The Evolution of Human Cognition* (Oxford: Blackwell, 2003).

erating primates: they are communities of persons, who live in mutual judgment, organizing their world in terms of moral concepts that arguably have no place in the thoughts of chimpanzees. It is possible that cognitive science will one day incorporate these moral concepts into a theory of the brain and its functions, and that theory will be a biological theory. But its truth will be tested against the distinctively human capacities that, according to Wallace, seem "superfluous to evolutionary requirements," and not against the features of our biological makeup that we share with other animals.

Now, any philosopher who argues in that way finds himself confronting a powerful current of opinion, which has flowed through all the channels of intellectual life since the publication of Richard Dawkins's *The Selfish Gene*.[25] Natural selection can account for all the difficult facts presented by human culture, Dawkins suggests, once we see culture as developing according to the same principles as the individual organism. Just as the human organism is "a survival machine" developed by self-replicating genes, so is a culture a machine developed by self-replicating "memes"—mental entities that use the energies of human brains to multiply, in the way that viruses use the energies of cells. Like genes, memes need *Lebensraum,* and their success depends upon finding the ecological niche that enables them to generate more examples of their kind. That niche is the human brain.[26]

A meme is a self-replicating cultural entity that, lodging in the brain of a human being, uses that brain to reproduce itself—in the way that a catchy tune reproduces itself in hums and whistles, so spreading like an epidemic through a human community, as did *"La donna è*

25. Richard Dawkins, *The Selfish Gene* (New York: Oxford University Press, 1976, rev. ed. 1989).

26. For various attempts to give a memetic theory of culture, see Robert Aunger, ed., *Darwinizing Culture: The Status of Memetics as a Science* (Cambridge: Cambridge University Press, 2000). The theory of the meme is dismissively criticized by David Stove in "Genetic Calvinisim, or Demons and Dawkins," in *Darwinian Fairytales: Selfish Genes, Errors of Heredity, and Other Fables of Evolution* (New York: Encounter Books, 2006).

mobile" the morning after the first performance of *Rigoletto*. Dawkins argues that ideas, beliefs, and attitudes are the conscious forms taken by self-replicating entities, which propagate themselves as diseases propagate themselves, by using the energies of their hosts: "Just as genes propagate themselves in the gene pool by leaping from body to body via sperm or eggs, so memes propagate themselves in the meme pool by leaping from brain to brain by a process which, in the broad sense of the term, can be called imitation." Dennett adds that this process is not necessarily harmful: there are, among parasitical organisms, both symbionts, which coexist harmlessly with their hosts, and mutualists, which positively amplify the host's ability to survive and flourish in its environment.[27]

To make the theory remotely plausible, Dawkins has to distinguish memes that belong to science from memes that are merely "cultural." Scientific memes are subject to effective policing by the brain that harbors them, which accepts ideas and theories only as part of its own truth-directed method. Merely cultural memes are outside the purview of scientific inference and can run riot, causing all kinds of cognitive and emotional disorders. They are subject to no external discipline, such as that contained in the concept of truth, but follow their own reproductive path, indifferent to the aims of the organism that they have invaded.

That idea is appealing at the level of metaphor, but what does it amount to in fact? From the point of view of memetics, absurd ideas have the same start in life as true theories, and assent is a retrospective honor bestowed on reproductive success. The only significant distinction to be made, when accounting for this success, is between memes that enhance the life of their hosts and memes that either destroy that life or co-exist symbiotically with it. It is one of the distinguishing characteristics of human beings, however, that they can distinguish an idea from the reality represented in it, can entertain

27. Daniel C. Dennett, *Breaking the Spell* (London: Allen Lane, 2006).

propositions from which they withhold their assent, and can move judge-like in the realm of ideas, calling each before the bar of rational argument, accepting them and rejecting them regardless of the reproductive cost. And it is not only in science that this attitude of critical reflection is maintained. Matthew Arnold famously described culture as "a pursuit of our total perfection by means of getting to know, on all matters which most concern us, the best which has been thought and said in the world, and, through this knowledge, turning a stream of fresh and free thought upon our stock notions and habits" (*Culture and Anarchy*, 1869). Like so many people wedded to the nineteenth-century view of science, Dawkins overlooks the nineteenth-century reaction—which said, "Wait a minute: science is not the only way to pursue knowledge. There is moral knowledge too, which is the province of practical reason; there is emotional knowledge, which is the province of art, literature, and music. And just possibly there is transcendental knowledge, which is the province of religion. Why privilege science, just because it sets out to *explain* the world? Why not give weight to the disciplines that *interpret* the world, and so help us to be at home in it?"

That reaction has lost none of its appeal. And it points to a fundamental weakness in "memetics." Even if there are units of memetic information, propagated from brain to brain by some replicating process, it is not they that come before the mind in conscious thinking. Memes stand to ideas as genes stand to organisms: if they exist at all (and no evidence has been given by Dawkins or anyone else for thinking that they do) then their sempiternal and purposeless reproduction is no concern of ours. Ideas, by contrast, form part of the conscious network of critical thinking. We assess them for their truth, their validity, their moral propriety, their elegance, completeness, and charm. We take them up and discard them, sometimes in the course of our search for truth and explanation, sometimes in our search for meaning and value. And both activities are essential to us. Although culture isn't science, it is nevertheless a conscious activity of the critical mind.

Culture—both the high culture of art and music and the wider culture embodied in a moral and religious tradition—sorts ideas by their intrinsic qualities, helps us to feel at home in the world and to resonate to its personal significance. The theory of the meme neither denies that truth nor undermines the nineteenth-century view that culture, understood in that way, is as much an activity of the rational mind as science.

The concept of the meme belongs with other subversive concepts—Marx's "ideology," Freud's unconscious, Foucault's "discourse"—in being aimed at discrediting common prejudice. It seeks to expose illusions, and to explain away our dreams. But it is itself a dream: a piece of ideology, accepted not for its truth but for the illusory power that it confers on the one who conjures with it. It has produced some striking arguments—not least those given by Dan Dennett in *Breaking the Spell*. But it possesses the very fault for which it purports to be a remedy: it is a spell, with which the scientistic mind seeks to conjure away the things that pose a threat to it.

In this connection Marx made a celebrated distinction between science and ideology.[28] An ideological belief, according to Marx, is explained by its social function: it exists *because* it benefits the social order in which it propagates; a scientific belief is explained by the evidence adduced in its favor, regardless of any benefit that might come from endorsing it. Ideology is a power-directed, science a truth-directed, device. That argument, which makes a crude but necessary distinction, does not translate into the theory of genetics, and does not treat ideas merely as self-replicating devices, with a strategic agenda of their own. It is we, rational beings, who are the engine of their expansion, and it is we who hold them up to the light and find them wanting.

Reflecting on this, it seems clear to me that Wallace had a point in the emphasis that he put on the features that seem to place humanity in a world apart, though he was surely wrong to think of those features as "surplus to evolutionary requirements," for if any of our attri-

28. For example, in *The German Ideology*, 1845, co-authored with Friedrich Engels.

butes is adaptive, rationality surely is. But then, rationality is, in one sense of that difficult expression, "of our essence." Wallace was therefore pointing to the fact that we human beings, even if we are animals, belong to a kind that does not occupy a place in the scheme of things comparable to the kinds under which we group the other animals. And it seems to me that the *philosophical* controversy here—a controversy adjacent to that among biologists and evolutionary psychologists concerning the significance of culture—is precisely a controversy about human nature: to what kind do we belong?

Dawkins sets out to explain goals and rational choices in terms of genetic materials that make no choices. He describes these materials as "selfish" entities, motivated by a reproductive "goal," but (at least in his less rhetorical moments) he recognizes that genes are not, and cannot be, selfish, since selfishness is a feature of people, to be characterized in terms of their dispositions and their rational projects.[29] In a cogent biological theory all such teleological idioms must be replaced with functional explanations.[30] And that is what the recourse to game theory and similar devices is supposed to authorize. A player wants to win and therefore adopts a winning strategy: that is a teleological explanation of his behavior. Natural selection tells us that winning strategies will be selected, even when they describe the behavior of genes that want nothing at all. That is a functional explanation, which says nothing about intentions, choices, or goals.

Functional explanations have a central place in biology.[31] The fact

29. Though David Stove takes Dawkins to task for his constant reference to "selfishness," and his failure to say what it could possibly mean in this context: see "Genetic Calvinism."

30. How teleological thinking can be replaced by functional explanation is one theme of Dawkins's subsequent book, *The Blind Watchmaker* (London: Longman, 1986). For an illuminating discussion of functional explanations, and their application outside biology, see G. A. Cohen, *Karl Marx's Theory of History: A Defence* (Princeton, N.J.: Princeton University Press, 1978).

31. See Ron Amundson and George V. Lauder, "Function without Purpose: The Use of Causal Role Function in Evolutionary Biology," in D. Hull and M. Ruse, *The Philosophy of Biology*, Oxford Readings in Philosophy (Oxford: Oxford University Press, 1998).

that birds have wings is explained by the function of wings, in enabling birds to fly. The process of random mutation at a certain point produces a winged creature: and in the competition for scarce resources, this creature has the decisive advantage over its rivals. Note, however, that this reference to function amounts to a causal explanation only because supplemented by the theory of random mutation—a theory that tells us *how* the existence of a trait is caused by its function. This point bears heavily on the "explanations" of altruism and morality advanced by Axelrod and Maynard Smith. A population genetically averse to cooperation, to parental affection, to self-sacrifice on behalf of children, to sexual restraint, and to the control of violence is a population endowed with traits that are dysfunctional relative to reproduction. Hence it will disappear. From this trivial truth, however, we can deduce nothing about the causes of moral conduct or moral thought, and nothing about their grounds. It does not follow that morality is the result of natural selection, rather than group selection within the species; nor does it follow that morality originates in our biological makeup rather than in the workings of rational thought. In fact nothing follows that would serve either to bypass or to undermine the work of philosophy in exploring the foundations of moral judgment and its place in the life of a rational being. It is a trivial truth that dysfunctional attributes disappear; it is a substantial theoretical claim that functional attributes exist *because of* their function.[32] And until the theory is produced, the claim is without intellectual weight.

You may think that genetics provides the needed theory: for it implies that altruism is the evolutionarily stable solution to genetic competition within our species. But that explanation gives only a *sufficient* condition for "altruism," and only by redescribing altruism in terms that bypass the higher realms of moral thought. If Kant is right about

32. A similar objection can be mounted, it seems to me, against the defense of Marx's theory of history presented by G. A. Cohen, *Karl Marx's Theory.* That dysfunctional institutions disappear is no ground for thinking that the existence of an institution is caused by its function.

the categorical imperative, then there is an independent sufficient condition, namely rationality. Moreover, practical reason explains not only altruism, in the minimalist description favored by geneticists, but also the superstructure of moral thought and emotion. It also suggests a theory of *the kind to which we belong,* and it is a theory at odds with that suggested by the game-theoretic account of genetic self-sacrifice. According to Kant, the kind to which we belong is that of *person,* and persons are by nature free, self-conscious, rational agents, obedient to reason and bound by the moral law. According to the theory of the selfish gene, the kind to which we belong is that of *human animal,* and humans are by nature complicated byproducts of their DNA. Kant's theory allows that non-human beings may nevertheless belong to the same kind as us: angels, for instance, maybe dolphins too. The selfish gene theory would dismiss the suggestion as nonsense.

Despite such difficulties, the idea that genetics can somehow replace the old studies which had human kind as their subject-matter is becoming an intellectual commonplace. In the hands of their popularizers, the biological sciences are used to reduce the human condition to some simpler archetype, on the assumption that what we are is what once we were and that the truth about man is contained in his genealogy. Here is an instance, from the critic John Carey, drawing on the applied ethology of Ellen Dissanayake:

> The violence and sensationalism that critics of popular art deplore can . . . be seen as answering biological imperatives programmed into us by evolution. A need for novelty and excitement, and the evasion of monotony, are basic human attributes, and are also observable in non-human primates, particularly when young. We seek intense emotions, because the purpose of emotion, in evolutionary terms, is to give focus and direction to our activities. Cognition is, so to speak, free-wheeling, until emotion (anger, fear, desire) selects something for it to home in on.[33]

33. John Carey, *What Good Are the Arts?* (London: Faber and Faber, 2005), 36, drawing on Ellen Dissanayake, *What Is Art For?* (Seattle: University of Washington Press, 1988).

That passage illustrates the place to which this premature generalization of evolutionary biology may lead us—namely, to the conclusion that we cannot judge the tastes, appetites, or values of our fellow human beings. Notice, however, the way in which *explicandum* is read back into *explicans:* the violence and sensationalism of popular art are "seen as answering" to certain biological "imperatives." *Autrement dit,* we are drawn to violence in art because we have a (biologically implanted) disposition to be drawn to violence. Moreover, Carey makes no attempt to replace teleological with functional explanations. According to him we "seek" emotions, which are in turn things with an evolutionary "purpose." These teleological idioms are supposed to excuse our emotional excesses, by tracing them to purposes outside ourselves. Thus, by a sleight of hand, Carey is able to avoid both the obvious truth that emotions are socially molded and informed by judgment and also the more pertinent truth, that emotions are *objects* of judgment. In this way he finds an easy route to his preferred stance as a critic, which is that "anything goes." And his argument depends on a deep misrepresentation of the kind to which we human beings belong.

One mark of bad science is the attempt to create a stir by offering to show some ordinary belief, on which we depend for our peace of mind, to be an illusion. Popularizers of physics such as Sir James Jeans have declared that tables aren't solid, that nothing is really colored, and that, if you make a tour of the universe, you will get back to where you started, only younger than you would have been had you stayed put. The previous wave of pop genetics, which called itself "sociobiology," came up with similar startling conclusions, such as this one: "morality has no other demonstrable ultimate purpose than to keep human genetic material intact."[34] Such conclusions depend upon using the language of common sense while at the same time canceling the presuppositions on which common-sense terms depend for their

34. E. O. Wilson, *On Human Nature* (Cambridge, Mass.: Harvard University Press, 1978), 168.

meaning. This trick can be played in almost any area of human think-ing, and is never more effective than when it is used to pour scorn on our moral and religious ideas. Ordinary people are in the unfortunate position of believing things that are true, but which they cannot de-fend by any rational argument that will withstand the force of scien-tific reasoning, however flawed that reasoning may be. Hence by tar-geting ordinary beliefs—beliefs that, if backed up at all, are backed up by religious faith and not by scientific argument—the scientist scores easy points, and conceals the weakness of his case.[35]

I do not deny that we are animals, nor do I dissent from the theo-logical doctrine that our biological functions are an integral part of our nature as human persons, and also the objects of fundamental moral choices.[36] But I want to take seriously the suggestion that we must be understood through another order of explanation than that offered by genetics and that we belong to a kind that is not defined by the biological organization of its members. The "selfish gene" theory may be a good account of the origin of the human being: but what a thing is, and how it came to be, are two different questions, and the answer to the second may not be an answer to the first. It may be as impossible to understand the human person by exploring the evo-lution of the human animal as it is to discover the significance of a Beethoven symphony by tracing the process of its composition.

Consider one of those features of people that set them apart from other species: laughter. No other animal laughs. What we call the laughter of the hyena is a species sound that happens to resemble hu-man laughter. To be real laughter it would have to be an expression of

35. This accusation was strongly made against Dawkins, in the context of the orig-inal TV series of *The Selfish Gene*, by Mary Midgley, *Beast and Man*, 102–3. Whether Midgley's objections are fair is a moot point; but she deserves credit for recognizing that the challenge presented by Dawkins goes to the heart of philosophical anthropol-ogy. Her criticisms of sociobiological writers are more pertinent, and have been ampli-fied in *Evolution as a Religion*, rev. ed. (London: Routledge, 2002).

36. This view is eloquently defended by Pope John Paul II in the encyclical *Veritatis Splendor*, sections 47 et seq.

amusement—laughter *at* something, founded in a complex pattern of thought. True, there is also "laughter at what ceases to amuse," as Eliot puts it. But we understand this "hollow" laughter as a deviation from the central case, which is the case of amusement. But what is amusement? No philosopher, it seems to me, has ever quite put his finger on it. Hobbes's description of laughter as "sudden glory" has a certain magical quality; but what does he mean by "glory"? Schopenhauer, Bergson, and Freud have attempted to identify the peculiar thought that lies at the heart of laughter: none, I think, with more than partial success.[37] Helmuth Plessner has seen laughing and crying as keys to the human condition, features that typify our distinctiveness.[38] But his phenomenological language is opaque, and leads to no clear analysis of either laughter or tears.

One contention, however, might reasonably be advanced, which is that laughter expresses our ability to accept our all-too-human inadequacies; and by laughing we attract the community of sentiment that inoculates us against despair. This fact about laughter—that it implies a community of sentiment—has been well brought out by Frank Buckley.[39] From that suggestion, however, another follows. Only a being who makes judgments can laugh. Typically we laugh at things that *fall short,* or at witticisms that place our actions side by side with the aspirations that they ridicule. If the laughter of children seems not to conform to that suggestion, it is largely because the judgments of children, like the laughter that springs from them, are embryonic—stages on the way to that full readiness of social assessment which is the basis of adult life. Insofar as children are amused by things it is because, in their own way, they are comparing those things with the

37. See R. Scruton, "Amusement," in *The Aesthetic Understanding* (London: Methuen, 1982).

38. Helmuth Plessner, *Laughing and Crying: A Study in the Limits of Human Behavior,* trans. J. Spencer Churchill and Marjorie Grene (Evanston, Ill.: Northwestern University Press, 1970).

39. F. H. Buckley, *The Morality of Laughter* (Ann Arbor: University of Michigan Press, 2003).

norms that they challenge. Putative cases of amusement in chimpanzees should, it seems to me, be understood in a similar way.[40] Creatures coaxed by their human masters to the verge of judgment are on the verge of amusement too. And by getting to the verge they reveal how wide for them is the chasm that children will cross with a single stride.

To explain laughter, therefore, we should have to explain the peculiar thought-processes involved in our judgments of others; we should have to explain the pleasure that we feel when ideal and reality conflict, and also the peculiar social intentionality of this pleasure. Of course, we can make a stab at this kind of explanation, postulating cognitive programs in the human brain, and biological "wetware" in which they are imprinted. But as yet the explanation will be a pure speculation, with little or no input from genetics. I envisage a sociobiologist offering the following account of laughter. By laughing together at our faults, he might say, we come to accept them, and this makes cooperation with our imperfect neighbors easier, since it neutralizes anger at our shared inadequacies. Hence a community of laughing people has a competitive advantage over a community of the humorless. But a moment's reflection will reveal the emptiness of that explanation. For it assumes what it needs to explain, namely that laughter promotes cooperation. Admittedly my way of describing laughter suggests that this is so. But it suggests it by quite another route from that presented by biology or the theory of genetics. I was describing a thought process, involving concepts, such as those of "fault" and "ideal," that can have no clear place in evolutionary biology, as we now know it. I was assuming that laughter is an expression of understanding, and that this understanding may be shared. And at no point did I assume that the sharing of laughter benefits anybody's genes in any of the ways that feature in the theory of genetics. Indeed, so far as my account was concerned, laughter might be an entirely redundant by-

40. For an example, see the case of Roger and Lucy—two chimpanzees with some competence in the "Ameslan" sign language—described in Linden, *Apes*, 97.

product of human life. It seems otherwise only because of my account, which is not a scientific account at all, but an exercise in what Dilthey called *Verstehen*—the understanding of human action in terms of its social meaning, rather than its biological cause.[41]

Suppose a group of zoologists were to come across a species that sat around in groups, pointing and emitting laughter-like sounds. How would they set about explaining this behavior? They would *first* have to know whether what they observed was real laughter. In other words they would have to know whether these creatures were laughing *at* something, and pointing *at* something. And this word "at" does not yield easily to scientific analysis. It is a marker of intentionality, the "mental direction upon an object," as Brentano described it,[42] and can be deciphered only if we are able to interpret the thought processes from which the behavior in question flows. All the work of explanation, therefore, depends upon a prior work of interpretation, the point of which is to settle the question whether these creatures are like us in being amused by things or whether, on the contrary, they are not like us at all, and their laughter-like behavior is something to be explained as resulting from a species-life already fully accessible to biological science. If we come to this second conclusion, the apparatus of ethology can indeed be imported into the case: we can begin to ask what function this laughter-like behavior might perform in securing an ecological niche for the genes of those who engage in it. If we come to the first conclusion, then we need to understand these creatures as we understand one another—in terms of the way they conceptualize the world, and the values that motivate their response to it.

I used the phrase "creatures like us," implying that amusement is one of our characteristics. And the question before us is how we should

41. See Rudolf Makkreel, *Dilthey: Philosopher of the Human Studies* (Princeton, N.J.: Princeton University Press, 1993). Makkreel is currently editing an accurate and scholarly English edition of Dilthey's works, which are in the course of publication by Princeton.

42. Franz Brentano, *Psychology from an Empirical Standpoint,* trans. L. McAlister (London: Routledge, 1974), 77.

unpack that phrase. What do we mean when we refer to "creatures like us"? Do we mean to include only humans? Or do we have some wider, or perhaps narrower, category in mind? Homer tells us of the "laughter of the gods," and Milton of laughter among the angels. Here is the beginning of a profound metaphysical problem. We belong to a natural kind, the kind: *Homo sapiens sapiens*, which is a biological species. But, when we talk of creatures like us, it seems that we do not necessarily refer to our species-membership. Our "glassy essence," as Shakespeare calls it, refuses to be contained in our species-life.

One last point about laughter. As I described it, laughter seems to have a beneficial effect on human communities: those who laugh together also grow together, and win through their laughter a mutual toleration of their all-too-human defects. But we should not confuse the social benefit of a habit with its social function. Functions are often attributed to human actions by anthropologists and evolutionary psychologists, since this is a first step toward explaining them. But not everything that confers a benefit has a function. Entirely redundant behavior—jumping for joy, listening to music, bird-watching, prayer—may yet confer enormous benefits. By calling it redundant I mean that those benefits are the effect of the behavior, not its cause. That is how it is with laughter. There are communities of the humorless in which laughter is perceived as a threat, and severely punished. But the humorless community is not for that reason dysfunctional; in itself it is as well equipped for survival as a community of comedians. It merely lacks a certain benefit, which is a benefit only for "creatures like us."

I turn now to another feature of the human condition that divides us from our simian relatives: the feature of responsibility. We hold each other accountable for what we do, and as a result we understand the world in ways that have no parallel in the lives of other species. Our world, unlike the environment of an animal, contains rights, obligations, and duties; it is a world of self-conscious subjects, in which events are divided into the free and the unfree, those that have reasons and those that are merely caused, those that stem from a rational subject and those that erupt into the stream of objects with no conscious design. Thinking of the world in this way, we respond to it with emotions that lie beyond the repertoire of other animals: indignation, resentment, and envy; admiration, commitment, and praise—all of which involve the thought of the other as an accountable subject, with rights and duties and a self-conscious vision of his future and his past. Only responsible beings can feel these emotions, and in feeling them, they situate themselves in some way outside the natural order, standing back from it in judgment. From Plato to Sartre philosophers have differed radically in their attempts to account for these peculiar features of the human condition: but almost all have agreed in searching for a philosophical rather than a scientific explanation.

There is one interesting historical exception to that claim, however, and that is Nietzsche, who, in *The Genealogy of Morals,* tries to explain the origins of responsibility, in a way that anticipates the more recent attempts of geneticists to account for the moral life in terms of survival strategies that benefit our genes. Nietzsche envisages a primeval human society, reduced to near universal slavery by the "beasts of prey" as he calls them—namely the strong, self-affirming, healthy egoists who impose their desires on others by the force of their nature. The master race maintains its position by punishing all deviation on the part of the slaves—just as we punish a disobedient horse. The slave, too timid and demoralized to rebel, receives this punishment as a retribution. Because he cannot exact revenge the slave expends his resentment on himself, coming to think of his condition as in some way deserved, a just recompense for his inner transgressions. Thus is born the sense of guilt and the idea of sin. From the *ressentiment,* as he calls it, of the slave, Nietzsche goes on to derive an explanation of the entire theological and moral vision of Christianity.

According to Nietzsche's genealogy, the master race benefits from the subjection of the slaves—and you can see this as the premise of a proto-biological, even proto-genetic, explanation of its social strategy.

The master-race secures its position by a regime of punishment, and in due course the punishment is internalized by the slave to engender ideas of guilt, blame, desert, and justice. But why should the slave understand punishment in these elaborate and moralized terms? Why should the internalization of punishment lead to *guilt,* rather than *fear?* A horse certainly fears the whip: but when has he felt guilty for provoking it? Why is the original exercise of force seen as a *punishment,* rather than a mere need on the part of the one who inflicts it? What, after all, is the distinction between suffering inflicted as a means to securing one's ends, and suffering inflicted as a punishment? Surely the difference lies in the mind of the agent. The trainer thinks that the suffering he inflicts is *needed,* the punisher thinks that it is *due.* That is due which is deserved, and that is deserved which may be rightly and justly inflicted. In short, punishment is a moral idea, to be unpacked in terms of those concepts of justice, desert, and responsibility that Nietzsche was supposed to be explaining. His genealogy of morals works only because he has read back into the cause all the unexplained features of the effect. In other words, it is not a genealogy at all, but a recognition that the human condition, in whatever primitive form you imagine it, is the condition of "creatures like us," who laugh and cry, praise and blame, reward and punish—that is, who live as responsible beings, accountable for their actions.

There are other momentous truths about the human condition which, while often overlooked or downplayed by biologically minded thinkers, occupy a central place in the outlook of ordinary people: for example, there is the fact that we are persons, who regulate our communities through laws ascribing duties and rights. Some philosophers—Aquinas notably, but also Locke and Kant—argue that it is "person," not "human being," that is the true name of our kind. And this prompts a metaphysical question brought to the fore by Locke and still disputed, which is that of personal identity. What is the relation between "same person" and "same human being" when both are said of Jill? Which description engages with the fundamental kind under which Jill is individuated and reidentified? I mention that question not so as to suggest an answer to it,[43] but in order to highlight the difficulties confronting the view that Jill is in some way reducible to the biological processes that explain her. Under what conditions do those processes reproduce the person who Jill *is*?

There is also the division that separates merely conscious creatures from *self*-conscious creatures like us. Only the second have a genuine "first-person" perspective, from which to distinguish how things seem to *me* from how they seem to *you*. The creature with "I" thoughts has an ability to relate to his kind in a way that sets him apart from the rest of nature, and many thinkers (Kant and Hegel preeminently) believe that it is this fact, not the fact of consciousness per se, that creates or reveals the central mysteries of the human condition. Although dogs are conscious, they do not reflect on their own consciousness as we do: they live, as Schopenhauer put it, in "a world of perception," their thoughts and desires turned outward to the perceivable world.

I have tried to illustrate the way in which, in order to construct vivid biological explanations of our mental life, we are tempted to read back into the biology all the things that it ought to be trying to explain. To aim for a plausible theory of human nature we must first of all resist that temptation. And we must be prepared to admit that such laws of species-being as we have established—the laws of genetics, and the functional account of inherited characteristics—are not yet adequate either to describe or to explain our normal behavior. They fall short of the target, for the very reason that what we are is not the thing that they assume us to be. We are animals certainly; but we are also incarnate persons, with cognitive capacities that are not shared by other animals and which endow us with an entirely distinctive emotional life—one dependent on the self-conscious thought-processes that are unique to our kind.

43. Moves toward an answer are given by David Wiggins, *Sameness and Substance Renewed* (Cambridge: Cambridge University Press, 2001), ch. 7.

This returns us to the problem of the relation between the human animal and the person. This problem, as I see it, is not biological but philosophical. I can make only a tentative suggestion in response to it—a suggestion that has something in common with what Aristotle meant when he described the soul as the form of the body, and with what Aquinas meant when he argued that while we are individuated through our bodies, *what* is individuated thereby is not the body but the person. I would suggest that we understand the person as an emergent entity, rooted in the human being, but belonging to another order of explanation than that explored by biology.

"Emergence" is accepted in modern physics as part of the natural order. The laws governing the motion and transformation of large entities are not always reducible to the laws governing the motion and transformation of their parts: new orders of explanation emerge as we move up the scale of entities from quarks to galaxies.[44] In referring to the person as an "emergent entity," however, I am not invoking the physicist's concept of emergence. Emergent entities in physics are governed by causal laws which, while irreducible to the laws governing the entities from which they "emerge," are nevertheless causal laws of the same logical kind, subsuming all relevant transformations under universal formulae. The laws through which we understand human beings, however, are of a different kind from the laws that govern their biological makeup. They import not a higher-level causality but only a higher-level understanding.

An analogy might help. When painters apply paint to canvas they create physical objects by purely physical means. Any such object is composed of areas and lines of paint, arranged on a surface that we can regard, for the sake of argument, as two-dimensional. When we look at the surface of the painting, we see those areas and lines of paint, and also the surface that contains them. But that is not all we see. We also see—for example—a face that looks out at us with smil-

44. See Philip Clayton and Paul Davies, eds., *The Re-Emergence of Emergence: The Emergentist Hypothesis from Science to Religion* (Oxford: Oxford University Press, 2007).

ing eyes. In one sense the face is a property of the canvas, over and above the blobs of paint; for you can observe the blobs and not see the face, and vice versa. And the face is really there: someone who does not see it is not seeing correctly. On the other hand, there is a sense in which the face is not an additional property of the canvas, over and above the lines and blobs. For as soon as the lines and blobs are there, so is the face. Nothing more needs to be added, in order to generate the face—and if nothing more needs to be added, the face is surely nothing more. Moreover, every process that produces just these blobs of paint, arranged in just this way, will produce just this face—even if the artist is unaware of the face. (Imagine how you would design a machine for producing Mona Lisas.)

Maybe personhood is an "emergent" feature of the body in that way: not something over and above the life and behavior in which we observe it, but not reducible to them either. Once personhood has emerged it is possible to relate to an organism in a new way—the way of personal relations. (In like manner we can relate to a picture in ways that we cannot relate to something that we see merely as a distribution of pigments.) With this new order of relation comes a new order of explanation, in which reasons and meanings, rather than causes, are sought in answer to the question "why?" With persons we are in dialogue: we call upon them to justify their conduct in our eyes, as we must justify our conduct in theirs. Central to this dialogue are concepts of freedom, choice, and accountability, and these concepts have no place in the description of animal behavior, just as the concept of a human being has no place in the description of the physical makeup of a picture, even though it is a picture in which a human being can be seen.

There is another thought that is helpful in describing the relation between persons and their bodies, a thought first given prominence by Kant, and thereafter emphasized by Fichte, Hegel, Schopenhauer, and a whole stream of thinkers down to Heidegger, Sartre, and Thomas Nagel. As a self-conscious subject I have a point of view on the

world. The world *seems* a certain way to me, and this "seeming" defines my unique perspective. Every self-conscious being has such a
perspective, since that is what it means to be a subject of consciousness. When I give a scientific account of the world, however, I am
describing objects only. I am describing the way things are, and the
causal laws that govern them. This description is given from no particular perspective. It does not contain words like "here," "now," and
"I"; and while it is meant to explain the way things seem, it does so by
giving a theory of how they are. In short, the subject is in principle
unobservable to science, not because it exists in another realm but because it is not part of the empirical world. It lies on the edge of things,
like a horizon, and could never be grasped "from the other side," the
side of subjectivity itself. Is it a real part of the real world? The question is surely wrongly phrased, since it misconstrues the deep grammar of self-reference and of the reflexive pronoun. When I refer to
myself I am not referring to another *object* that is, as it were, hidden
in the lining of the observable Roger Scruton. Self-reference is not
reference to a Cartesian self, but reference to this thing, the thing that
I am, namely an object with a subjective view.

We are not entitled to reify the "self" as a distinct object of reference. Nor can we accept—given the force of Wittgenstein's anti–private
language argument—that our mental states exhibit publicly inaccessible features that somehow define what they really and essentially
are.[45] Nevertheless, it is still the case that self-reference radically af-

45. Though we should note the tenacity of the view that the felt "quale" of a mental
state is a *fact* about it, inwardly but not outwardly observable, and bound up with its essential nature. It seems to me that the notion of qualia is an empty hypothesis, a wheel
that turns nothing in the mechanism, as Wittgenstein would put it. In an interesting
paper, however, Ned Block—one of the most sophisticated defenders of qualia in the
current literature—argues that Wittgenstein inadvertently commits himself to the existence of qualia, in a form that goes against the tenor of his philosophy. ("Wittgenstein
and Qualia," forthcoming, and available on-line: see Ned Block's website.) The debate
here goes so far beyond the scope of this paper that I can only refer the reader to the
brilliant summary by Michael Tye (an equally sophisticated defender of qualia) in the
Stanford Encyclopedia of Philosophy: http://plato.stanford.edu/entries/qualia. The posi-

fects the way in which people relate to one another. Once in place, self-attribution and self-reference become the primary avenues to what we think, intend, and are. They permit us to relate to each other as subjects and not as objects only: and that is what lies at the heart of those ideas for which Nietzsche gave his pseudo-scientific genealogy: ideas of responsibility, accountability, guilt, praise, and blame. By relating to May in this way, I come face to face with her: her essential being as a person "emerges" from her bodily reality, in the way that the face emerges from the colored blobs on the canvas.

The subject/object distinction, which I have briefly sketched in a paragraph, is the theme of German philosophy from Fichte to Heidegger, and not one that I can elaborate upon here. But it is important to link what I have said to the recent developments in philosophy of mind and cognitive psychology. In a series of books and papers Daniel Dennett has argued for the view that human beings are "intentional systems"—organisms that exhibit intentional states, which are systematically connected.[46] The behavior of intentional systems can be explained or predicted by attributing "propositional attitudes": by describing them as both representing the world and seeking to change it. Not all intentional systems are human: some animals exhibit intentional states; maybe computers, when sophisticated in the way that Turing foretold, can exhibit them too. Dennett himself takes an easygoing attitude, allowing anything to be an intentional system if our treating it as such gives us some ability to predict its behavior—so that even a thermostat is an intentional system on Dennett's view.[47] His motive in taking this line is to make way for a "genealogy" of intentionality, building toward "aboutness" from simple feedback mechanisms that operate unmysteriously in the ordinary physical world.

tion I take can be gleaned from "The Unobservable Mind," in *Technology Review,* February 2005 (MIT's online journal).

46. D. C. Dennett, "Intentional Systems," *Journal of Philosophy* 68 (1971): 87–106, reprinted in *Brainstorms: Philosophical Essays on Mind and Psychology* (Brighton: Bradford, 1978), 3–22.

47. See, for example, *Kinds of Minds* (London: Weidenfeld, 1996), 34.

But it is not necessary to follow Dennett in this. Whatever the genealogy of the intentional, we must recognize the very real difference that exists between behavior that is caused by and expressive of an intentional state and behavior that is not.

Brentano's original insight implies that an intentional state is founded on a reference that may fail or a thought that may be false. We can attribute such a state only where there is the possibility of referential failure. Animals exhibit intentionality through their beliefs and desires; they may even exhibit the kind of non-propositional intentionality in which an object is "before the mind" and mentally targeted—as when a dog barks *at* an intruder, whether or not an intruder is there. It is certainly true that we are intentional systems and that this is a feature of our biological organization. Our brains are not merely devices for mediating between stimulus and response, but instruments that enable us to think about and perceive the world, and which lead us at times to think about it and perceive it wrongly.

In referring to the emergence of personality and self-consciousness, however, I am not referring only to this familiar feature of the human condition. I am referring, as Dennett has pointed out,[48] to a higher level of intentionality, one that is only doubtfully exhibited by other animals and which has certainly not been simulated by a computer. A dog sees his master as a living thing, capable of eye-contact; but there is no place in his mental repertoire for the thought of his master as a "subject of consciousness," capable also of I-contact. By contrast, we humans respond to each other and to other animals *as* intentional systems, recognizing a distinction between how things are in the world and how they seem to other observers, and adopting the "intentional stance" that Dennett again has emphasized in a series of books and papers.[49] But once we admit the existence of the intentional stance—the stance that interprets the behavior of other creatures in terms of the propositional attitudes expressed in it—we must recognize this higher

48. *Consciousness Explained* (London: Allen Lane, 1991).
49. D. C. Dennett, *The Intentional Stance* (Cambridge, Mass.: MIT Press, 1987).

(because more conceptually complex) level of intentionality. Our attitude to a dog is toward a creature with beliefs and desires; our attitude toward a normal human being is toward a creature that *attributes* beliefs and desires, to itself and to others, and therefore to us. Recognizing that others take this perspective upon us, we become accountable for what we think and do, and try to understand and relate to one another as responsible subjects of consciousness, each of whom has a unique perspective that informs his thoughts and actions. By describing this personal perspective as an "emergent" feature of the organism I am offering no theory of its nature—any more than I am offering a theory of pictures when I say that they emerge from the physical marks in which we see them. Rather, I am saying that, at a certain level of complexity, a way of seeing others and ourselves becomes available to us, and through this way of seeing we are confronted with another world than that described by evolutionary biology. This other world is the world in which we live—the *Lebenswelt,* to use Husserl's term—the world of interpersonal attitudes.[50]

Hard-line reductionists might respond in the following way: emergent properties, they might argue, are nothing "over and above" the physical properties in which we perceive them. The aspect of a picture, for example, emerges automatically when the shapes and colors are laid down on the canvas, and any other production of those same shapes and colors produces just that aspect. The aspect is "a mere appearance," with no reality beyond that of the colored patches

50. The view I am arguing for has some connection with that defended by P. F. Strawson in "Freedom and Resentment," in his *Freedom and Resentment and Other Essays* (London: Methuen, 1974). Unlike Strawson, however, I believe that the human being is truly represented in our interpersonal attitudes, and falsely represented in those attitudes he calls "objective." The higher-order intentionality to which I refer—which is the ability to form mental representations of mental representations (one's own and other people's)—has been described, in important psychological studies by Alan Leslie and others, as "metarepresentation." See, e.g., A. Leslie and D. Roth, "What Autism Teaches Us about Metarepresentation," in *Understanding Other Minds: Perspectives from Autism,* ed. S. Baron-Cohen, H. Tager Flusberg, and D. Cohen (Oxford: Oxford University Press, 1993).

in which it is seen. Likewise with personality, which is nothing over and above the biological organization in which we perceive it, since all its features are generated by the biology of the body, and no other input is required.

That response is in fact irrelevant. For the argument concerns what Hegel would call a "transition from quantity to quality." Incremental additions of colored patches to a canvas at a certain point produce a human face: and we are presented with the experience that Wittgenstein describes as "the dawning of an aspect."[51] From this point on we do not merely see the picture differently: we respond to it in another way. We find reasons for the disposition of colored patches that could not have been pertinent before; and we make a distinction between those who understand the picture and those who do not. The picture takes its place in *another context,* under another order of understanding and another order of explanation, from that which pertains to colored patches on a canvas. And that is what happens to an organism when, as the result of whatever incremental steps, it crosses the chasm from the animal to the personal, and the aspect of free self-consciousness dawns. Everything in its behavior then appears in a new light. It not only can but must be understood in a new way, through concepts that situate it in the web of personal accountability.

There is an interesting response that might be made to the position I have adopted, concerning the emergent nature of the human person—a response that picks up on an argument of Churchland's, in favor of "eliminative materialism."[52] Churchland believes that "folk psychology," in which propositional attitudes play a major role, is a genuine *theory* of human behavior, and one that might turn out to be false. After all, folk psychology accounts for only a small segment of human mentality, contains no theory of memory retrieval, of image construction, of visual-motor coordination, of sleep, and of a thou-

51. See *Philosophical Investigations* (Oxford: Blackwell, 1953), part 2, section xi.

52. Paul Churchland, "Eliminative Materialism and the Propositional Attitudes," in *Mind and Cognition,* ed. W. Lycan (Oxford: Basil Blackwell, 1990), 206–21.

sand other vital aspects of the mind. Any theory that offered to explain those things, while also matching or outstripping the predictive power of our ordinary mental concepts, would replace folk psychology in the same way that relativity theory replaced Newtonian mechanics. We might hold on to folk psychology for simplicity's sake, as we hold on to Newtonian mechanics; but this would not alter the fact that its ontological presuppositions might no longer be tenable. There are brain processes and their information-carrying potential. But maybe there are no such things as beliefs, desires, intentions, and perceptions. Churchland gives reasons for thinking that we might come to this conclusion, and that it is in fact the way in which cognitive science is going. Folk psychology might end up as a mere *façon de parler.*

It seems to me that the developments predicted by Churchland would no more rid our world of propositional attitudes than the physical theory of the picture, in terms of the disposition of pigments, rids our world of the painted image. Suppose the true theory of Jill's motive, when she helps me out of compassion, mentions only digital processes in her brain and the muscular response to them. To those brain processes I have no emotional reaction: they are of no account in my relation to Jill, and are an object at best of scientific curiosity. The intentional object of my own response to her—that toward which I *feel, think,* and *intend* on encountering her behavior—must be described in terms of folk psychology. It is only *as so described* that her behavior awakens my emotions. And these in turn are objects for Jill, *only as so described.* Now a third party, observing the relations between us, may be better placed to explain them in neurophysiological terms than by attributing propositional attitudes. However, we ourselves are not in the position of that third party. I understand Jill as motivated in just the way that I am motivated, and my own motives are given to me in consciousness only in folk-psychological terms. The pattern of my relations with Jill is built on the supposition that we conceptualize our own and the other's behavior in personal terms. The neurophysiology may give the *true* theory of what we so conceptualize, but we could deploy that theory only with the effect of changing our behavior, so that the theory is strictly useless to *us* in understanding and reacting to each other. What we are trying to describe, in describing personal relations, is revealed *only* on the surface of personal interaction. The personal eludes biology in just the way that the face in the picture eludes pigmentology. The personal is not an *addition* to the biological: it emerges *from* it.

There is another and more interesting reason for thinking that the person, though an emergent feature of a biologically determined being, cannot be eliminated from our account of human nature, which is the interconnectedness that I referred to earlier between the concept of the person and that of the subject. My reaction to you is dependent on the knowledge that you identify yourself in the first person, just as I do. The practice of giving, receiving, and criticizing reasons for action depends upon the self-attribution of those reasons, and in general all our interpersonal responses are dependent on the belief that others attribute beliefs, attitudes, reasons, and emotions to themselves. I react to you with resentment because you consciously intended to hurt me, and that means that you consciously attributed to yourself just such an intention. I express my resentment with accusations of *you,* which I expect you to meet with a confession or plea phrased in terms of "I." Someone who responded to an accusation by describing himself in the third-person case would either be insane or be avoiding the issue.

If we are to relate to each other as I to I, then our self-attributions must obey the logic of the first-person case. We must ascribe intentional states to ourselves immediately, on no basis and with first-person privilege if we are really to identify ourselves as "I" and not as "he."[53] But this first-person privilege is contained in the logic of folk psychol-

53. Precisely what is meant by this is a deep and difficult point in the philosophy of mind: I have tried to elucidate it in *Sexual Desire* (New York: Free Press, 1986), Appendix 1.

ogy. It is a feature of the concept of belief that someone knows immediately and on no basis what his ordinary beliefs are. This is not a feature of any of the concepts deployed by a brain science: hence brain science could not replace folk psychology in first-person awareness, without that awareness ceasing to be a genuine awareness of self. It follows that brain science cannot play the role in interpersonal relations that self-knowledge irreplaceably plays. Were brain science to replace folk psychology the whole world of interpersonal relations would disintegrate. The concept of the person, and its attendant idea of first-person awareness, is part of the *phenomenon,* and not to be eliminated by the science that explains it.

Personality, as I have described it, is an adaptive trait, and all those studies that argue for a cultural input into the evolutionary process can be seen as recognizing this truth.[54] A creature with personality has ways of calling on the help and cooperation of others, ways of influencing them, ways of learning from and teaching them, which are maximally responsive to changes in external circumstances and internal goals. If, by incremental steps, a set of genes can make the "transition from quantity to quality" that has personality as its endpoint, it has scored an enormous evolutionary advantage. It now has fighting for it, in the sunlit world of rational agency, a knight in armor who has his own compelling reasons for advancing the cause of friends, family, and offspring. He does not need to rely on the strategies implanted in his genes in order to be motivated toward altruism, forgiveness, and the pursuit of virtue: if Kant is right, the motive toward these things is implicit in the very fact of self-consciousness.[55]

Taking a sober look at the many attempts to describe some part of what is distinctive of the human condition—the use of language

54. For example, Boyd and Richerson, *Not by Genes Alone,* and Sterelny, *Thought.*

55. If it were *only* Kant who thought this, then of course there is an opening here for the skeptic. The thought is, however, common to Kant, Fichte, Hegel, and Schopenhauer; to Shaftesbury, Smith, Hutcheson, and Hume; and to countless contemporary thinkers.

(Chomsky, Bennett), second-order desires (Frankfurt), second-order intentions (Grice), convention (Lewis), freedom (Kant, Sartre), self-consciousness (Kant, Fichte, Hegel), laughing and crying (Plessner), the capacity for cultural learning (Tomasello)—you will surely be persuaded that each is tracing some part of a single holistic accomplishment.[56] Now there is nothing in the theory of evolution, either in its original Darwinian form or in the form of Fisherian genetics, that forbids the jump from one mode of explanation and understanding to another. To believe that incremental change is incompatible with radical divides is precisely to misunderstand what Hegel meant by the transition from quantity to quality. You won't find intermediate stages between the conscious and the self-conscious animal, any more than there are intermediate stages between patterns in which you cannot see a face and patterns in which you can. Once arrived on the scene, however, the self-conscious creature has an adaptation that will cause him to populate the earth and bend it to his purposes. And, as we know all too well, not all those purposes will be adaptive.

If we now turn back to the question of human nature, we find ourselves equipped to say something about the kind to which we belong. We are the kind of thing that relates to members of its kind through interpersonal attitudes and through the self-predication of its own mental states. Now the intentional states of a creature reflect its conceptual repertoire. To understand your emotions I must know how you conceptualize the world. I cannot simply describe your behavior as though it were a response to the-world-as-science-would-describe-it. There are concepts that direct our mental states but which can play no role in an explanatory theory, because they divide the world into

56. Chomsky, *Language and Mind*; Jonathan Bennett, *Linguistic Behaviour* (Cambridge: Cambridge University Press, 1976); Harry G. Frankfurt, "Freedom of the Will and the Concept of the Person," *Journal of Philosophy* 68 (1971): 5–20; H. P. Grice, "On Meaning," *Philosophical Review* 66 (1957): 377–88 and its many sequels; David Lewis, *Convention: A Philosophical Study* (Cambridge: Cambridge University Press, 1969); Michael Tomasello, *The Cultural Origins of Human Cognition* (Cambridge, Mass.: Harvard University Press, 2000).

the wrong kinds of kind—concepts such as those of ornament, melody, duty, freedom. The concept of the person is such a concept, which means not that there are no persons, but only that a scientific theory of persons will classify them with other things—for example, with apes or mammals—and will not be a scientific theory of every kind of person. (For example, it will not be a theory of corporate persons, of angels, or of God.) Hence the kind to which we belong is defined through a concept that does not feature in the science of human biology. That science sees us as objects rather than subjects, and its descriptions of our responses are not descriptions of what we feel. The study of our *kind* is the business of the *Geisteswissenschaften,* which are not sciences at all, but "humanities"—in other words, exercises in the kind of understanding exhibited in my account of laughter.

The kind-concept under which we assemble human beings influences our understanding of their psychological states. These are understood as the states of persons, and not as states that non-personal animals might equally exhibit. And the way we understand them influences the way we experience them. The example of sexual feelings provides a vivid illustration of what I mean. Sexual relations, the biologist might argue, are to be explained in terms of genetic strategies. There is no difficulty in accounting for phenomena such as jealousy, female modesty, male predatoriness, and the well-known typologies of attraction, once we see these things as aspects of genetic "investment." Evolutionary psychology has made great strides in these areas, and the work by Bowlby provides a cross-species comparative analysis that explains all our attachments—parental, filial, and sexual—as control mechanisms that we share with our nearest neighbors on the evolutionary tree.[57] My response to this is to say: that is fine, so far as it goes. But the explanations given underdetermine the behavior to be explained. The feature that most needs explaining is precisely the interpersonal intentionality that distinguishes us from our evolutionary

57. J. Bowlby, *Attachment and Loss.*

neighbors and causes our attachments to "reach through" the empirical circumstances that give rise to them toward the free subject who is their target. Sexual jealousy in a person is not like its simulacrum in a bonobo, since it involves the thought of betrayal, for which another person is answerable. Monogamy in a person is not like the monogamy of geese or gibbons, in that it involves a lifelong vow of devotion, often conceived in sacramental terms.[58] The comparisons given by Bowlby bring human sexual behavior within the ambit of evolutionary psychology only by leaving its interpersonal intentionality out of account.

This is not to deny the truth of Bowlby's theory, conceived as a phylogenetic explanation of our disposition toward affectionate ties. So understood, the theory conceives attachment as a general feature of the species, manifested by human beings as well as by other animals, and one that helps the survival of our genes. But what is shared across species is precisely what is not distinctive of our condition. We could give a general theory of arithmetical competence—manifest, for example, in the ability to assess the number of predators in one's environment. Many birds have this ability, and some mammals too. The ethological explanation is clear: if a group of predators enters a covert, and a group subsequently departs from it, you need to know whether the number of the second group is less than the number of the first. That kind of explanation applies to humans too. But it falls short of what is distinctive of the human condition, which is the ability to engage in every kind of abstract mathematical reasoning—even mathematical reasoning about mathematical reasoning, as in proofs of consistency and completeness. In like manner the general disposition to attachment, which is explained in Bowlby's way, and which must always be borne in mind when we consider fundamental disorders of the personality that seem to spring from childhood abuse,

58. On the connection between sexual desire and the idea of sacrament, see R. Scruton, *Death-Devoted Heart: Sex and the Sacred in Wagner's* Tristan und Isolde (New York: Oxford University Press, 2004).

falls short of what is distinctive of our condition, which is love for and grief over another individual, whose place in our affections stems from his being exactly the person he is. Once fixated on biological explanations, people find themselves tempted to eliminate the individualizing intentionality from human emotions, and especially from those emotions, such as sexual desire, that express our leaning toward another moral subject. For this intentionality is the real obstacle to what is so often the undisclosed aim—which is to expose "what we really are," by describing us as less than human.

There is another lamentable effect of the belief that we should explain human behavior in exactly the same way, and in terms of the same variables, as animal behavior, which is that people begin to transfer to the animals the concepts that they have downgraded or debunked in their human use—concepts of right, justice, dignity, and so on. Quite suddenly the conceptual barrier is breached, and the moral privileges of humans flood into the animal kingdom. Thus arises the movement for animal rights, which refuses to countenance any morally significant distinction of kind between humans and other animals. This movement takes the side of Darwin against Wallace, not by denying to humans those moral attributes that are so fundamental to the traditional conception of human destiny, but by affirming them promiscuously of just about everything that moves.

In 1970 Richard Ryder coined the word "speciesism" to describe the sin of making moral distinctions between people and other animals, implying that this habit of discrimination is like racism and sexism—a habit of moral discrimination, on the basis of morally irrelevant facts. Thanks to Peter Singer the word has caught on, and perhaps it is worth pausing to consider just how utterly misleading it is. It is not the difference of species that I endow with moral significance, when I distinguish people from other animals. It is rather the difference between a moral being, who lives as the subject and object of judgment, and a non-moral being, who merely lives. Maybe all moral beings belong to a single species: but, as I have argued, it is not the species that I consider when I distinguish the life and fulfill-ment of a person from the life and fulfillment of a dog. And if any dis-tinctions are morally relevant, then surely the distinction between the moral and the non-moral being is one of them.

It is often objected that we do in fact make discriminations on grounds of species membership, since we afford to "marginal hu-mans," who lack the capacities that distinguish the moral being from the rest of nature, some, although not all, of the privileges of fully re-sponsible people. For example, we regard the killing of an idiot as a crime comparable to the killing of a normal person; we extend a duty of care and protection to the retarded, the brain-damaged, and the vegetative that we withhold from animals more intelligent and more capable than they. To this I would respond that we do this because the human form is, for us, the outward sign and symbol of the moral life, and because we never wish to foreclose the possibility that each hu-man body harbors, in whatever embryonic form, a personality. This reaction is part of piety; it may be hard to justify it in terms of the cold, hard, utilitarian reasoning that appeals to Peter Singer; but the fault lies in that cold, hard form of reasoning. Utilitarianism overlooks precisely what is distinctive of our condition, which is our rooted dis-position to understand ourselves as moral beings, bound in relations of accountability to others of our kind. We define human nature in terms of its normal development, along the trajectory of the person-al and responsible life. That is the kind of thing that we are; and it is the kind to which even the tragically abnormal human being belongs, and from which dogs, cats, horses, and all other animals with which we habitually have dealings are by their nature excluded.

I have argued that, while we human beings belong to a kind, that kind cannot be characterized merely in biological terms, but only in terms that make essential reference to the web of interpersonal re-actions. These reactions bind us to each other and also reach out to (even if they may not connect with) persons who are not of this world, and not of the flesh. This thought may produce metaphysical qualms in the reader. After all, how can I be a member of a species, while belonging to a kind that is defined not in terms of its biological constitution but in terms of its psychosocial capacities? It is helpful here to turn back to the case of the picture. A picture is a surface, which presents to the normal educated eye an aspect of a thing depicted. That is the kind to which pictures belong, and we know that members of this kind include an enormous variety of objects: canvases, sheets of paper, computer screens, holographs, and so on. The behavioral complexity required to exemplify interpersonal responses, to entertain "I"-thoughts, and to hold oneself and others accountable for changes in the world is something that we witness only in members of a particular natural kind—the kind *Homo sapiens sapiens*. But could we not envisage other beings, members of some other species or of no biological species at all, who exhibit the same complexity and are able to engage with us, I to I? If so, they belong with us in the order of things, and there is a kind that includes us both.

Religious people, by holding on to their faith, hold on to that kind of deep, but metaphysically unsettling, truth about the human condition. They have no difficulty in understanding that human beings are distinguished from other animals by their freedom, self-consciousness, and responsibility. And they have a ready supply of stories and doctrines that make sense of those truths. But those truths would be truths even without religion, and it is one task of philosophy in our time to show this. On the other hand, how philosophical reasoning can filter through to the lives of ordinary mortals, without the open channels afforded by faith, I do not know.

The problem here is not a new one. Plato had an inkling of it, and it is Plato's influence that can be discerned in al-Fârâbî, when he claims that the truths furnished to the intellect by philosophy are made available to the imagination by religious faith.[59] This thought, developed by Avicenna and Averroës, entered the consciousness of medieval Europe.

59. Al-Fârâbî, *Fî Tahsîl as-Sa'âdah*, quoted in Lenn E. Goodman, *Islamic Humanism* (Oxford: Oxford University Press, 2003), 9.

In the writings of Averroës it borders on the heresy of "double truth": the heresy of believing that reason may justify one thing, faith another and incompatible thing. This idea, ascribed to the troublemaker Siger of Brabant, called forth a round condemnation from Aquinas. And it is one that no modern philosopher is likely to find congenial. The point made by al-Fârâbî is the more measured one, that truths discoverable to reason may also be revealed—but in another, more imagistic, more metaphorical form—to the eye of faith. Those incapable of reasoning their way to the intricate truths of theology may nevertheless grasp them imaginatively in ritual and prayer, living by a knowledge that they lack the intellect to translate into rational arguments.

The work of philosophy that I have sketched stands to be completed by a work of the imagination. For the person with religious faith this work has already been accomplished; for skeptics, however, it must begin anew. The philosophical truth, that our kind is not a biological category, is swept out of view by scientistic "clairantism" (to use J. L. Austin's felicitous word). It can be conjured back by stories, images, and evocations, in something like the way that Milton conjured the truth of our condition from the wonderful raw materials of *Genesis*. Milton's allegory is not just a portrait of our kind; it is an invitation to kindness. It shows us what we are, and what we must live up to. And it sets a standard for art. Take away religion, however; take away philosophy, take away the higher aims of art, and you deprive ordinary people of the ways in which they can represent their apartness. Human nature, once something to live up to, becomes something to live down to instead. Biological reductionism nurtures this "living down," which is why people so readily fall for it. It makes cynicism respectable and degeneracy chic. It abolishes our kind; and with it our kindness.

five

Ceslas Bernard Bourdin

RELIGIOUS FREEDOM AND THE
SEPARATION OF CHURCH AND STATE

A Lesson from Post-revolutionary France

There are people in France who look on republican institutions as a tempo-rary expedient for their own aggrandizement. (. . .) [I]t is not to such as they that I speak, but there are others who look forward to a republican form of government as a permanent and tranquil state and as the required aim to which ideas and mores are constantly steering modern societies. Such men sincerely wish to prepare mankind for liberty. When such as these attack religious beliefs, they obey the dictates of their passions, not their interests. Despotism may be able to do without faith, but freedom cannot. Religion is much more needed in the republic they advocate than in the monarchy they attack, and in democratic republics most of all. How could society escape de-struction if, when political ties are relaxed, moral ties are not tightened? And what can be done with a people master of itself if it is not subject to God?

Alexis de Tocqueville, *Democracy in America*

The author would like to express his gratitude to the Institute for the Psychological Sciences and its authorities, especially Dr. Gladys Sweeney, for providing the opportu-nity to conduct this research at its Centre for Philosophical Psychology in Oxford. He would like to heartily thank Gregory Vincent for translating this article.

To deal with the French view of religious freedom for an Anglo-American public is bold and relevant at the same time. It is bold in that the United States and Great Britain do not see religious freedom the way that France does, because of each country's specific history. From the point of view of the United States, a young nation, God and religion are the friends of liberty. For France, an old nation (like Great Britain), liberty was wrought out of a conflict with religion (more than with God as such); more precisely, the conflict was with the Roman Catholic Church and also with the monarchy. What is at stake here is the very idea of human rights (claimed in the name of God the creator in the United States, but in the name of the Supreme Being in France);[1] correlatively this affects also the way the universality of mankind—common to everyone—is perceived.

Consequently the result is the divergent way in which our two countries view republic:[2] on the one hand, human rights in America arose, so it seems to me, from a combination of peculiarities due to the gradual granting of rights to the multitude, as the American republic[3] extended geographically; on the other hand, human rights in France were, as early as 1789, part of a political scheme meant to express the connection between man and the citizen: man, that is the individual as an abstraction, not the empirical man, is freed from all particular loyalties that would hinder the constitution of the nation.[4] This double divergence (on human rights and republic) implies a third one: the French notion of what a nation is derives from the theological-political legacy of the monarchy's institutions and of

1. Blandine Barret-Kriegel, *Les droits de l'homme et le droit naturel* (Paris: Presses Universitaires de France, Quadrige, 1989).

2. Denis Lacorne, "La séparation de l'Église et de l'État aux Etats-Unis. Les paradoxes d'une laïcité philo-cléricale," in *Le Débat* (Paris: Gallimard, 2003), 63–79; Jefferson's letter to the Baptists of Danbury after his election as president (71–72); by the same author, *L'invention de la République. Le modèle américain* (Paris: Hachette, "Pluriel," 1991).

3. It is exactly Hannah Arendt's philosophical approach in *On Revolution* (New York: Viking Press, 1963).

4. Marcel Gauchet, *La Révolution des Droits de l'Homme* (Paris: Gallimard, 1989).

the French Roman Catholic Church, a legacy that was echoed in the nineteenth century by the lay republican scheme of a separation between the state and the Church.

On the contrary, the way the American nation emerged laid the grounds for its independence: it broke with the British monarchy and called for a republican scheme of a separation between the state and the churches that is very different from the French one, due to the absence of—and opposition to—any established church in America.

Hence both our countries share common values such as religious freedom, human rights, the republic, and the nation; but the logic and the history of each are so different that they cause many misunderstandings.

This is what makes the handling of the religious freedom problem relevant, especially at the moment when the French commemorate the one-hundredth anniversary of the law that separated the state from the churches on the 9th of December 1905.

The British, the Americans, and the French all agree on the fact that there is no religious liberty if politics (as expressed by the state) is not severed from religion (as expressed by the churches). Yet they disagree on how to separate the state from the churches and on the meaning of this separation for the political philosophy of a modern state, which can be defined by its autonomy with regard to religious laws. To me, in addition to the divergences on what is at the root of human rights, republic, democracy, and nation, this problem of the modalities of the separation of the state from the churches is the central problem on which the American and French visions differ: the philosophy of autonomy, from which all the other notions derive, doesn't have the same meaning in both countries and other European countries.[5]

5. John Courtney Murray, "Leo XIII: Separation of Church and State," *Theological Studies* 14, no. 2 (1953): 146. In his work *Institutiones iuris publici ecclesiastici*, II (Rome: Typis Polyglottis Vaticanis, 1948), 82, Cardinal Ottaviani states that the "most common system of separation is that which is enunciated in the well-known formula, 'A free Church in a free state'"; he adds (ibid., note 1) that this system was proclaimed in Ita-

As yet, in order to overcome those misunderstandings—if not those caricatures—we should consider our national histories as a whole, and not just focus on the epoch-making events that signal the entrance of Britain, America, and France into modernity—that is, respectively, the glorious revolution of 1688–89, the independence of 1776, and the revolution of 1789. If time permitted, a precise and penetrating historical as well as philosophical-political analysis should allow us to go as far back as the sixteenth and above all the seventeenth century, thanks to a comparative study of the relationship between Christianity and politics in Great Britain and France.

Although France played a decisive part in the American war for independence, Great Britain no doubt played a no less decisive part in the making of the Anglo-American notion of "enlightenment," because of the influence the religious Reformation had on some of the American colonies.

---

ly by Count Cavour in 1861, but has "obtained in the United States since Sept. 17, 1787." (This is the date of the signing of the Constitution by the Constitutional Convention, which did not become operative till June 1788, when nine states had ratified it; the Bill of Rights, which settled the relation of church and state, did not become law till 1791.) Surely this is a misleading statement; one knows what Cavour meant by his famous formula, and an American knows what the First Amendment means. Cavour's formula cannot be used to describe the situation of the Church in the United States. The differences between the Italian republican system and the American system are profound. The difference derives from what Cavour and the United States Constitution respectively mean by the "state," and from what Cavour means by a "free" state and what the United States Constitution means by a "limited" state, or better, government. Again it is said (ibid., 83, and note 1) that in the United States the system of the *ius commune* obtains. This is quite unwarrantedly to overlook the fact, to which I shall later advert, that the Continental *ius commune* and the American First Amendment have hardly at all the same juridical meaning, since they respectively repose on widely divergent political theories. Later (ibid., 91) it is said: "The formula, 'A free Church in a free state,' established indeed the Church's right to freedom before the state, but it reserves to the state the determination of the sphere of activity within which the Church may freely act." This was indeed the mind of Cavour, in accordance with his concept of state sovereignty; it is not at all the mind of the United States Constitution, which is premised on a very different concept of sovereignty. It is unfortunate that European canonists should intrude European political concepts into the American system, where they have no place.

Since I have to limit myself to the study of the French vision of religious freedom, and more precisely to the study of the reasons why the Holy See opposed the lay republican scheme of the late nineteenth and early twentieth centuries, I will just sketch the problem with which both the French and the British monarchies were confronted: they both faced the crisis of the Christian medieval notion of the universal, which itself was fuelled by the crisis of the understanding and transmission of the Christian truth in the sixteenth and seventeenth centuries. Yet this crisis allowed the theological-political genesis of the modern state to take place by asserting the absolute monarchy by divine right.[6] Having painted this historical and philosophical-political picture, I will get to the core of this essay: the French singularity of a lay republican state acting as a prerequisite for religious freedom in a traditionally Catholic country, this singularity pointing to the difference with the Anglo-American approach in order to make clear what lies behind such concepts as human rights, republic, nation, and autonomy.

Religious Tolerance as a Theological-Political Problem of the Monarchical State in Great Britain and France

Since it is, I think, agreed upon that to speak of the modern state in the singular cannot but be an inadequate formula, we will have to examine at least roughly the different ways in which modern states came into being, with a special emphasis on the concepts of legitimacy and sovereignty, and their implications with respect to the tension between unity and the openness to the universal. Without such openness there can be no tolerance toward ecclesial minorities, let alone

---

6. Bernard Bourdin, *La genèse théologico-politique de l'État moderne: La controverse de Jacques Ier d'Angleterre avec le cardinal Bellarmin* (Paris: Presses Universitaires de France, 2004). See also "Le droit divin et les sources théologico-politiques de la modernité," in Actes du colloque: Degré de modernité des États en Europe, *Revue d'Éthique et de la Théologie Morale* (Paris: Cerf, 2004): 119–42.

religious freedom, because then the "openness to the universal" is basically reduced to a univocal unity.

Great Britain and France are exemplary in this respect. If, despite very specific and divergent histories, those two great northwestern monarchies equally generated absolutism by divine right, it is because, on the one hand, Britain broke with the Holy See, and, on the other hand, France experienced civil religious wars between Catholicism and Calvinism. Those two historical examples are emblematic of how deep the crisis of the medieval universal was and how urgent it was to install a new connection with that universal. As yet there can be no universal unless there emerges a principle of unity around which hinges the setting up of a common civic life.

Now if the religious crisis that affects sixteenth century Europe is no doubt a crisis of the universal, it is because its center of unity, the Holy See, has ceased to be a source of universalism, for it is no longer the mediator of the medieval Ecclesia. The same is true of the Holy Roman Empire, whose mission it was to incarnate, on the temporal side, the Christian universal. Very emblematic, in this respect, is the double failure of Emperor Charles V and of the Holy See to face a double challenge, first that of Luther, then that of Calvin. From thence the center of unity shifts toward political powers, the monarchies. The result is, after several decades of religious reforms in England and of edicts of tolerance in France, the rise of the monarchical power, itself proportional to the absoluteness of the delegation of sovereignty by God to the king. If the political and religious histories of those kingdoms are undoubtedly specific, what they have in common is their determination to keep the temporal power of the crown independent. In other words, whether there is a break with or a distancing from the Holy See, the secular monarchy is the new institutional way of expressing unity, and hence, a "particular" universal circumscribed within the limits of the royal state. The parallel between the two monarchies is worth being pointed out because of the influence the French monarchy of the Valois and its political ideas had on the

British monarchy of the Tudors, as the British historian Salmon has amply shown.[7] Within those parallel and specific histories, the common emphasis laid by both the new dynasty of the Stuarts and that of the Bourbons on the absoluteness of the royal power represents the perfect expression of that new institutional figure: the sovereign unity. The royal power is fully sovereign because it proceeds from a delegation by God.[8] In this respect the royal power is the legitimate warrant of the theological-political unity of Christian societies within a delineated territory. Hence the Christian universality derives from the peculiarity of the royal state, within which "heretical" religious differences can be integrated.

At the same time the ambivalence of the monarchical state shows through, in that it can consent to religious otherness only if this religious otherness remains politically loyal. Political or civil tolerance toward ecclesial minorities hence depends upon the theological-political shift of the unity of the Christian universal. If the sovereign and universal unity of the papal monarchy crumbles, it is nonetheless the monarchical principle that presides over the future of the *corpus christianorum*. What has been called a "metaphysical mutation," in addition to religious, political, and anthropological transformations, results— on an institutional plane—in a change in the status and metaphysical meaning of the very idea of monarchy. The absoluteness of the royal: power by divine right (or delegation by God) enhances this shift of the unity.

The center of gravity now is the secular monarchy, which is an

7. J. H. M. Salmon, "Gallicanism and Anglicanism in the Age of the Counter-Reformation," in *Renaissance and Revolt: Essays in the Intellectual and Social History of Early Modern France* (Cambridge: Cambridge University Press, 1987), 155–88.

8. Bernard Bourdin, "James VI and I—Divine Right, the Doctrine of the Two Kingdoms and the legitimizing of Royal Power," in *The Struggle for the Succession in Late Elisabethan England, Politics, Polemics and Cultural Representations,* ed. Jean-Christophe Mayer (Montpellier: Université Paul-Valéry, 2004), 119–41; see also Glenn Burgess, *Becoming English? Becoming British? The Political Thought of James VI before and after 1603* (Montpellier: Institut de Recherche sur la Renaissance, Université Paul-Valéry, 2004), 143–75.

ambivalent form of "modern" state, in that this type of state, such as expressed in the thought of the jurist-consultants who theorized it, gave birth to the "modern" notion of sovereignty. "Absolute" and "perennial" as it is in its major elements, this state is in no way arbitrary and must in fine account for its actions before God. This "direct" reference to the judgment of God, ultimately the sole Sovereign ruling over the political community, is the best illustration of the shift of meaning of such concepts as religious sacrality and metaphysical unity. As yet, since the monarchy fully expresses a theological-political metaphysic that hinges upon the sacred, it continues to uphold the demands of a Christian society, and, as a result, tolerates dissidence only conditionally, at the risk of falling back into intolerance and violence.[9] Such is the ambivalence of the theological-political genesis of the modern state: it is modern in the sense that it puts the concept of sovereignty into practice, but it doesn't break with the transcendent dimension of the theological-political and metaphysical unity. The center of this unity is simply shifted, and the monarchical universality ends up being the minimal tolerance toward ecclesiastical minorities, hence indirectly—rather than directly—connected with the unity incarnated by the king. A testimony of this is given by the comparatively early crisis of the English[10]—as opposed to the French—version of the monarchy by divine right. The religious disruption caused by the schisms of 1534 and 1559 produced its full effects in the middle of the seventeenth century[11] and came to its end only with the glorious revolution of 1688 and the fall of absolutism.

French absolutism lived longer, but it raised the same problems and triggered the radicalism of the revolutionary years of the late eighteenth century. The Jansenism crisis, the quashing of the edict of Nant-

9. Bernard Bourdin, "Le droit divin royal en Angleterre," 207–34.

10. Franck Lessay, "Jacques II roi révolutionnaire?" in *Espace des révolutions: Paris-Londres 1688–1848*, ed. Jacques Six (Villeneuve d'Ascq: Université d'Ascq, Université Lille III, 1991), 27–51.

11. Conrad Russell, *The Causes of the English Civil War* (Oxford: Clarendon Press, 1990).

es, and the influence of Richerism show the extent to which many religious circles had already resisted the absolute sovereignty of a monarch by divine right.[12] In other words, the comparative study of those two monarchies points out what I call the theological-political paradigm of sixteenth and seventeenth century Europe: an ambivalent, highly unstable period that inaugurated a new form of Christian sacredness, and appears—short as it may be—as an indispensable and clarifying link between medieval Christendom and secular and democratic Europe. Enhanced and at the same time carried away by the religious reformations, this paradigmatic historical turning point is both a religious way out of medieval politics and a political way out of medieval religion.

The all-encompassing Christendom, splintered as early as the sixteenth century into multiple ecclesial orthodoxies, is still able to redefine a new concept of universality through local and national ecclesiologies; but since those local and national churches are more or less coextensive with the secular power, the path is made for intolerance and religious violence that will ultimately destabilize the monarchies and prevent them from maintaining the unity they so badly want.

Hence when a political society fails to secure the earthly order by its transcendent heteronymous legitimacy, it has to fall back on other sources of legitimacy to do the job.

The revolutionary process creeps into this gap left by the inherent flaw and ambivalence of the absolute monarchy by divine right: although it is critical of the sovereignty of this other monarchy, the roman pontificate, the absoluteness of the royal divine right contests heteronymous transcendence only insofar as it jeopardizes its full independence with regard to any ecclesiastical attempt to intrude upon its legitimacy and political action. Still the king, because of his vicarious function of "lieutenant of god on earth,"[13] is all the more eager to

12. Dale K. Van Kley, *The Religious Origins of the French Revolution: From Calvin to the Civil Constitution, 1560–1791* (New Haven, Conn.: Yale University Press, 1996).

13. J. Montagu, R. Barker, and J. Bill, eds., *The Trew Law of Free Monarchies: or The Reciprock and Mutuall Duetie Betwixt A Free King, And His naturall Subjects in The Workes of the Most High and Mightie Prince, James by the grace of God, King of Great*

make his this heteronymous transcendence. The root of the conflict with papacy revolves therefore on the question of who has institutional precedence over whom in terms of sovereign unity; it is not the principle of this sovereign unity as such that causes the fight. As soon as the king has taken over the transcendent heteronymous origin of the unity of the earthly order, the political power is all the more liable to act as a regulator and—if need be—as a censor of the diversified religious expressions. British history is very telling with respect to this unsolved problem. The Stuart monarchy will pay the price for it by its downfall; and so will the Bourbon monarchy as I have already mentioned. The British and French models of absolutism by divine right are equally possessed with the same ambivalence: sovereign power, intolerance, and violence are the hallmark of an inability to combine the otherness of religious dissidence with the oneness of the political community.

The divine right of the royal state with its transcendent heteronymous origin is a power with feet of clay that can't but refer to a normative religious truth. If the ecclesiastical mediation (which is a token of both salvation and universal truth) is now explicitly taken on by the royal state and enables it to be free of all church intrusions upon its temporal action, this nevertheless implies the rise of another sacred norm (the heteronymous transcendence by divine right) in which the individual conscience is restricted to the sphere of intimacy.

All the contractual political philosophies have aimed to answer the religious reformations and the shift within the order of the sacred and in the metaphysical status of politico-religious heteronomy. The absoluteness of the royal power by divine delegation only temporarily settled the matter; philosophical rationality purports to give a final solution to the problem of the source of political power by laying the grounds of a new anthropology centered on the individual and

Britaines, France and Ireland. Defensor of the Faith, etc (London, 1616), 191–210. See my critical edition and translation: Bernard Bourdin, *La Vraie loi des libres monarchies ou Les devoirs réciproques et mutuels entre un roi libre et ses sujets naturels*, Astraea Texts no. 2 (Montpellier: Presses Universitaires de la Méditerranée, 2008).

on a representative state. The philosophical endeavor of the classical period is thus concerned not just with a shift of power within a sacral representation of the world, but rather with an inversion of the source from which stems the legitimacy of any sovereign power: the emphasis is now on the autonomy of man, which stands for the basis of the political society. "Civilization" has become a secular value in which the theological-political all-encompassing of European societies, whatever form it takes, has lost all its justifications. The universal criteria that lay the foundations of a common citizenship are the "law" and the "contract" as determined by the individuals and not by a norm coming from above. What is at stake here is nothing less than the emergence of the paradigm of classical humanism put forward by philosophers such as Hobbes and Locke in England, Spinoza in the Netherlands, and Montesquieu and Rousseau in France.[14] It is not possible here to analyze the complex theories of rationalist philosophies. Let us be reminded that this philosophical stream deeply influenced the Anglo-Saxon as well as—although in a different perspective—the French culture as concerns the relationship between Christianity and the contractual foundations of the modern representative state. It is precisely "philosophy" that the Holy See opposes, the "philosophy" of the classical humanist paradigm, the legacy of which (especially in Rousseau's version) has fuelled the French revolution. The political, moral, and religious consequences of "philosophy" are that there isn't any more an analogical connection between the earthly and the religious order.

To a metaphysical, religious, and moral order centered on the concepts of common good *(bonum commune)* and beatitude *(beatitudo)* artfully developed by St. Thomas Aquinas's scholastic philosophy, succeeded an order in which there is a disconnection between religious and political ends. The ethic of contractual philosophies is a

14. On some aspects of the philosophies of the contract, see Bernard Bourdin, "Aux origines de la modernité politique ou l'art de produire du neuf à partir de l'ancien," *Revue d'Éthique et de Théologie Morale* 226 (September 2003): 75–91.

utilitarian one and is valid only within the scope of common interests with no ultimate spiritual purpose. In a similar way, Hobbes refuses to sever the soul from the body, hence his inability to think of God in any other way but a corporal one.[15] The political society has thus a purpose of its own, devoid of any religious consideration, which coalesces with the purpose of mankind in general. The liberal philosophy of Locke, because he adheres to the notion of separation between churches and the state, only confirms the fact that medieval philosophy has been relinquished.[16]

In another perspective the Rousseauist attempt to "bypass" Christianity by setting up a civil and civic religion will play a decisive part in the emergence of the French notion of a "civil religion," quite different from the American one. Rousseau is certainly the philosopher who makes it possible to grasp the diverging way in which the United States and France understand the relationship of politics with religion.

Furthermore, from a purely historical point of view, the French revolution has made two epoch-making steps that illustrate how divergent the two countries' views are on subjects like republic or religious liberty: the first of these steps is the fusion as early as 1789 of the three orders of the Etats Généraux into a national assembly. The new principle that now lays the foundations of politics is the sovereignty of the people by means of the sovereignty of the nation. The people and the nation, made up of individuals, such as the individualistic philosophy of human rights conceives them, the transformation of the royal sovereignty (theological-political heteronomy) into a sovereignty that stems from the people (secular autonomy), are the ma-

15. On the Hobbesian critique of religion, see Leo Strauss, *La critique de la religion chez Hobbes, Une contribution à la compréhension des Lumières (1933–1934)* (Paris: Presses Universitaires de France, 2005).

16. Yves Charles Zarka, Franck Lessay, and John Rogers, *Les fondements philosophiques de la tolérance en France et en Angleterre au XVII͏ᵉ siècle* (Paris: Presses Universitaires de France, 2002), 3 tomes, see specially the first tome about the geneses of the separation between church and state in the thought of John Locke.

jor legal grounds for democracy and a posteriori liberal democracy, which presupposes a secular unity.

The second step—in fact a logical consequence of the first—is *the civil constitution of the clergy*,[17] which is nothing but the expression of the national sovereignty of the people on an ecclesial plane. From those two epoch-making steps, one can see how the French conception of secular autonomy, hence of a separation between religion and the state, differs from the American one.

Introduction to the Conflict between France and the Holy See

To start with, I will put forward the general philosophical grounds for the clash between modern society as emerging from 1789 with its basic tenets—public liberties and equality—and the Holy See, whose mechanisms of thought can be called post–theological-political in two different areas: the relationship between the church, the state, and society on the one hand, and the relationship between revelation and reason on the other hand. Our concern here is of course primarily the relation between the church, the state, and society; but one cannot omit to mention—at least briefly—the problematic relationship between revelation and reason, with its theological-political touchstone: the conflicting concepts of freedom and truth. The opposition of papacy toward the civil constitution of the clergy will be decisive in this respect.

The second part of my contribution will mainly comment on Leo XIII's encyclical *Immortale Dei* and Pius X's encyclical *Vehementer Nos*; the subject of the later being precisely France, one year after the law of the 9th of November 1905 had been promulgated. No matter its historical interest, *Vehementer Nos* doesn't add anything to the

17. See Charles (†) et Luce Pietri, André Vauchez, and Marc Venard, "Histoire de Christianisme des origines à nos jours, sous la direction de Jean-Marie Mayeur," tome 10: *Les Défis de la modernité (1750–1840)*, under the direction of Bernard Plongeron (Paris: Desclée, 1997), 307–44.

mechanisms of thought already at work in *Immortale Dei*. The former, though, outlines the radical incompatibility—not even to mention the laicist republican agenda—between the revolution of the sixteenth and seventeenth century in philosophy, that of 1789 in politics,
and the thought of the Holy See as concerns the extremely delicate
subject of the relations between the Church, the state, and modern
society. There is a thread of permanence and change in history that
is especially enlightening in view of the current French controversies,
at a time when it has been suggested that religions should be granted
public recognition and be no more relegated to the so-called private
sphere. The opposition between what is "public" and what is "private"
is still of crucial importance, in the future, for the relations between
the churches (religions), the state, and modern society; but what is at
stake is different, and the meaning of these words has changed. Let us
not fall into the trap of anachronism. To stick to the laicist agenda of
the late nineteenth and early twentieth centuries, the major conflict between the modern scheme of autonomy-separation and the politico-
theological scheme of heteronomy-concord of the Holy See lies in this
semantic strife over the concept of "public" and "private." This strife has
been initiated by the philosophical revolution of the seventeenth and
eighteenth centuries and the French revolution.

At the Root of the Conflict between the French Modern State
and the Holy See: A Philosophical Divergence

The law of the 9th December 1905, the so-called laicity law, inaugurated this word of "laicity" to designate the separation of the churches
by the state. I agree with Emile Poulat in saying that the separation of
the churches by the state already existed from Bonaparte's concordat of
1801, since France had then abandoned the principle of a state church.
As yet the law of 1905, which lays the ground for French laicity, as it
has commonly been called, is not only the result of the implementation of a philosophical, moral, and political agenda starting with the

setting up of the third republic and developed further in the 1880s; it is a thrice-fold project fuelled by the revolutionary ideals of 1789, and because of that is all the more the heir of the Enlightenment philosophy of the seventeenth century, which is truly a European one. As we know, there are many sides to the Enlightenment philosophy: it is German, English, and French; more precisely, it is a German from the far-off east Prussia, Immanuel Kant, who best defined the goal of Enlightenment: let man attain his majority.[18]

Laicist and republican France will not forget the Kantian message. The laicist agenda of the Republic includes freeing consciences and reason from the control of the Roman Catholic Church as well as freeing the state of any concordat with the Holy See. The separation of the Church from the state closes the period opened by the separation of the Church from the school. To phrase it in more conceptual terms, the breaking of the post–theological-ecclesial-political bond between the state and the Church supplements the separation of reason from the Christian revelation initiated twenty-five years before by the distinction between civic, moral, and religious instruction. It is thus necessary to study the documents produced by the Church during this period in order to understand what are—viewed from a Roman Catholic standpoint—the intellectual roots of the conflict between "republican laicity" and the Holy See.

Let us now examine the nature of the historical strife between the Holy See and European societies, and especially France. What are the ideas that the papacy reckons as downright incompatible with the "Christian order"? One single philosophical concept allows one to grasp the dispute in its entirety: autonomy. Because the republican-laicist agenda aims to free children (and by means of children, women) from a school education controlled by the Church and dictated by authoritarian dogmas preventing the use of free judgment, because laicity intends to rid the state of any theological creed (which the 1801 con-

18. Immanuel Kant, "Qu'est ce que les Lumières?" *Oeuvres philosophiques* (Paris: Ed. de la Pléiade, 1986), 2:209.

cordat for instance indirectly supported), for those reasons the central concept that stands for the philosophical touchstone of the conflict between Rome and the modern democratic state is autonomy. The core of autonomy is separation, as the etymology of the word indicates: the modern order of things resulting from the French revolution doesn't come from above, it fundamentally denies that heaven should organize the earth; it is not opposed to God as such, but it will not acknowledge any allegedly divine right to cater for the organization of man's society. In other words the medieval analogy between divine and human government is no longer the prevailing notion that determines how secular society is to be ruled. Autonomy, which philosophically is at the root of the emergence of modernity throughout centuries, emptied this medieval analogy of its meaning. Politically speaking, autonomy, which originates in Kantian philosophy, inevitably leads men to rule themselves according to their own will: this is democracy. Now democracy can be implemented only by universal suffrage, which itself cannot be effective unless society is "enlightened," thus educated enough to have a collective clear conscience of itself. An example of this is given by the French republican idea of nation. Lastly, autonomy has a moral dimension, which I have already underlined speaking of the school: autonomy promotes an ethic that holds all by itself, without God, at least not by God such as "lexicalized" by the Church. One thing is hence clear: separation, this magical word, almost unanimously accepted in its legal sense ever since 1905, is only a small part of the philosophical agenda of the age of Enlightenment; it is the prerequisite for all the other separations—scientific, moral, political, as well as legal—from the theological rhetoric. Without the concept of autonomy, it is impossible to understand the cultural landslide that caused a new turn in the policy of the elder daughter of the Church in the late nineteenth and early twentieth century. The law of 1905 consequently aspires to go a lot further than Bonaparte's concordat, which, like its author, swayed between the legacy of the revolution and the Enlightenment period and that of the theological-political conceptions of the Ancien Regime. If the term "laicity" is absent from the 1905 law, its philosophical purpose is to untie the spiritual from the temporal. I have recourse to this medieval vocabulary to point to the incompatibility between the republican-laicist agenda and the stance of the papacy in the late nineteenth and early twentieth centuries.

To the policy of autonomy supported by the republican laicists, the Holy See replies by reasserting a policy of heteronomy; to the promotion of individual liberties and equality for all and everyone, Rome replies by a praise of the ancient hierarchical, theological-political order, in which inequality coalesces with social justice, with an emphasis on unity and obedience to the Roman pontiff, the keystone of this order of concord. The popes accordingly have repeatedly stressed throughout the nineteenth century that separation—be it that of reason from revelation or that of the Church from the state—can only lead to disorder and hence to the decadence of Christian, Roman Catholic, European societies.

This defense of heteronomy is coupled with a discourse on concord that stands in total opposition with the so badly connoted word of "separation." I will try to demonstrate this by showing that this nostalgia for an Ancien Regime–style concordat is a recurrent *topos* of the Church's rhetoric concerning the relations of reason with revelation as well as those of the state with the Church. I insist on this last point because there is a link in the papal thought between the impossibility of a complete autonomy of the state with regard to the Church and the limited autonomy of reason with regard to revelation: the former illustrates the latter. The metaphysical coherence of the modern aspiration to autonomy-separation finds its symmetrical opposite and paradoxical illustration in the metaphysical coherence of the Roman Catholic counterview. The First Vatican Council and its syllabus will show it clearly.[19] I suggest (and historical facts compel me) to bring

---

19. One could not forget the attempt to develop a plan "De Ecclesia" on the relationship between church and state during the Vatican I Council. See G. H. Baudry, "L'Église et l'État au 1ᵉʳ concile du Vatican," *M.S.R. XLIV*, n°2/2/3 (1987): 71–77.

this metaphysical coherence to light starting with the document that initiated the conflict between autonomy-separation on the one hand and heteronomy-concord on the other hand: Pius VI's letter *Quod Aliquantum,* in which the pope puts forward his arguments against the civil constitution of the clergy.[20]

The Civil Constitution of the Clergy and the Letter *Quod Aliquantum* (1791): At the Root of the Strife between Roman Catholicism and French Political Modernity

Starting with the beginning is self-evident since what proceeds sheds light on what follows. True, between the letter *Quod Aliquantum* and the encyclical *Vehementer Nos* there elapsed a hundred and fifteen years of French and European history. The context of the two texts is thus different; but you shouldn't overly rely on the context if you want to make the subject of your study intelligible.

From the beginning of the revolution to the Third Republic, France had fifteen constitutions, like other European nations it went through two other revolutions in 1830 and 1848; between the restoration of the monarchy and the Third Republic the effects of the shock caused by revolutions were felt to their full as an intellectual U-turn was brought about by two major ideas, that of liberty on the one hand, and on the other hand the idea of reversing of the origin of sovereignty: no longer a theological-political one (God and the king), it became popular. In other words with the collapse of the Ancien Regime

20. The topical arguments in the teaching of the Roman See (brief *Quod Aliquantum* during the First Vatican Council) seek to ensure unfailing continuity in the attachment of the papacy to an Ancien Regime "Christian order." Furthermore, the two encyclicals *Immortale Dei* and *Vehementer Nos* represent a turning point in comparison with the previous Roman teaching of the first half of the nineteenth century. See my comment on the encyclical of Leo XIII since the pope himself refers to the encyclical *Mirari Vos* (1832) and to the Syllabus (1864). On the papal teaching until 1864, see Adrien Le Clere et al., *Recueil des allocutions consistoriales encycliques et autres lettres apostoliques des souverains pontifes Clément XII, Benoît XIV, Pie VI, Pie VII, Léon XII, Grégoire XVI, Pie IX* (Paris: Libraire, 1865).

the legitimacy of the political order stopped coming from "above" (God and the Church); it now came from "below" (the people). What I earlier made clear regarding the philosophical concept of autonomy had its political counterpart regarding three other concepts: liberty, equality, and democratic sovereignty. Thus the costly re-foundation of the social order, which the revolution was confronted with and failed to achieve, was tackled anew by the Third Republic, although it stumbled on two major problems.

The first is that of "national representation": individuals have formed by means of contract a political society, which represents them; in other words some men "represent" other men without having recourse to a sovereign authority, the origin of which would have to be theological. This society is a whole made up by its constituent parts (and not the other way round), which cannot tolerate any intermediary body in order to preserve its unity.[21] This new conception of social organization stems from the idea that society, which now forms a nation, has a full command over itself and hence cannot acknowledge any exterior authority within itself (the king by divine right) nor any exterior authority parallel to itself, the Church—the clergy was the first order of the Ancien Regime—whose unity has a warrant, the Roman pontiff, himself a sovereign. All the elements of "nationalization" of the Church via the civil constitution of the clergy are thus gathered.

This short experience of nationalization points to a second problem raised by and posed to the French revolution; this second problem has itself two aspects: to start with there is a first experience of almost total separation from papacy in order to strengthen the link between the Church and the state representing the nation.[22] The Church, within this new political and philosophical framework, takes part in the national sovereignty, is one with the nation, and allows the

21. See the law Le Chapelier of 1791.
22. Plongeron, *Les Défis de la Modernité (1750–1840)*, 307–44.

latter to gain full mastery over itself. The Church stands no more in the way, and one can even speak of a rising "momentum" of the political sovereignty, with its terrible consequences under the terror of 1793–94. The second aspect of this second problem is almost a natural consequence of the collapse of the former theological-political order: it is the question of the social status not just of the Roman Catholic Church but of religion altogether.

There again two aspects have to be distinguished: from a political point of view can the rise of an autonomous society—through liberty, equality of the individuals detached from all intermediary bodies, and popular sovereignty—be, as it were, summarized by the sole "social contract"?[23] No, answered the revolutionaries, whatever meaning their ideological chapel gave to the expression social contract. The society of autonomy is not incompatible with a reference to a philosophical or religious transcendence; even more, it requires it, but in another way.

This resulted in experiences that all failed, from the civil constitution of the clergy to the worship of the Supreme Being; lastly there was a first separation of the Church from the state at the very end of the revolution.

From a religious point of view I would raise the following question: can the Roman Catholic Church acknowledge the liberal and equalitarian society of democratic autonomy, or even better, make its jurisdictional and sacramental mediation for salvation compatible with this recognition?

If we stick to historical events from the French revolution up to the Second Vatican Council, the answer is no. The answer would be quite different if the question concerned the very principle of the Church's ecclesiastical jurisdiction and sacramentality. With respect to this, Vatican II made a valuable contribution, especially *Gaudium*

23. See Ghislain Waterlot, *Rousseau, Religion et Politique* (Paris: Presses Universitaires de France, 2004).

et Spes and the *Declaration on Religious Freedom (Dignitatis Humanae).*[24]

However, in the epoch-making context of the French revolution and its nineteenth-century aftermath, the answer is no because from Pius VI to Pius X the pontifical teaching is unable to get out of the framework of the theological-political way of thinking, which itself relies upon a metaphysical conception of the here below world. The main feature of this way of thinking is, as I have already underlined, the mutual concord between the temporal and the spiritual. Only then can the mediation of the Church take place both on a jurisdictional and on a sacramental plane.[25] Locked up in this view, papacy couldn't but frontally reject the new political philosophy that takes over France during the revolution, and that the Third Republic will implement with those three great ideas: republic, democracy, and laicity of the school and the state. Undoubtedly the revolution was the occasion of a frontal opposition between two views of the organization of society: the violence induced by what came out of the revolution is primarily a conceptual one; the revolution implies a break that constitutes the political society as such, and hence, determines its relationship with religion. The revolution is the initial and founding stage of the process of separation of religion from politics, that is, in Roman Catholic terms, of the Church from the state. Pope Pius VI understood it well not only in the objections he formulated against the civil constitution of the clergy, but also in the excursus he introduces speaking of the philosophy of human rights:[26] the latter has of

24. See *The Teachings of the Second Vatican Council,* intro. Gregory Baum (Westminster, Md.: Newman Press, 1966).

25. On what is at stake on the historical and theological aspects of these questions, see Gérard Pelletier, *Rome et la Révolution Française: La Théologie et la Politique du Saint-Siège devant la Révolution Française (1789–1799)* (Rome: École française de Rome, 2004).

26. According to Pius VI, there is a close link between *The Civil Constitution of Clergy* and the French declaration of human rights. This link is not false. The question that is more problematic is the incompatibility as such between the rights of man and

necessity influenced the principles that presided over the new ecclesiastical organization.

This is a topos of the pontifical teaching of the nineteenth century and an epitome of the Holy See's hostility against "modern ideas" such as were gathered in the 1864 Syllabus and confirmed by the First Vatican Council. This teaching continued, with a few time-related inflections, in Leo XIII's encyclical *Immortale Dei*.

The Encyclical *Immortale Dei* (1885): A Theological-Political Conception of the Relationship between the Church, the State, and Society

Between the 1791 brief *Quod Aliquantum* and the 1885 encyclical *Immortale Dei* the Holy See obviously staggered under the blow, which is testified by the many documents issued during that period, like the Syllabus, a doctrinal synthesis, and the First Vatican Council (1869–70),[27] which stands for the final expression of the Church's authority. Was the year 1885 a turning point? I would say no as concerns the basic argumentative structure developed by Leo XIII, which doesn't mean that the encyclical is void of interest or that the pope isn't somehow reserved about the Syllabus. Yet the interest of the encyclical doesn't lie where it is generally assumed to do: it doesn't display any kind of openness, judging from a "pre–Vatican II" point of view. *Immortale Dei* is not a balanced, moderate text; it is not an extremist one either. Such adjectives have no meaning. Leo XIII, who is well perceived as a nice personality because he is the author of the first social encyclical, *Rerum Novarum,* and because he recognized the republic, is nonetheless representative of an uncompromising, al-

---

the rights of God. It is the Second Vatican Council that has resolved this fundamental problem in the *Declaration on Religious Freedom (Dignitatis Humanae).*

27. Marcel Gauchet, *La Religion dans la Démocratie, parcours de la laïcité* (Paris: Gallimard, 1998), 53. Concerning the *Syllabus* as such, see Paul Christophe and Roland Minnerath, *Le "Syllabus" de Pie IX* (Paris: Cerf, 2000).

beit moderate,[28] type of Catholicism. It would be pointless and anach-
ronistic to reproach him with it. It is just a fact that has to be acknowledged in order not to be misled about his innermost ideas concerning
the role of Catholicism and its place in modern society. It should
be remembered that Leo XIII was the first pope without a temporal
state; he was struggling with the Kuturkampf in Germany and with
the laicization of education in France. All this is felt in the ideas developed in his encyclical; no wonder thus that the pope makes use
of the classical pontifical discourse already held by his predecessors,
Gregory XVI and Pius IX, whom he explicitly quotes. For Leo XIII
the "already quite old"[29] accusations against the Church that it runs
counter to "the interests of civil society"[30] are absolutely groundless.
This criticism is not new; it can be traced back to the early times of
the Church, which for that reason were called times of persecution.
Pius VI had already had recourse to this kind of arguments, and all
the more so did the popes of the nineteenth century; but we might
just as well go back to the sixteenth and seventeenth centuries. The
discourse on "persecution," which has little to do with serious scientific
history, is always indicative of a crisis. In this respect Leo XIII is quite
in the wake of what Pius VI said in the brief *Quod Aliquantum;* the per-
secutor now is the "new right that is allegedly the fruit of maturity."[31]

28. For a general presentation of Leo XIII's ideas, see Yves-Marie Hilaire, *Histoire de
la papauté, 1000 ans de mission de tribulations* (Paris: Tallandier, 1996), 415–28. Leo XIII
published five encyclicals on the relationship between church and state, which shows the
importance he gave theological and political thought. On the rallying to the Republic,
see: *Au milieu des solicitudes,* 111–22, and the *Lettre Encyclique aux cardinaux français,*
123–27, in *Lettres Apostoliques de S.S. Leo XIII,* t. 3 (Paris: La bonne presse, 1892). In this
encyclical, Leo XIII explains on several occasions that his call to rallying the Republic
does not mean supporting a philosophical-political regime absolutely incompatible with
the teaching of the Roman See. It only means rallying a new constitutional order: in this
prospect, the pope distinguishes in particular the respect due to the power, which can
come only from God, from legislative measures that the power takes against the Church
(see in particular 125–26).

29. Leo XIII, *Immortale Dei, Lettres Apostoliques de S.S. Léon XIII,* 17.

30. Ibid.

31. Ibid., 19. The possibility that Leo XIII refers to Kant's assertion, which says man
attains his majority with "the Enlightenment," cannot be ruled out.

Having examined the current state of modern society and thus that of the Church, Leo XIII carries on with his line of reasoning, relying on two very classical postulates; the first one originates in the philosophy of Aristotle:

> Man's natural instinct moves him to live in civil society, for he cannot, if dwelling apart, provide himself with the necessary requirements of life, nor procure the means of developing his mental and moral faculties. Hence, it is ordained that he should lead his life—be it family, or civil—with his fellow men, amongst whom alone his several wants can be adequately supplied. But, as no society can hold together unless some one be over all, directing all to strive earnestly for the common good, every body politic must have a ruling authority, and this authority, no less than society itself, has its source in nature, and has consequently, God for its author.[32]

The second comes from the New Testament (Rom 13:1–8): "hence it follows that public power must proceed from God."[33] True, and that is possibly one of the new ideas of the encyclical that caught the attention of commentators: "the right to rule is not necessarily bound up with any special form of government."[34] Yet the encyclical doesn't deal with the different types of regimes. Leo XIII writes: "rulers must set God before themselves as their exemplar and law in the administration of the State."[35] This is the central point of the pope: the world, when society is organized on the basis of autonomy, turns away from God, who stands for the metaphysical and theological-political principle that had been presiding over Christian Europe for centuries.

Accordingly Leo XIII stresses the necessity for a "public profession of religion." Religious liberty shouldn't be tolerated precisely be-

32. Ibid.

33. Ibid. Leo XIII here refers to Saint Paul's epistle to the Romans, 13:1–8.

34. Ibid. Leo XIII's point of view on this question differs from the traditional problematic of the best of regimes, that is to say monarchy, and that of the indirect temporal power of popes; these theories are defended by Cardinal Bellarmine, to cite only the best known example.

35. Ibid., 19–21.

cause it abolishes the very notion of "public profession of religion." The argument is not new; it had already been used during the sixteenth century's religious crisis. Leo XIII objects to people's choosing their religion, "no such religion they may have preference for,"[36] for this would ruin the public profession of religion, which can only worship the true God, the sole warrant for the strong and necessary unity of the political order. There can be no legitimate authority unless it is grounded on truth, and there can be no lasting human society if it is separated from this truth; but also there can be no public profession of religion without recognition of the true God, of whom the Church—with the pope as its head together with the episcopate—is the mediator. In that Leo XIII sticks to the traditional ecclesiology of the Church as perfect society:

> This society is made up of men, just as civil society is, and yet is supernatural and spiritual, on account of the end for which it was founded, and of the means by which it aims at attaining that end. Hence, it is distinguished and differs from civil society, and, what is of highest moment, it is a society chartered as of right divine, perfect in its nature and in its title, to possess in itself and by itself, through the will and loving kindness of its Founder, all needful provision for its maintenance and action. And just as the end at which the Church aims is by far the noblest of ends, so is its authority the most exalted of all authority, nor can it be looked upon as inferior to the civil power, or in any manner dependent upon it.[37]

It is thus clear that Leo XIII, like his predecessors of the first half of the nineteenth century, can only dismiss "the philosophy that truckles to the state,"[38] a philosophy that proved so harmful to the jurisdictional and sacramental order of the Church, especially with the civil constitution of the clergy. At the core of this attack on the Church was the discredit it brought on the papacy, the keystone of Roman ecclesiology. Leo XIII reminds us that "it was not without a singu-

36. Ibid., 23.   37. Ibid., 25.
38. Ibid.

lar disposition of God's providence that this power of the Church was provided with a civil sovereignty as the surest safeguard of her independence."[39]

It is this power to power—spiritual and temporal—relationship that a laicist thinker such as Renouvier firmly contests.[40] To think the relationship between the state and the Church in terms of that of two powers ordained by God can only lead to a conflict between the French republicans-laicists and the papal teaching. On the one hand the origin of the conflict is metaphysical; Leo XIII has recourse to the analogy between "body and soul"[41] to account for the concord[42] that should exist between the two powers, the spiritual and the temporal. Yet on the other hand the object of this metaphysical dispute is the practical relations between the state and the Church. In this respect the analogy between "body and soul" doesn't make sense for the republicans-laicists. Thus it is the logic of separation that prevails, even though around 1885 no one yet talks of denouncing the concordat. At the time the main thing on the political agenda of the republicans is the laicization of teaching; but, in order to free the minds of people from this metaphysical order, you have in the long run to go as far as a legal separation of the state from the Church. There is no way in

39. Ibid., 27.

40. See Marie-Claude Blais, *Au principe de la République, le cas Renouvier* (Paris: Gallimard, 2000), 325: "The influence of words together with the pressure of facts have always exerted leads us to consider any regulation of the contacts between the two powers as a contract; and it will be noticed that the separation appears in the same light as the union to those who claim it; because they readily conceive of them as a recognition of the independence of the Church and giving what it calls its liberty is a way of dealing with it while keeping, however badly, the freedom of the civil powers." This text is an extract from an article by Renouvier entitled "The Dilemma of the Liberal Principle and the Clerical Principle," *Critique Philosophique* (28 August 1875): 51. The author refers to "The letter on Tolerance" drawn from an extract of the French edition of 1710, in the philosophical criticism, *Un passage de Locke* (27 June 1872), 311–14.

41. Leo XIII, *Immortale Dei*, 27; "A system of well-ordered relations between the two powers, not without analogy with that which in man forms the union of soul and body, is therefore necessary."

42. Ibid., 29.

which the democratic republican autonomy can come to terms with such a statement as: "[T]he ruling powers are invested with a sacredness more than human, and are withheld from deviating from the path of duty, and from overstepping the bounds of rightful authority; and the obedience is not the servitude of man to man, but submission to the will of God, exercising His sovereignty through the medium of men."[43] Leo XIII is very clear about it when he says further: "[N]ow, when the State rests on foundations like those just named—and for the time being they are greatly in favor—it readily appears into what and how unrightfully a position the Church is driven."[44]

The result is that "when the management of public business is in harmony with doctrines of such a kind, the Catholic religion is allowed a standing in civil society equal only, or inferior, to societies alien from it."[45] It is significant that Leo XIII pleads that one should stick to the 1801 concordat,[46] but let us not be misled by the word. In concordat, there is concord; and for the author of *Immortale Dei,* concord, as I have shown earlier, corresponds to a medieval metaphysical and theological-ecclesio-political status that neither Bonaparte nor the drafters of this international treaty had in mind. Portalis doesn't expound any theory of the two powers, nor does he reject religious liberty in the name of a public profession of religion to be offered to God! For Leo XIII, like for Pius VI, the hierarchical mediation of the Church for the salvation of man can take place only if the civil power is on its side. Concord is necessary for the good of the temporal as well as of the spiritual. The society of autonomy accepts divine transcendence, but in the way of the deism of spiritualists such as Jules Si-

43. Ibid., 31; in other words, the forms of devolution of power can change, but their foundation cannot, because their divine origin makes them eternal. See *Au milieu des sollicitudes,* 118.

44. Leo XIII, *Immortale Dei,* 35.

45. Ibid.

46. It must be said that the concordat is still maintained today in Alsace and the North of Lorraine. Another system of worship also exists in the French overseas countries.

mon, who advocates a God without the ecclesial mediation of clerics separated from the rest of society. Significantly Jules Simon ends his book, *La religion naturelle,* saying that a state which would deny the existence of God would cause society to collapse.[47] Leo XIII would have subscribed to such a clear-cut assertion, yet he is not talking of the same God: "[N]ow, natural reason itself proves convincingly that such concepts of the government of a State are wholly at variance with the truth. Nature itself bears witness that all power, of every kind, has its origin from God, who is its chief and most august source."[48]

The same is true of liberty, a theme that indicates that there is a turn in the ideas developed in the encyclical: the Christian order that comes from God doesn't reject liberty, but this liberty is "an element of perfection for man which must be applied to what is true and good."[49] The liberty of heteronomy-concord regulated by truth utterly differs from that of autonomy-separation, which is self-indulgence for the mind.[50] God and liberty the Catholic way are not the God and liberty of the laicists. Starting from this insuperable opposition, the question of the school is one of paramount importance.[51] In this context Leo XIII makes use of Gregory XVI's encyclical *Mirari Vos* and the Syllabus, two major texts that had condemned the liberal Catholics without naming them.[52]

Lastly democracy within a society of autonomy-separation radically differs from what Leo XIII suggests it is. The word as such doesn't appear; it is negatively alluded to when Leo XIII explicitly expresses the fear that with democracy, and because of the freedom of opinion it entails, "seditions might be rightfully fostered."[53] What matters

47. Jules Simon, *La religion naturelle* (Paris: Hachette, 1856); also by the same author, *Dieu, Patrie, Liberté* (Paris: Calman Lévy, 1883).

48. Leo XIII, *Immortale Dei,* 39.   49. Ibid.

50. Ibid.   51. Ibid.

52. Ibid., 39–41. See in the *Syllabus* the propositions 19, 39, 56 and 76. In the encyclical *Au Milieu des Solicitudes,* op. cit., 121, Leo XIII may refer to the American idea of separation.

53. Ibid., 41.

to Leo XIII is the political status granted to the "people" who "more or less takes part in the ruling of affairs," which, he adds, "is not only an advantage, but also a duty for the citizens."[54] As yet nothing is said about the way the people "takes part in the ruling of affairs," which is understandable since an encyclical is not a treatise of political philosophy. To me there is here an implicit reference to St. Thomas Aquinas's theory of mixed government.[55] Leo XIII's "balanced" conception of the participation of the people in public affairs is coupled with a balanced view on religious tolerance, which he calls "just tolerance":

> The Church, indeed, deems it unlawful to place the various forms of divine worship on the same footing as the true religion, but does not, on that account, condemn those rulers who, for the sake of securing some great good or of hindering some great evil, allow patiently custom or usage to be a kind of sanction for each kind of religion having its place in the State. And, in fact, the Church is wont to take earnest heed that no one shall be forced to embrace the Catholic faith against his will, for, as St. Augustine wisely reminds us, "Man cannot believe otherwise than of his own will."[56]

In substance Leo XIII puts forward the famous theory of the "thesis" and "hypothesis."[57] Quoting St. Augustine, who had supported the no

54. Ibid., 41.

55. St. Thomas Aquinas, *Selected Political Writings*, ed. with an intro. by A. P. D'Entrèves, trans. J. G. Dawson (Oxford: Basil Blackwell, 1948).

56. Leo XIII, *Immortale Dei*, 43.

57. We must mention that the distinction of thesis and hypothesis was born after a conflict between liberal Catholics and the intransigents. It appears for the first time in an article by a Roman journalist giving an account of the Congress of Malines (see the *Civilta Cattolica*, 2 October 2 1863, that is to say, shortly before the Syllabus). The distinction explains that it is at the same time possible to accept papal condemnation of modern liberties and Montalembert's praise of them. "These modern liberties as a thesis, that is to say as universal principles concerning human nature in itself and the divine order of the world, must definitely be condemned.... But as a hypothesis, that is to say as measures appropriate to special conditions of such or such country, they can be rightful and Catholics can love them and defend them." In a word, the "thesis" represents the rule of ideal behavior; the "hypothesis" the rule of conduct that takes into

less famous interpretation of the *Compelle intrare* of St. Luke's Gospel,[58] the pope acknowledges that man's conscience has to be respected. Yet the theory of the thesis and hypothesis, because of its postulate, doesn't contradict the ideal necessity for a public profession of religion offered to the sole true God. Unlike *Dignitatis Humanae* of the Vatican II Council, Leo XIII's encyclical makes only a concession—although a non-negligible one—to the new context. His point is to acknowledge what is good in the liberty of conscience, whilst averting its devastating effects: "In the same way the Church cannot approve of that liberty which begets a contempt of the most sacred laws of God, and casts off the obedience due to lawful authority, for this is not liberty so much as license, and is most correctly styled by St. Augustine the 'liberty of self-ruin,' and by the Apostle St. Peter the 'cloak of malice.'"[59]

The task of the Church is to regulate this liberty in view of its possible dangers for the state:

> This honorable liberty, alone worthy of human beings, the Church approves most highly and has never slackened her endeavor to preserve, strong and unchanged, among nations. And, in truth, whatever in the State is of chief avail for the common welfare; whatever

account circumstances and time. The distinction was applied to the proposals of the Syllabus by Mgr. Dupanloup, bishop of Orleans, in a leaflet entitled *La convention du 15 septembre et l'encyclique du 8 décembre* (January 1865). After the exegesis of the prelate, most Catholics, living in accord with a hypothesis, continued to follow modern liberties in all security of mind and to grant them to others (including the freedom of non-Catholic cults), it was enough to admit that this situation was not ideal. The leaflet of the bishop of Orléans achieved its goal perfectly; it imposed a sweetened interpretation of the Syllabus on a large audience. Besides, the American reader will not fail to notice the important part played by the Jesuit theologian J. C. Murray concerning his interpretation of the thought of Leo XIII, as well as his influence at the Second Vatican Council in the redaction of *Dignitatis Humanae (The Declaration on Religious Freedom)*.

58. Lk 14:23.

59. Leo XIII, *Immortale Dei*, 43. On the question of relation between religion and freedom, see Agnès Antoine, *L'Impensé de la démocratie. Tocqueville, la citoyenneté et la religion* (Paris: Fayard, 2003).

has been usefully established to curb the license of rulers who are opposed to the true interests of the people, or to keep in check the leading authorities from unwarrantably interfering in municipal or family affairs; whatever tends to uphold the honor, manhood, and equal rights of individual citizens—of all these things, as the monuments of past ages bear witness, the Catholic Church has always been the originator, the promoter, or the guardian. Ever, therefore, consistent with herself, while on the one hand she rejects that exorbitant liberty which in individuals and in nations ends in license or in thralldom, on the other hand, she willingly and most gladly welcomes whatever improvements the age brings forth, if these really secure the prosperity of life here below, which is, as it were, a stage in the journey to the life that will know no ending.[60]

In accordance with the teaching of Vatican I, in the constitution *Dei Filius* (1870) on faith and reason, Leo XIII unfailingly stresses: "And as all truth in the natural order is powerless to destroy belief in the teachings of revelation, but can do much to confirm it, and as every newly discovered truth may serve to further the knowledge or the praise of God, it follows that whatsoever spreads the range of knowledge will always be willingly and even joyfully welcomed by the Church."[61]

The autonomy of sciences is "just" on condition that "natural truth" doesn't invalidate the faith in revealed truths. This pontifical epistemological stance quite reassembles the subtle balance that needs to exist in the relations between the state and the Church, or between liberty and the acknowledgement of the truth professed by Rome. Hence Leo XIII deplores the discredit into which Catholic thought has fallen: "All this, though so reasonable and full of counsel, finds little favour nowadays when States not only refuse to conform to the rules of Christian wisdom, but seem even anxious to recede from them further and further on each successive day."[62]

60. Leo XIII, *Immortale Dei*, 43–45. Leo XIII distances himself from the *Syllabus* on this point.

61. Ibid., 45.

62. Ibid.

Consequently Leo XIII calls Catholics "to stick to the judgment of the Holy See" and comply with its decisions. Starting from this teaching Catholics must get involved in the affairs of society in view of the "public good,"[63] be it in the field of moral and religious education, or even outside the field of education, which Leo XIII finds overly limited. To keep away from this duty would mean leaving it to the "enemies of the Church"[64] to run public affairs. As in the beginning of the encyclical, there is a historical argument recalling that the early Christians, while being hostile to heathen society, were good citizens respectful of authorities. That is how Christian institutions penetrated the heathen world. Again and again it is the task of the Christians to civilize people. This recurrent reference to Christian antiquity is quite telling; it points to a context in which the Church was a persecuted minority. As I have already noted, this nonscientific way of dealing with history introduces confusion between the pagan context of the early Christians and the evil doing of a society of autonomy that separates itself from the civilizing Christian institutions.[65] Since concord with the new society no longer exists, it is all the more necessary that it prevail, and even be reinforced, within the Church.

"In the endeavor to secure interests of the highest order there is no room for intestine strife or party rivalries; since all should aim with one mind and purpose to make safe that which is the common object of all—the maintenance of religion and of the State."[66] In other words, the encyclical *Immortale Dei* takes place in the context of a conflict with several European states trying to get free from the control of the papacy, and especially France at the time of the strife over laicity at school. Yet Leo XIII is moderate in order to adapt to the new situation. To this end, it is of the interest of Catholics not to become marginal, although the bulk of the doctrine developed in the encyclical still abides by metaphysical premises—with their theological-political implications—that are identical with those of Leo XIII's predecessors.

63. Ibid., 47.
64. Ibid., 49.
65. Ibid.
66. Ibid., 51.

This kind of thinking is what I would call an Ancien Regime–style line of reasoning since it implies that the Church is coextensive with the state and society: it is an organic way of thinking based on concord and characteristic of the theological-political age that precedes the philosophy of Enlightenment.

Although there is no denying that Leo XIII made concessions, the type of thought he sets as a model for the Catholics can only clash with the republican laicist philosophy of autonomy-separation as concerns teaching. In the long run the separation of the Church from the state will follow logically.

The ideas developed by Pius X in *Vehementer Nos* can be understood only in the light of the process of formulation for the 1905 law. Although the logic of this encyclical is identical with that of Leo XIII's *Immortale Dei,* Pius X's text is exclusively concerned with France; it is therefore much more limited in scope, but it is quite telling as to the nature of the conflict between the republican laicists and papacy as concerns the social status of religion.

The Encyclical *Vehementer Nos* (1906): Wrestling with the Laicity of the Republican State

The encyclical *Vehementer Nos,* which is addressed to "the Archbishops and Bishops, and to all the Clergy and People of France," perfectly illustrates a conception according to which the Church is coextensive and in concordance with the state and society: the encyclical addresses both the ecclesiastical hierarchy within the Church and the people, that is, lay people outside the Church.[67] Yet unlike Leo XIII, Pius X more precisely addresses the people of France. This papal text is thus very much dependent on the conflict between the republican France around 1900 and the Roman Church. Let us keep in mind another major fact that is very much linked to France: the modernist

---

67. Pius X, *Vehementer Nos,* in *Actes de S.S. Pie X,* t. 3 (Paris: La bonne presse, 1906), 123–49. Cardinal Merry del Val was the principal writer of this encyclical.

crisis that occurred in the same context and that has also been the subject of an encyclical. "For Pius X and the people around him both result from a malevolent conspiracy and call for the same vigilance and condemnation," says Jean-Marie Mayeur in his book *La séparation de l'Eglise et de l'Etat.*[68]

Once again for the Holy See, the conflict of faith with reason and that of the Church with the modern state are inseparably linked. From a historical point of view Pius X's intervention takes place in the middle of the crisis caused by the inventories of the ecclesiastical properties on the 11th of February 1906. Those inventories have been decided by the government in order "to prevent any theft of antiques"[69] in accordance with article 3 of the law of separation voted on the 9th of December 1905. As this crisis resulted in violent incidents, Pius X couldn't ignore it and intervened publicly.

However, in the course of the two previous years a number of discussions had been going on among the republicans. There was a clash between three stances;[70] to start with, between that of the "petit père Combes," aggressively anticlerical, which aimed at dismantling the churches by imposing upon them a departmental structure, and the democratic stance, which compelled the churches to adopt the rules of the French democracy, not the specific rules of the Roman Church.[71] This second stance, as well as the first, was criticized by the bishops (actually by every church), who feared that separation might lead to a schism. Inevitably the equalitarian legal and political principles of the society of autonomy had to clash with the *ius gentium*[72] advocated by the Church for centuries prior to the philosophy of hu-

---

68. Jean-Marie Mayeur, *La séparation de l'Église et de l'État* (Paris: Julliard, collection Archives, 1966), 104. See the encyclical *Pascendi Dominici Gregis,* in *Actes de S.S. Pie X* (Paris: La bonne presse, 1906), 85–187.

69. See Jean Baubérot, *Vers un nouveau pacte laïque* (Paris: Seuil, 1990), 76.

70. I am highly indebted to the French sociologist Jean Baubérot concerning his theories of the three models of separation.

71. Baubérot, *Vers un nouveau pacte laïque,* 69.

72. Pius X, *Vehementer Nos,* 131.

man rights, and to an even greater extent, with the hierarchical, non-egalitarian type of the Roman ecclesiology:

> For the provisions of the new law are contrary to the constitution on which the Church was founded by Jesus Christ. The Scripture teaches us, and the tradition of the Fathers confirms the teaching, that the Church is the mystical body of Christ, ruled by the Pastors and Doctors (Ephes. 4:11–16)—a society of men containing within its own fold chiefs who have full and perfect powers for ruling, teaching and judging (Matt. 28:18–20; 16:18–19; 18:17; Tit. 2:15; 2 Cor. 10:6; 13:10, etc.). It follows that the Church is essentially an unequal society, that is, a society comprising two categories of persons, the Pastors and the flock, those who occupy a rank in the different degrees of the hierarchy and the multitude of the faithful. So distinct are these categories that with the pastoral body only rests the necessary right and authority for promoting the end of the society and directing all its members towards that end; the one duty of the multitude is to allow themselves to be led, and, like a docile flock, to follow the Pastors.[73]

The reaction of the bishop of Quimper, Bishop Dubillard, points to the incompatibility of the Roman ecclesiology with the aforementioned democratic stance of some republicans: "[T]he separation will inevitably lead to a schism. . . . It is the very negation of the hierarchical power, and, what is more, it suppresses the leadership of the holy Father: it is the world upside down, instead of having the authoritative voice come from above, they want to have it come from below. . . . It is the annihilation of any hierarchy, it is the destruction of the needed authority, it is a schism!"[74]

"Instead of having the authoritative voice come from above, they want to have it come from below"; at least the intervention of the bishop of Quimper underlines a gap that cannot be bridged between two notions of authority, that—heteronymous—of the Roman Church, based on a hierarchical structure, and that, based on autonomy and

---

73. Ibid., 133–135.
74. Baubérot, *Vers un nouveau pacte laïque*, 69–70.

separation, which derives from the Enlightenment, the French revolution, and has been taken over by republican laicists.

In other words, for the ecclesiastical hierarchy the Catholic Church cannot fit in with the common law of the republic. The rejection by the Church of this republican idea of separation, which is reminiscent of the civil constitution of the clergy and which more resembles an intervention of the state in the Church affairs than a real separation, could only reinforce the attitude of some republicans, who thought that no "neutral" separation was possible.[75] The resignation of the "petit père Combes" from the cabinet for something that had nothing to do with the Church affairs helped in finding a way out of the crisis.[76] This resignation was a turning point in the making of the law of separation.[77] There appeared a more liberal and respectful stance on separation, that is, the third of the three stances I was alluding to earlier: this third stance was respectful of the rules peculiar to each church. This was, to a large extent, the main contribution of Jean Jaurès, whose concern was to bring the conflict between the two Frances to an end and not make things worse. Accordingly the law of separation of the 9th of December 1905, which was voted after many controversial debates in parliament,[78] clearly showed that the republican state had given up on any interference with the internal affairs of churches. The law of separation thus is a compromise with the Catholic Church.[79] As yet the problem of the inventories momentarily jeopardized this compromise and truce.

In his encyclical Pius X strictly forbids the constitution of the "associations of worship" stipulated by Title II of the law:

75. Ibid., 70.

76. His resignation concerned the files that had been established in order to control the activities of Catholic officers; see Jean Baubérot, *Laïcité 1905–2005, entre passion et raison* (Paris: Seuil, 2004), 96.

77. Baubérot, *Vers un nouveau pacte laïque*, 71.

78. Ibid., 71–73, 72–76.

79. See Guy Bedouelle and Jean-Paul Costa, *Les laïcités à la française* (Paris: Puf, politique d'aujourd'hui, 1998), 51–52.

Besides, nothing more hostile to the liberty of the Church than this Law could well be conceived. For, with the existence of the associations of worship, the Law of Separation hinders the Pastors from exercising the plenitude of their authority and of their office over the faithful; when it attributes to the Council of State supreme jurisdiction over these associations and submits them to a whole series of prescriptions not contained in the common law, rendering their formation difficult and their continued existence more difficult still.[80]

The result is that the Catholics use the places of worship illegally. The French government doesn't react, and Aristide Briand declares that willy-nilly the Church will abide by the law (such is the meaning of the law of the 2nd of January 1907) after having considered a recourse to the law of 1881 on public reunions.[81] This strife, technically a legal one but in fact ecclesiological and political in its implications, which hinged on the "associations of worship," will only be settled with the institution of diocesan associations presided by the bishop. This way the Catholic Church is no longer granted official recognition, but its internal ecclesial structure is respected. Pius XI in his encyclical *Maximam Gravissimamque* in January 1924 says that diocesan associations are a good solution.[82] The council of state will reckon them as "compatible with the associations of worship" devised by the 1905 law.

So three models of separation have been considered; the last one—

80. Pius X, *Gravissimo officili* (10 August 1906), 137, 139–41; Pius X confirms his refusal of any compromise with the religious organizations. See on the notion of cult, the article by Pierre Vallin, *Lumière et Vie* 190 (1989): 74. In his book *Vers un nouveau pacte laïqu* 78, Jean Baubérot mentions Aristide Briand's statement concerning the law of 2 January 1907: "This law will have the effect of making it impossible for the Catholic Church to go beyond the law, even if it wanted it strongly." This situation will last until 1924.

81. Concerning the parliamentary debates about the elaboration of the 1905 law, see Aristide Briand, *La Séparation Application du régime nouveau (1906–1908)* (Paris: Fasquelle, 1909).

82. Bedouelle and Costa, *Les laïcités à la française*, 56 and 62; Baubérot, *Vers un nouveau pacte laïque*, 78.

liberal and respectful—has been put into practice by the 1905 law. As yet the incompatibility between the republican policy of separation and the Roman notion of "public worship" such as expounded under Pius X remains. If everyone agrees that there can be no neutral separation, an agreement has yet to be found as to the meaning of non-neutrality, speaking of free Catholic public worship.

For the Roman Church free public worship implies that only Catholic worship is true because only the Catholic Church holds religious truth. Symmetrically the goal of political societies is "the everlasting blissfulness offered to man when this so short life comes to an end." This theological-political conception of public worship and the spiritual end assigned to political societies can only dismiss the idea of separation because this idea implies that the secular coextensive relationship of the temporal with the spiritual has been broken. From a Roman point of view none of these models of separation are neutral. Pius X has spoken several times about this in his encyclical, showing incidentally how attached he was to the doctrine of the two powers— civil and ecclesiastical—upheld by Leo XIII. Only in this sense can there be a separation, which in fact is just a distinction since the point is still to maintain concord between temporal and spiritual powers.

This Ancien Régime view implies that the Church has a legal status in its relations with the state. The ecclesiastical public law (canon law) can in no way come to terms with the lay secular public law, which doesn't grant churches any public status: they are confined to the private sphere; worship is free but officially not recognized.

Freedom of worship in the laicist sense of the word isn't derived from any theological-political conceptions, hence the republican emphasis on the private character of religion and the impossibility of any concordat. The non-neutrality of the laicist agenda echoes the non-neutrality of the Church's notion of public worship. So the dispute hinges on what public worship is, not just from a legal but also from a philosophical standpoint.[83] In this dispute neither of the two parties

83. See Patrick Valdrini, *Droit canonique* (Paris: Dalloz, 1989), 573.

can be neutral: either freedom of worship is based on the recognition of the Church by the state, hence its public character; or it is based on the non-recognition of the Church by the state, hence its private character. Although the 1905 law was inspired by a liberal and respectful attitude, it doesn't change the main issue: what is at stake in the idea of separation is the removal from the public sphere of the Ancien Régime–style freedom of worship. Such is the difference between the status of the Church in the 1905 law and in the concordat of 1801. Separation presupposes that the conflict between "law" and "freedom" has been solved. The *ius gentium* doesn't metaphysically correspond to human rights; freedom within the public recognition of the Church is not freedom within the public non-recognition of the Church.[84] Autonomy lies at the bottom of the philosophy of laicists: it is the autonomy of the school first, then that of the state.

If the lawmakers of 1905 didn't have in mind this philosophy, there would have been no reason to abolish Bonaparte's concordat. Freedom of worship already existed, but the Church was publicly recognized according to the public law of Catholicism, that is, as "the religion of the majority of the French people." We have returned to the inventories crisis and to the very delicate problem of the respect given to the inner organization of the Church,[85] in other words, to its ecclesiology in a society that has rid itself of all theological-political grounds in view of its democratic-autonomous principles.

The arguments of the encyclical *Vehementer Nos* undoubtedly echo the debates that took place between 1904 and 1905.[86] From the Holy See's point of view (at least under Pius X) there is no difference between the three republican stances on the non-recognition of the public worship of the Catholic Church. The three of them are by nature unacceptable because Rome insists that there is concord between

84. Pius X, *Vehementer Nos*, 129.

85. See Title II of the 1905 law.

86. Bedouelle and Costa, *Les laïcités à la* française, 62; Baubérot, *Vers un nouveau pacte laïque*, 78.

the state, society, and the Church. Besides, a concordat is a contract that "binds both parties,"[87] and moreover, as it has already been mentioned, the law of separation clashes with the hierarchical constitution of the Church.[88]

Conclusion

In this decisive conflict between the state and the Church, which led to the separation of the Church by the state and not of the Church from the state—which would presuppose that both parties agreed—the different opinions among the republican laicists are worth noting at least schematically. They show that the notion of separation is polysemic rather than univocal. There is a wide gap between the invasive conception of the state, reminiscent of the philosophical-political premises that presided over the civil constitution of the clergy, and the more liberal stance that prevailed in the 1905 law.

From a Roman Catholic point of view it is perfectly understandable that the Church defended its autonomy. It's indeed a fallacy to believe that the law of separation aims at preserving the freedom of worship when the state dictates to the Church what ideally it should be. The legal and administrative sides of the conflict have to be analyzed in the light of the philosophical, political, and theological-ecclesiological problems at stake: the former are outlined by the latter in a very telling way.

From a laicist point of view the 1905 law epitomizes the republican agenda of the second half of the nineteenth century, that is to say, the implementation of a policy of autonomy-separation. More generally, a modern state cannot let its social order be structured by re-

---

87. Pius X, *Vehementer Nos,* 131.

88. Ibid., 133. It is particularly judicious to compare the position of Pius VI on this matter in his encyclical *Quod Aliquantum* with that of Pius X a little more than a century later; the Church as an institution that mediates salvation is conceivable only if its cult is public and therefore acknowledged by the state.

ligion, in this particular instance Roman Catholicism. The problem is not so much the reference to divine transcendence as the dogmatic way in which it is asserted by the Church, itself a hierarchical institution whose organization and mechanisms of thought are in all respects opposed to the secular-autonomous and democratic organization of modern societies. In the background of this frontal opposition, the seventeenth and eighteenth centuries' philosophy and the French revolution have laid the foundations of the transformation of a heteronomy-concord order into one of autonomy-separation, and of a coextensive relationship between politics and religion into one in which politics and religion belong to two different spheres, on the basis of a separation-dissociation. Such is the logic of the republican-laicist agenda, yet its radicality is not to be seen elsewhere in Europe. It allows France to define itself as a fatherland, a nation, and a state by means of the school and the laicist ethics. The ambition of republicans is to combine freedom with secular public rules; hence the Church is relegated to the so-called private sphere. It doesn't fit ordinary standards; it is an institution among others, but with a specific history and culture.[89]

This is precisely what the Catholic Church, or at least most of it, and at any rate the Holy See, didn't accept. Can the society of men exist without the public worship offered to the sole true God whose mediator is the Church united around the sovereign pontiff? Certainly not in the mind of Leo XIII, Pius X, and their predecessors. However, through the logic of separation it is the whole theological-political status of truth and authority that was called into question.[90] It was the task of Vatican II, and noticeably of *Gaudium et Spes* and *Dignita-*

89. We must note that for the founders of French secularity, especially during the 1870s, the American model is the subject of true admiration. For example, the case of Ferdinand Buisson on coming back from the Philadelphia 1876 universal exhibition. It is exactly Jules Ferry's position. See Baubérot, *Laïcité 1905–2005*, 165–66.

90. See Danièle Hervieu-Léger, *Catholicisme, la fin d'un monde* (Paris: Bayard, 2003), 285–311, in particular the last chapter, on the status of authority in the Catholic Church.

tis Humanae, to give a new perspective to this unprecedented status of truth and authority. As yet the logic of separation mustn't be confused with dissociation between politics, ethics, and religion, or between reason and truth. In the same way that the divinity of Christ is power within kenosis, the autonomy-separation is not an immanence circumscribed within it. It is maybe the herald of a new humanism in which the peculiarities of the nations may be combined with a notion of the universal of which religions are fully part.[91]

That's why I think the European countries and the United States must work together to define a new understanding of universality. Although we have organized in a specific way our conception of democracy, republic, human rights, nation, and autonomy-separation with religion, we have nevertheless common values that determine our conception of society and the proper status of religion in democracy. It is a very important debate, which also determines the promotion of our values in today's world, where the link between religion and politics still means, very often, hostility against a democratic conception of nations.

However, democracy is a collective identity in which freedom and religion are the lost allies that need to actively participate in order to promote a new universal humanism.

91. See Claude Lefort, "Permanences du théologico-politique?" in *Essai sur le politique, XIXème-XXème siècles* (Paris: Esprit/Seuil, 1986), 251–300. The reflection of Claude Lefort illustrates well the disconnection of theology and politics in the 19th century and the advent of democracy.

six

Aidan Nichols

THE REBELLIOUS DISCIPLESHIP

OF FATHER VICTOR WHITE

Theology and Psychology in a Critic of C. G. Jung

Some few years ago I received a letter from Washington, D.C., asking me about none other than Father Victor White, born 1902, died 1960. The letter was from the Catholic University of America Press, which had been offered for publication a doctoral thesis on this subject. The question they put was, Could Fr. Victor's name be regarded as sufficiently well-known in modern Catholic theology to justify the publication of the thesis at their hands? My answer was to the effect that Fr. Victor's name was by no means as familiar as it ought to be but that, for good or ill, the name of Carl Gustav Jung was certainly celebrated. Indeed, the last decade or so has seen the appearance of three major English-language biographies, all door-stoppers for size: specifically, Frank McLynn's *Carl Gustav Jung* of 1996,[1] Ronald Hayman's *A Life of Jung* in 1999,[2] and more recently Deirdre Bair's *Jung: A Biography* in 2004. I was able to tell the acquisitions editor at the press that, on the very morning his letter arrived, the London quality daily *The Independent* had devoted half a page to the vicissitudes of the German translation of Bair's sober and responsible study since her text had drawn down on itself the wrath of Jung's extended family.[3] This testified, I pointed out, not only to his family's zeal for his honor, for which purposes they are organized as the C. G. Jung *Erbengemeinschaft*, with lawyers ever ready. It also witnessed to a continuing public interest in the sage of Zurich and his thought. What I could not do was put my hand on my heart and claim that Fr. Victor's was a household name among the Catholic intelligentsia of two continents, and this despite my devoting a chapter to him in a survey of what I called the English Dominican common culture of the period from the 1930s to the Second Vatican Council.[4] However, as I added with pardonable exaggeration, no Jung biography could pass muster that did not devote at any rate half a chapter to Jung's relations with Fr. Victor White. This act of advocacy, I noticed, did not prevail, but soon after, another American university press snapped up the book, written by a lay student at Blackfriars Oxford, Clodagh Brett.[5]

In my own book, *Dominican Gallery*, I approached the issue of White and Jung's collaboration, its dramatic collapse, the ensuing bitterness, and, finally, deathbed reconciliation (of a sort) very much

1. Frank McLynn, *Carl Gustav Jung* (London: Bantam Press, 1996).

2. Ronald Hayman, *A Life of Jung* (London: Bloomsbury, 1999).

3. Deirdre Bair, *Jung: A Biography* (London: Little and Brown, 2004). Unfortunately, the *Independent* article gave the author's name as "Blair" throughout. In contemporary "New Labour"–dominated England, that would presumably count as a Freudian slip.

4. Aidan Nichols, O.P., *Dominican Gallery: Portrait of a Culture* (Leominster: Gracewing, 1996), 53–123.

5. Now Clodagh Weldon. See Clodagh Weldon, *Fr. Victor White, O.P.: The Story of Jung's "White Raven"* (Scranton, Pa., and London: University of Scranton Press, 2007).

from an English Dominican perspective. I looked at it from the angle of Fr. Victor's personal search as an orthodox Catholic, a Dominican, and, philosophically and theologically speaking, a Thomist, if an adventurous one, who was seeking to engage with contemporary culture. As Fr. Victor envisaged it, this involved a two-way process. Using the intellectual resources of Thomism, it should be possible to lend to a major movement in the then contemporary culture, namely Jungian psychology, the natural and supernatural context that alone would make full sense of it. At the same time, by drawing critically yet generously on elements of Jung's writings and therapeutic practice, one might hope to release more effectively the transformative power hidden in the Christian imagination, in classical Christian thought, and in the Church's worship. That combination of intellectual confidence and a universalism of interests, motivated pastorally and apostolically by the desire to make English Catholicism home to a rich and vibrant culture, was what I saw as the hallmark of the seven figures I discussed. And it was all modeled on the historic synthetic achievement of St. Thomas.

What I wish to do in this presentation is to consider Fr. Victor's intervention in the life and, as he vainly hoped, the spiritual aeneid of Jung from a dual perspective—not only in terms of what the English Dominican expected but of what the Swiss psychologist wanted as well. Fr. Victor thought he saw an ally for Catholic truth in a way that was full of hope for the future. Jung too was seeking something in this encounter. That alone can explain the unusual degree of encouragement he gave this almost unknown priest, whom at one time he considered declaring officially his intellectual heir. Unfortunately—though the consequences were more serious for Fr. Victor than for Jung—their trajectories were set from the start on a collision course, and not toward the *hieros gamos,* the "sacred marriage," of heaven and earth that they assumed.[6]

---

6. To this extent, the lecture is comparable in approach to the "binocular" method used in the only existing book-length study of its topic, Ann C. Lammers, *In God's Shadow: The Collaboration of Victor White and C. G. Jung* (Mahwah, N. J.: Paulist, 1994).

The Development of Jung's Religious Views

I start with Jung. Had Fr. Victor known more of Jung's biography and the development of what for a want of a better word we must call his religious outlook, it is unlikely that he would have pitched his expectations so high. But Jung's autobiographical memoir *Memories, Dreams, Reflections* was published, more or less simultaneously in English and German, only in 1961, the year after the Dominican's death from cancer of the bowel at the age of fifty-seven.[7] Jung, born in 1875, was the son of a pastor in the Swiss Reformed Church who, whether through temperamental difficulties or owing to intellectual reservations about the truth of Christianity or—as is more likely—both of these together, had become disenchanted with his own calling. In the Basle of the turn of the nineteenth and twentieth centuries, it was customary for the sons of the professional classes to follow their father's calling. Jung, negatively impressed by his own father's unwillingness to engage with him about central Christian doctrines such as the Trinity, was disposed to do nothing of the sort, even without his father's urging to study anything at all so long as it was not theology. One of Jung's earliest dreams was of the Almighty figured in a seated position above the roof of Basle's medieval cathedral, subsequently its principal Protestant church, and letting drop an enormous turd, which crashed through the roof of the building. Here not only was the wish the father to the thought. The wisher was son to the father.

Jung's mother, a more confident figure than his father, was possessed of paranormal psychic powers. This appears to have been a feature of the womenfolk in the family. During his student years in the faculty of medicine at the University of Basle, Jung organized séances centering on his cousin Hélène, whose mediumistic gifts, if that is the correct expression, he sought to develop through experimenting with hypnosis. The too diaphanous disguise with which he cloaked her identity in the notes he wrote up for his first published work may

7. C. G. Jung, *Memories, Dreams, Reflections* (New York: Random House, 1961).

have ruined her life, but in fairness it can be remarked that psychoanalytic practice had not yet developed conventions of confidentiality.
More widely, Ronald Hayman sums up the Jung of this early period:
"He tried to reconcile science with spiritualism while rejecting orthodox Christianity."[8]

Jung told the fellow-members of his university fraternity at Basle
that the scientific investigation of psychic phenomena was a responsibility institutions of higher learning were currently shirking. That was
not the case in the United States, where no less an academic figure
than William James, professor successively of psychology and philosophy at Harvard, had founded the American branch of the Society for
Psychical Research. (Jung met James, who was dying, on his first academic visit to the United States and was probably influenced to a mild
degree by Jamesian pragmatism.) But where poltergeists, spooks, and
things that go bump in the night were concerned, conditions in Europe were certainly different, and in Britain have remained so.[9] When
the essayist and political philosopher Arthur Koestler left in his will a
substantial sum to establish a chair of parapsychology, no British university could be found willing to accept the risk to its reputation that
was involved, and the moneys—not normally regarded with such in-
souciance by academic administrators—passed instead to the University of Utrecht, in the Netherlands. It is hard to overestimate the influence on his development of Jung's early dabblings in parapsychology,
which continued in mediumistic séances held in Zurich in 1921–23,
suppressed in his autobiography, as well as in a lifelong interest in
ghosts. They set the spiritual tone of his mature psychological theory
and his later therapeutic practice, which was more interested in the
marvels to be found in the collective unconscious than in the personal situation of his patients. They also anticipate his resolutely natural-

---

8. Hayman, *A Life of Jung*, 43.

9. An exception should be made for the classicist Gilbert Murray, who acted for
some years as president of the Society in Britain: see Duncan Wilson, *Gilbert Murray,
O.M., 1866–1957* (Oxford: Oxford University Press, 1987), 273–82.

istic attitude to religion in general and Christian faith in particular, and—especially—his antipathy to doctrines of divine transcendence. It is tempting, but a little unfair, to compare his fascination with the paranormal to his later absorbing interest in flying saucers.[10]

A second discouraging element in Jung's intellectual makeup so far as an eventual meeting with Catholic theology was concerned derives from his avid devouring of the German philosophers, notably Kant and Nietzsche. While this does him honor as an enquiring mind, his choice of intellectual mentors was hardly propitious in the context of dialogue with Catholic orthodoxy, especially of a Thomistic kind. As Marilyn Nagy has shown in her study *Philosophical Influences in the Psychology of C. G. Jung,* the philosophical framework Jung acquired through serious but untutored reading was essentially the neo-Kantianism dominant in the main German universities just before and after the First World War.[11] From Kant himself, Jung took one maieutically helpful notion for his psychological thought, namely, the distinction between analytic judgments, which do not convey any new information to the hearer, and synthetic judgments, which do. It has been noted that the contrast between Freudian and Jungian psychologies can be summarized in these Kantian terms. Focusing on the origins of a neurosis, Freudian psychoanalysis could provide no new information, but Jung would "deal with the trajectory of the neurosis and its implications for the future development of the patient."[12] In his book *Symbols of Transformation* Jung will use the term "synthesis" for what can be predicted on the basis of dreams.[13] More widely, however, neo-Kantianism, not only emphasizing the way Kant eliminated classical metaphysics but also going further than the master of Königs-

10. Bair, *Jung: A Biography,* 571–72.

11. Marilyn J. Nagy, *Philosophical Issues in the Psychology of C. G. Jung* (Albany: State University of New York Press, 1991).

12. Hayman, *A Life of Jung,* 109.

13. Carl G. Jung, *Symbols of Transformation: An Analysis of the Prelude to a Case of Schizophrenia* (Princeton, N.J.: Princeton University Press, 1956; 1967).

berg and eradicating the last relics of transcendence-oriented thinking from his thought, had the effect of rendering Jung theologically color-blind. He himself called his academic method "empiricism," though it was hardly the empiricism of the British empiricist philosophers, as his inclusion of parapsychic phenomena goes to show. Nonetheless, "epistemologically," Jung declared, "I take my stand on Kant."[14] If so, this was not the Kant of history but the Kant of faith: what Jung called "psychic facts," to him the most interesting thing about the world, simply do not enter the historical Kant's discussion.

I mentioned that the young medic's other philosophical enthusiasm was Nietzsche. Unfortunately, as Fr. Victor was to discover, the facet of Nietzsche's thought that fascinated Jung was that which gave its name to his *Beyond Good and Evil*. Jung questioned traditional ideas of good and evil, asking: "Do we not have to love evil if we are to escape from the obsession with virtue that sickens us and prohibits the enjoyment of life?"[15] That is a particularly strong statement, whose making might not have survived Jung's so-called creative illness of 1913–15. But all his life he considered we should offload at least part of the responsibility for the shadow side of human nature onto the gods, that is, onto powers beyond the human ego, the individual, with his or her moral responsibility. An unsympathetic interpreter might conclude with Ronald Hayman that "[i]n childhood Jung's precarious sense of identity had made impulses to blasphemy and obscenity seem so dangerous that he externalised them with the paranoid image of a God who was himself guilty of aggression, blasphemy and obscenity."[16]

In the bizarre notebook filled during his Great War illness with "Seven Sermons Addressed to the Dead," the *Septem Sermones ad*

14. Cited in Hayman, *A Life of Jung*, 219. He also stated that whoever did not understand Kant's theory of cognition "cannot understand my psychology," cited in Bair, *Jung: A Biography*, 508.

15. Cited in Hayman, *A Life of Jung*, 127.

16. Ibid., 204.

mortuos, Jung envisaged an *Uebermensch* commissioned with the symbolic task of uniting the divine and the diabolical—a notion that inspired Herman Hesse's novel *Demian.* (Hesse underwent therapy with Jung in the years immediately following the end of the Kaiser's War.) The *Septem Sermones* are perhaps the earliest place in which one can find Jung explicitly rejecting the view of evil as a lack or distortion of the good—the *privatio boni* doctrine common to the ancient philosophers and medieval Schoolmen alike.[17]

Of course if neo-Kantian subjectivism and Nietzschean amoralism were all that could be said for the intellectual temper of Jungian psychology, the attraction of an apostolically minded, doctrinally solid Dominican friar priest to its lures would be quite inexplicable. True, by 1935 Ezra Pound was declaring himself the only sane—that is, non-analyzed—writer left in Europe. But this was not a period when being fashionable—or what the later decades of the twentieth century would call "trendy"—was much of a concern of the Catholic clergy. So surely even in the formative stages of Jungianism there must be more to it than this. And indeed there was. The notion of the collective unconscious, which is probably Jung's greatest achievement, opened the way to showing the relevance of the treasury of symbols of religious man to the wholeness of the human psyche. As Jung explained in a lecture of 1936, whereas the personal unconscious, already recognized by Freud and in fact by earlier nineteenth century psychologists under the influence of Romanticism, consists for the most part of complexes, bundles of psychic elements that function to some degree as sub-personalities, this is not the entire story of life below the psychological surface. There is also a collective unconscious consisting of—and here Jung borrowed a term from the Platonist tradition—"archetypes."[18]

Jung's notion of the collective unconscious was triggered by his psychiatric work at Zurich's Burghölzli Hospital, where he had his

17. Ibid., 200–202.
18. Cited in ibid., 122–23.

early hands-on experience as assistant to the director of that asylum. But its intellectual ancestry was more complicated, owing something, in all probability, to Nietzsche's suggestion in *Human, All Too Human,* that when dreaming we traverse the thought of earlier generations, and also to the theory of the biologist Ernst Haeckel that the human body in its lifelong development goes through the same stages as the evolution of the race as a whole. There is something here that chimes—at a natural level—with the Catholic concept of Tradition in the theological, rather than simply cultural, sense of that word. The archetypes are "pathways" that have traced themselves out by way of the cumulative experience of our ancestors.[19] This is, one might say, an adumbration of the Catholic understanding of appeal to the communion of saints as part and parcel of *sentire cum Ecclesia*—a constitutive dimension of sharing the mind of the Church. For Jung, interestingly, the mind is not self-contained, nor is it wholly individual.

Jungian archetypes have been described—less diachronically and more synchronically—as patterns of order superimposed on the chaos of our unconscious psychic materials. They have been compared in this respect to a viewfinder of the sort that, as you look down it and through it, is marked at the lens with a cross or a circle divided into four, thus rendering manageable, if not fully intelligible, what is being looked at. A theologian might ask, Could the great biblical and liturgical symbols that had functioned as imaginative viewfinders for the psychology of grace in the "mystagogical catecheses" of such Church fathers as St. Cyril of Jerusalem be more persuasively presented in such a light? Especially appealing to a pastorally minded priest of Thomistic temper would be Jung's conviction that the integration of these archetypes by an exposure that was possibly dangerous but, more importantly, potentially healing to the psyche could lead to the goal of personal completeness, a goal never achieved before death but asymptotically approached under the name of what Jung termed "in-

19. Ibid., 227–28.

dividuation." Thomism, after all, is nothing if not a teleologically ori-
ented manner of thought. It looks to future beatitude as that which
makes sense of human striving. As Frank McLynn writes: "Whereas
Freudianism interpreted symbols as a sign of something repressed or
concealed, Jung saw them as an attempt to point the way to [the] further psychological development of the individual."[20] Over and again,
Jung stressed that the chief function of dreams is to permit the unconscious to "process material compensating some deficiency in the
conscious state."[21]

A theologian might say that Jung described individuation in terms
both "apophatic" and "staurological"—in terms, that is, reminiscent
of the language of the holy silence (*apophasis*) of the God known
through the *stauros,* the Cross. Individuation, wrote Jung, is "a mystery one will never understand." Moving toward it is "a lonely search"
akin to the "process of dying," since one has to give oneself "over to
the impersonal, in order to seek it."[22] Any priest wishing to help people in the ascetic dimension of Christian living, and in particular a
priest-disciple of Thomas inclined to see the chief point of something
in its final cause—the goal toward which it is moving—would natu-
rally prick up his ears at language such as this.

Up until the eve of the Second World War Jung's religious interests were highly eclectic. Of course, to flesh out the concept of the
collective unconscious necessitated study of the world religions and
the mythologies their various sacred writings contained, as well as the
religious literature of the past and the findings of social anthropologists in the present. But Jung's attitude was less detached than such a
statement might insinuate. At the time of his break with Freud he was
wondering whether it might be feasible to revive a long-dead rival
of Christianity in the Late Antique world, namely Mithraism. In the
1920s his attention was given to Hinduism and Buddhism. He devel-

20. McLynn, *Carl Gustav Jung,* 213.   21. Ibid., 373.
22. Bair, *Jung: A Biography,* 429.

oped a habit of grading religions on the basis, it must be said, of very limited acquaintance with them. What value, for instance, can we give to the following report: "Islam seemed to him a superior, more spiritual and advanced religion than Hinduism and he often rated it highly, second only to Buddhism and certain forms of Christianity, though well ahead of the Greek Orthodox Church."[23]

His anthropological expedition to British East Africa in the early 1930s was fired by a somewhat romantic attraction to what were then called "primitive" religions. He was vehemently opposed to Christian mission among such peoples and once delivered himself of the judgment that it would be "more humane to go to Africa and massacre its native peoples rather than visit Christianity on them."[24]

Perhaps through unfinished business with his father's memory, churches were among his least favored religious communities. In 1937, when giving the Terry Lectures at Yale, he asserted, "Life has gone out of the Church and it will never go back."[25] Only with his journey to India in 1938 did he change his mind. Like many people who have looked into the Upanishads, or the Gita, or even the Vedic hymns from the comfort of an armchair, say on the edge of Lake Zurich, and subsequently had to struggle with the crowds at Delhi railway station, the dirt, the flies, the unsafe drinking water, Jung decided that his mission was not to the East after all.

In a dream he had in Calcutta (notoriously the most difficult of the Indian cities for any Westerner to come to terms with, let alone a bourgeois Swiss), he found himself on an island divided by a channel. In fact he was swimming across this channel so as to reach an uninhabited dwelling that housed the Grail—the chalice of the Last Supper, the vessel in which, in later legend, the bloody flux flowing

---

23. McLynn, *Carl Gustav Jung*, 400.

24. Ibid., 413, referring to James L. Jarrett, ed., *Nietzsche's Zarathustra: Notes of a Seminar Given in 1934–1939 by C. G. Jung* (Princeton, N.J.: Princeton University Press, 1988), I, 98.

25. Hayman, *A Life of Jung*, 357.

from the side of Christ, symbol of the life of Baptism and the Eucharist, had been collected. On this rather slight basis, Jung inferred that his mission was to save Christianity from itself. As one of his biographers puts it: "Never entirely jettisoning orthodox Christianity [he remained a non-attending member of the Reformed Church], he had not given it precedence over the other belief systems he had studied. But for the next twenty-four years, his formidable (but dwindling) energy would be focused mainly on the history, traditions, symbols and rituals of Christianity."[26] The final outcome of the rise of Nazism in the horrors of the Second World War, which not only reduced Switzerland to the previously unheard of straits of food and petrol rationing but threatened to overspill its borders, convinced him he must act. In a spiritually sick world, neo-paganism, such as National Socialism had espoused, was likely to make the disease worse. The Eastern religions, whatever their merits, were too culturally alien to endure a successful graft. The only thing to do was to attempt to reverse the retreating tide of historic Christianity. Jung was convinced he was the man for the job. The Church's own leaders, he was persuaded, were mere administrators. Unlike him they lacked direct contact with the God-archetype. This contact, combined with the skills and the knowledge he had acquired in the course of his psychiatric practice and the production of his literary corpus, should enable him to reach what he thought of as the "other side of the island." He would revive the convalescent Church by translating dogma into the terms of psychological theory. A book by an enthusiastic Protestant cleric was so closely monitored by Jung as to be partly "ghosted" by him. The upshot is well-expressed in the title of a more recent work, *Jung's Treatment of Christianity*. We should note the ambivalent meaning there of the word "treatment," brought out in Murray Stein's subtitle, *The Psychotherapy of a Religious Tradition*.[27]

26. Ibid.

27. Murray Stein, *Jung's Treatment of Christianity: The Psychotherapy of a Religious Tradition* (Wilmette, Ill.: Chiron Publications, 1985).

Even when, with the Second World War, Jung developed these somewhat messianic convictions about his future role, it is important to note that his fundamental convictions did not in any way move closer to those of Christianity as such. In 1940, his Eranos lecture "A Psychological Approach to the Trinity"—eventually published in 1948—would prefigure the notorious *Answer to Job,* on which his relations with Fr. Victor were going to founder. In 1951, in his study *Aion,* he regretted that neither the historic figure of Jesus as reconstructed by exegetes on the basis of the Gospels nor the symbolic Christ-figure of the Church's liturgies and creeds was remotely adequate when considered as a symbol of the successfully individuated *Selbst* or "self." Christianity had not—that is, not yet—allowed Christ to have a "dark side." Its short-sighted insistence on not only the omnipotence but also the unmitigated goodness of God did not permit an archetype of the shadow to exist. But no archetype could possibly be complete unless it allowed for the expression of both good and evil within at once the conscious and the unconscious states.[28] Creeds and dogmas, the mature Jung considered, were necessary fictions. But then they should at least be helpful fictions. The highest stage of faith in God is when the world is understood not as creation, the fruit of divine agency, but as a "projected psychic structure" in which the only God is what Jung termed "the God image" or "the God within":[29] a phrase later to be modified by New Age feminism as "the Goddess within." Interestingly, Jung appears to have been the first person to speak of a coming "Age of Aquarius," when ancient credenda would metamorphose into a "New Age" belief system. In this at any rate he was gifted with one of the paranormal faculties that interested him: precognition. His fellow psychologist Erich Fromm remarked acerbically: "With his blend of outmoded superstition, indeterminate heathen idol-worship, and vague talk about God and with the allegation that he is building a bridge between religion and psychology, Jung has

---

28. Thus Bair, *Jung: A Biography,* 526.
29. McLynn, *Carl Gustav Jung,* 410.

presented exactly the right mix to an age which possesses but little faith and judgment."[30]

Enter Fr. Victor White

For the purposes of this essay, what chiefly concerns us are the implications for the eventually abortive negotiations Jung established with a Catholic theologian who was in one sense atypical—an Englishman, and therefore a member of a minority Church, a convert (his father had been an Anglican clergyman), and a thinker keen to expand the boundaries of Christian doctrinal awareness. In another sense, however, Fr. Victor was typical, typical not only of the culturally alert English Dominicans of the 1930s and '40s, but in his commitment to St. Thomas, then almost universally recognized, at least by lip service, as the classic theologian of the Latin church, and typical to some extent even in his desire to replace the neo-scholastic manuals with a different version of Thomism, more Platonist in its philosophical underpinnings, more conscious of its debt to the Fathers of the Church, Eastern as well as Western, and more sensitive to Thomas's own affinities with the monastic theologians of Christian experience who had preceded Aquinas in the twelfth century.[31] Fr. Victor stressed how Thomas had allowed direct knowledge of God by the soul, through connaturality, by means of love: what he termed, on Aquinas's behalf, "affective knowledge."[32] He was very much his own man. But he was also located in a historical conjuncture, when

30. Cited in ibid., 434.

31. Thus in "The Platonic Tradition in St. Thomas Aquinas," originally published in *Eastern Churches Quarterly* for 1941, but reprinted as chapter 5 of *God the Unknown;* he wrote: "The Platonic worldview consists essentially in its interpretation of this world as an imitation, a participation, a shadow, and thus as a symbol, a sign, a sacramental, of a transcendental world of pure intelligibility and immateriality"; Victor White, O.P., *God the Unknown and Other Essays* (London: Harvill Press, 1956), 63.

32. Victor White, O.P., "Thomism and 'Affective Knowledge,'" *Blackfriars* 24, no. 274 (1943): 8–16; 24, no. 277: 126–31; 25, no. 294: 321–28.

theological antennae were attuned to both the difference between the historical St. Thomas and the more systematized positions of the later Commentators and to that medley of concerns—spiritual, existential, ecumenical—that were in the process of acquiring the sobriquet "la nouvelle théologie."

There is no doubt Jung was in deadly earnest about the importance of this encounter. In the years since the end of World War II, he had come to the settled conviction that, as he put it in a letter of 1948, "The Church would have its *raison d'être* if it could save humanity or at least civilisation." By this date when Jung wrote "the Church" he tended to mean the Catholic Church. To some extent this emerging preference was aspectual. Catholicism did more justice to the feminine, maternal side of human nature: it had the Mother of God and a plethora of women saints. By denying the teaching of the magisterial Reformers of the sixteenth century that salvation came about *fide sola,* through faith alone, it showed itself the more warmly human, and less abstractly confessional, version of the Gospel. More generally, it was because "the Catholic Church codified the memories and lessons of history so much better and conserved so much of classical paganism [that] it had good claims to be considered *the* Christian church *par excellence.*"[33] The rituals and beliefs of Catholicism "co-opted" aspects of the older religions and were better able, accordingly, to answer human beings' deeply rooted psychological needs. Auricular confession, Jung noted or at least claimed, made Catholics less neurotic than Protestants. Writing on this subject, Jung somehow bears an uncanny resemblance to another European intellectual who suffered in this period from the accusation of sympathies with fascism, Charles Maurras; this is so not least when Jung is found remarking that at bottom Catholicism has little to do with Christianity proper and must be considered a religion of its own, comparable in this regard with Confucianism, Taoism, or whatever.[34] Somehow,

---

33. McLynn, *Carl Gustav Jung,* 413.
34. Ibid., 414, citing Gerhard Adler and Aniela Jaffé, eds., *Carl Gustav Jung: Letters,*

then, given the latitude of its appeal and its equal broadness of access to the masses, Jung had to find a collaborator in this Church. By that date, 1948, he believed he had succeeded. Soon after his seventieth birthday he received a packet through the post. Fr. Victor White enclosed a paper on "The Frontiers of Theology and Psychology" along with two articles and a review of a book by a psychoanalyst. One article bore the title "St Thomas Aquinas and Jung's Psychology," and the other, called "Psychotherapy and Ethics," proposed a synthesis between Thomism and analytic psychology.[35]

What had brought Fr. Victor to make this unusual offer? Conscious of some malaise, he had, a few years previously, undergone Jungian-style analysis with an Oxford man, John Layard, a minor literary figure of the inter-war cultural scene in England (before his marriage he had been one of the numerous lovers of Christopher Isherwood).[36] Fr. Victor had found it not only beneficial but extraordinarily cognate with his theological education to date. In an essay written in 1953 but not published, owing to its autobiographical nature, until after his death, he had this to say, with an evident reference to St. Thomas's rather subtle account of the consequences of the Fall of man:

> I have it on record that at my very first analytical interview, I was told that the *whole* psyche was alright, and so were its several parts and functions, but that my dreams showed (as indeed they did) that these parts and functions were disordered, un-balanced, unintegrated. Whether or not I understood my analyst correctly, the penny dropped: this was exactly what my theological mentors had told me was evil in fallen man—a disorder, a disintegration of the parts and

vol. 1: *1906–1950* (Princeton, N.J.: Princeton University Press, 1973), 133–34 (to H. Oberhausli, 16 December 1933).

35. Victor White, O.P., *The Frontiers of Psychology and Theology* (London: Guild of Pastoral Psychology, 1942); "St Thomas Aquinas and Jung's Psychology," *Blackfriars* 25, no. 290 (1944): 209–19; "Psychotherapy and Ethics," *Blackfriars* 25, no. 305 (1945): 287–300.

36. A. Cunningham, "Victor White, John Layard, and C. G. Jung," *Harvest* 38 (1992): 44–57.

functions of the soul. The Fall had brought it about, not that there was anything wrong with them in themselves, but that they were deprived of harmony, order and integration.[37]

He adds that precisely this predisposed him to see the unacknowledged "shadow" side of his soul not as something evil in itself and to be embraced as such (though this, so Jung now insisted, was indispensable), but rather as "basically good, the holder of the most precious values." He concluded:

> What was evil, harmful and dangerous about it sprang not from its positive content, but from its privations, its lack of consciousness, light, attention, love, justice to its rightful claims and function within the life of the whole personality.[38]

But in any case his initiative in seeking out Jung himself did not arise from a desire for more analysis from the master himself, as was the manner of various millionaire Americans charmed by Jung's charisma. It was the openings he thought he saw in the words of the response to the *Orate fratres* of the Roman Liturgy for the "utility of all [God's] holy Church," *ad utilitatem ... totiusque Ecclesiae suae sanctae*. He had picked up from Jung's immediately postwar writings that here was someone who "viewed Christianity as the only remedy for the soul-sickness and self-destructive tendencies of the modern world" and "cared deeply about revitalizing the central symbols of Christian life in Western culture."[39] For his part Jung was—something rare for him—bowled over. He found in Fr. Victor a scholar-theologian who (as Jung wrote) "really understood something of what the problem of psychology in our present world means" and recognized its "enormous implications." As Deirdre Bair writes:

> His handwritten letters filled many pages, as he overflowed with enthusiasm to find a younger man who shared his interests. In a very

37. Victor White, "Good and Evil," *Harvest* 12 (1966): 31.
38. Ibid.
39. Lammers, *In God's Shadow*, 36.

short while their intimacy was such that White became one of the special few invited to share Jung's vocations at the tower [a reference to the study-cum-hermitage Jung built at Bollingen on the shore of Lake Zurich as a sort of personal sanctuary dedicated to his vision of man].[40]

It is only in the last decade that the *Jung-Erbengemeinschaft*, in agreement with the English Dominican Province, have made all Fr. Victor's letters to Jung available to approved students, whereas Jung's replies have long been in the public forum.[41] The letters hitherto withheld concern the priest's vocational difficulties in the English Province, while the annotations to Jung's side of the correspondence and his own citations from Fr. Victor's missives enable us to understand everything at stake in the realm of theological principle.

By an optimistic selective reading in Jung's works Fr. Victor had convinced himself that Jung was the Aristotle of the twentieth century, the scientist-philosopher whose insights, duly corrected, could greatly enhance Thomism's appeal in the contemporary period. He began the correspondence confident that no danger existed of Jungianism replacing traditional ascetical theology with a new religion. While, to be sure, Jung's psychology aspired toward spiritual wholeness on its own terms, it had to call a "halt at the limits of finitude."[42] As he put it in *The Frontiers of Theology and Psychology*: "When [Jung] writes that 'The Personality as a full realisation of the wholeness of our being is an unattainable ideal,' he confirms—though necessarily only negatively—the Christian teaching that the fulfilment of this process awaits an eschatological realisation, and is consequently beyond the sphere observable by this-worldly psychology."[43] Had not Jung gone

40. Bair, *Jung: A Biography*, 544.

41. Adler and Jaffé, *Carl Gustav Jung: Letters*, vol. 1: *1906–1950*; also, ibid., vol. 2: *1951–1961* (Princeton, N.J.: Princeton University Press, 1973), passim. There is a short study by F.-X. Charet, "A Dialogue between Psychology and Theology: The Correspondence of C. G. Jung and Victor White," *Journal of Analytical Psychology* 35, no. 4 (1990): 421–42.

42. Lammers, *In God's Shadow*, 74.

43. Victor White, *The Frontiers of Psychology and Theology* (London: Guild of Pastoral Psychology, 1942), 22.

out of his way to demonstrate his respect for Catholic Christianity, and its liturgy, for instance in his 1928 article "Psychoanalysis and the Cure of Souls," where he wrote that "[t]he Catholic Church has at her disposal ways and means which have served since olden times to gather the lower, instinctual forces of the psyche into symbols and in this way integrate them into a hierarchy of the spirit"?[44] And he had shown a like sympathy for her priesthood, suggesting in another essay, "Psychotherapists or the Clergy," this time from 1932, that much of what psychotherapists were doing could be done as well by priests if the latter only acknowledged the full reality of the psyche and more people could trust them with disclosures of their inner lives.[45]

Moreover, had not Jung, to beneficent effect, reversed Freud's disastrous devaluation of culture and symbol? As one commentator has put it: "Freud sees language, art and religion as 'disguises' for the repressed incestuous instinct, whereas Jung sees these symbolic expressions as generated by a spiritual drive. The spirit is a primary 'instinctive' reality of human existence . . . , equal in power to sexuality."[46]

Fr. Victor rejoiced to find that Jung's theory of the archetypes gives all emotional life, including the sexual, a spiritual meaning. That finite acts and feelings partake of the infinite is what St. Thomas's doctrine of participation (much stressed in Fr. Victor's reading of Aquinas) would lead us to expect. The notion that human instinctual drives derive their ultimate meaning from a relation to the infinite spiritual reality of the God-image, the image of wholeness, parallels in its own realm St. Thomas's picture of God as *causa causarum*, the Cause of causes. In all these ways, so Fr. Victor convinced himself, Jung was an *anima naturaliter catholica atque thomistica*.

Into these placid waters of mutually congratulatory contentment

44. Carl G. Jung, "Psycho-analysis and the Cure of Souls," in *Psychology and Religion: West and East* (Princeton, N.J.: Princeton University Press, 1958; 1969), 547.

45. Carl G. Jung, "Psychotherapists or the Clergy," in *Modern Man in Search of a Soul* (New York: Harcourt, Brace, Jovanovich, 1933), 255–82.

46. Lammers, *In God's Shadow*, 76.

Jung's 1952 *Antwort auf Hiob*, translated in 1954 as *Answer to Job*, dropped with the effect not so much of a pebble as of a meteorite.

Answer to Job

It has to be said that, rather after the manner of George Bernard Shaw's *The Black Girl in Search of God*, Jung's *Answer to Job* is a very humorous book. But the humor, like the girl, is black. The biblical God is pinned down to the couch, and his psyche is subjected to a thorough and devastating analysis. With willing assistants on hand to scour the Zurich libraries and gut their contents, Jung made some attempt to place the Book of Job in historical context, opting with the majority of critical of scholars for a relatively late dating, but prior to the year 300 B.C.E. On Jung's view, then, the author of Job was able to profit, if that is the word, from an already substantial corpus of Hebrew religious texts. He was thus presented with a portrait of the divinity explicable, comments Jung, only if we assume God to be a highly undeveloped and consequently amoral self, who has failed to put in the necessary psychological work on his own unconscious. Only so can we explain a God who "knew no moderation in his emotions and suffered precisely from this lack of moderation. He himself admitted [so Jung continues, summing up as he believes the basic Old Testament doctrine of God] that he was eaten up with rage and jealousy and that this knowledge was painful to him. Insight existed along with obtuseness, loving-kindness along with cruelty, creative power along with destructiveness."[47]

Jung does not claim that most of ancient Israel found this a problem in the way the author of Job and he himself did. But he maintains that it is most certainly a problem for us today. He proposes to respond "fearlessly and ruthlessly," searching out the reasons *why* Job— the personage, not the book—was "wounded," and what the con-

47. Carl G. Jung, *Answer to Job* (London: Routledge and Kegan Paul, 1954), 3.

sequences of this proved to be both for the God of Israel, whom he names by the Tetragrammaton, YHWH, "Yahweh," and also for mankind.[48] Not only Job's speeches but even more strikingly the situation in which the Lord deliberately places him attest the antinomic, "split," character of God. This is a God who is "at odds with himself," and Job is equally persuaded, so Jung informs us, with little textual warrant, that there is evil in God quite as much as there is good.[49] As a consequence the divine attributes in expressing themselves "fall apart into mutually contradictory acts."[50] The Lord, seeking to shore up a fragile sense of identity, had bound the people to himself by covenant, and yet, in the testing of Job, breaks his own oath of fidelity "quite gratuitously" and, adds Jung, despite the information contained in the prologue and epilogue of the book, "to no purpose."[51] What can be the explanation? Jung proposes jealousy.

An intolerable surmise has grown up in God, aware of his own lack of reflectiveness: "man possesses an infinitely small yet more concentrated light than he."[52] But God fails to consult his own omniscience, preferring to let rip his omnipotence instead. He projects his shadow side, remaining unconscious at man's expense. He "behaves as irrationally as a cataclysm," writes Jung. God is a classic case of a "divided attitude," which, on the one hand, tramples ruthlessly on human life and happiness and, on the other, "must have man" for a covenant partner, wanting to be "loved, honoured, worshipped, and praised as just."[53] Although all commentators until Jung have missed this point, so Jung with his customary braggadocio tells us, the Book of Job sets man up as judge over God, who is tried and found wanting.[54] It is now as plain as daylight: God has a dual nature, the Satan of book's opening and closing chapters is as much his "son" as will be

48. Ibid., 5.
50. Ibid., 15.
52. Ibid., 21.

49. Ibid., 10.
51. Ibid., 20.
53. Ibid., 35.

54. Ibid., 36. The fullest account of the exegetical tradition is G. Ravasi, *Giobbe: Traduzione e commento*, 3rd ed. (Rome: Borla, 1993).

Jesus Christ. This became public knowledge with the composition of Job, and, remarks Jung, such knowledge could hardly become "public property and remain hidden from [God] himself alone." The consequences are dramatic. The Lord had not consulted his "total knowledge and was accordingly surprised by the result." At this juncture in the unfolding of the divine being, "self-reflection becomes an imperative necessity, and for this wisdom is needed."[55] God remembers, shamefacedly, that he once had a consort, the heavenly Wisdom, Sophia. In a renewal of the *hieros gamos,* the sacred nuptials, he regenerates himself and becomes man. This is unavoidable if he is to catch up with humankind, whose consciousness is so much more advanced than his own: a state of affairs in intolerable contradiction to God's omniscience. Summing up, then: "The immediate cause of the Incarnation lies in Job's elevation, and its purpose is the differentiation of Yahweh's consciousness."[56]

In the ministry of Jesus Satan is neutralized, or in the words of the Gospels, "falls from heaven" (Luke 10:18), which Jung takes to mean Yahweh identifies with his own "light aspect" becoming the good and loving Father. He *intends* to become the *Summum Bonum,* but, from what a student of the Hebrew Bible knows of his past record, it would be as well to stay alert for signs of recidivism. Not only is it unlikely that Satan, the manifestation of God's shadow and brother of Jesus, will accept permanent relegation (in fact, he returns at least prospectively in the New Testament writings as the Antichrist) but even for the divine Father himself it would be, comments Jung, "contrary to all reasonable expectation to suppose that a God who, for all his lavish generosity, had been subject to fits of rage ever since time began could suddenly become the epitome of everything good."[57] The Incarnation is "reparation for a wrong done by God to man,"[58] but its climax, the Atonement, shows that God is still the "dangerous Yahweh who has to

55. Jung, *Answer to Job,* 45.   56. Ibid., 70.
57. Ibid., 80.   58. Ibid., 91.

be propitiated," demanding an appalling satisfaction from his "light" son, Jesus.[59] All in all, then, to hold that God is the Supreme Good is, Jung concludes, "impossible for a reflecting consciousness."[60]

Jung's *Answer to Job* reaches its own climax in an account of the Johannine Apocalypse that demonstrates God to be a wolf in sheep's clothing, or, were we to keep closer to St. John's imagery, a lion in lamb's clothing. It was fitting, he held, that the Apocalypse, of all books, should close the biblical canon. The entire preceding New Testament points to it by revealing a God who, in the struggle against Satan, continually hesitates to use coercion. Jung takes this to mean that even after the Incarnation and Atonement, God "still does not know how much his own dark side favours the evil angel."[61] This ambivalence is summed up in the book's central figure of the avenging Lamb. It was mirrored, Jung speculates, in St. John himself. Chronically virtuous people, writes Jung, are given to negative outbursts of rage and resentment. The author of the Johannine Epistles, whom he takes to be the same as the author of the Apocalypse, was consciously obsessed by the love of God, but unconsciously he was fixated on God's "fierce and terrible side."[62]

Only at this juncture, it seems to me, when *Answer to Job* is on the point of ending, does Jung remember that he is supposed to be not a metaphysician or a dogmatic theologian but an empirical psychologist whose subject is not extra-human divine agency at all but the God-image. The reconciliation of the antinomic aspects of the divine being must take place, Jung now insists, in the human psyche, for which the self is "always a *complexio oppositorum*," and, warns Jung: "the more consciousness insists on its light nature and lays claim to moral authority, the more the self will appear as something dark and

59. Ibid., 86.
60. Ibid., 93. That is, the manner of the Atonement denies the *Summum Bonum* itself: ibid., 111.
61. Ibid., 118.
62. Ibid., 145.

menacing."[63] The belatedness of Jung's recognition that what he has been investigating are merely inner-psychic symbolics tends to confirm what the passion with which this book is written already suggests, namely that he is actually reacting with all the force of his own personality to the God of the Swiss Reformed Church—the Bible plus liberal preaching—as he had known it in his childhood.

This would be small comfort to Fr. Victor White. *Answer to Job*, he maintained, Jung had assured him would circulate privately, as an experimental reading intended for the members of their own affinity. Its publication not only spelled the end of his project of uniting Thomism and analytic psychology. It also came at the worst possible time in his own Dominican life and "career." He had just been given the highest academic accolade the Order of Preachers confers, the degree of master in sacred theology. This was a prelude to his being appointed regent of Blackfriars, Oxford: head of the studium of the English Dominican Province and its senior theologian. For some time he had struggled as a matter of conscience with the ecclesiastical oaths that would need to be taken before he could enter on that goodly inheritance. The difficulty was not so much the draconian "anti-Modernist oath," laid down by Pope Pius X in the doctrinal crisis of the early years of the twentieth century. Fr. Victor was strongly anti-Modernist. He held with vigor to two principles all good Modernists abhorred: the utter objectivity of theological realities, and the reliability—though not sufficiency—of the concepts used to describe them. The difficulty for him was the much milder "Thomist oath" required by the Order of Preachers. What he objected to, apart from the historical incongruity of oath-taking in support of so open a mind as Thomas's, was the reference to Thomas's *school*. That he should be committed in advance to the scholasticism of Cajetan, and the theologians of Salamanca, the Baroque and the Leonine revival, went against the grain of the sort of renewal of Thomasian teaching which he himself sought, and whose

63. Ibid., 133.

character I indicated earlier in this essay. But now all was lost, his *sacrificium intellectus* in vain. *Answer to Job* had appeared in the public arena and, mark you, not merely published in German, which language might have thrown a *cordon sanitaire* around him in an English Province the run of whose superiors either were monoglot or, at best, might get by in French. The publication of the English translation was Fr. Victor's downfall. His nomination as regent was set aside in favor of an amiable canon lawyer not over-endowed in the upper story. Fr. Victor received a letter from the prior provincial. He would not be returning to Oxford as regent. He would be going for a sabbatical to California instead. Father Hilary Carpenter was unaware of the element of irony in his choice. California had always been Jung's least favorite state of the Union. When asked why he had never visited Los Angeles, Jung replied, "I don't need to go there since so many of my patients come from there."[64] There is no reason to think the Californians did not treat Fr. Victor well. But the anger at the biographical implications for him of Jung's—as he saw it—indiscretion boiled over in the intemperate review he wrote of *Answer to Job*, where he did not hesitate to speak of Jung's "religious development" as "fixated at the kindergarten level." Jung's response to the Jewish-Christian tradition in *Answer to Job* was, he said, that of a "spoiled child."[65] Not surprisingly, this effusion ruptured his friendship with Jung, the feeble remaining strands of which would not be brought together again until he was dying. Jung's book richly deserved a riposte from a Christian theologian. Whether the bitterness of Fr. Victor's disappointment at deprivation of the regency was wise is another matter. Saint Theresa says somewhere that we should pray God that we may never get in this world what we consider our heart's desire. It usually turns to dust and ashes.

64. Cited in McLynn, *Carl Gustav Jung*, 391.
65. Victor White, O.P., "Jung on Job," *Blackfriars* 36, no. 420 (1955): 52–60, and here at 58.

Conclusion

What of Fr. Victor's wider project of a reclamation of Jung's ideas to enrich the Thomist synthesis? I do not think his aspirations were entirely hopeless, only hopeless in the direction in which he attempted to realize them. It is not possible to bridge the gap between orthodox Catholicism of a Thomist stamp, and Jung's thought as a whole. Fr. Victor's hope for a perfect union of a revised Jungianism with St. Thomas and the Church was a chimera. The Jewish philosopher Martin Buber had already judged Jungianism a new religion of pure psychic immanence that obliterated the otherness of God. But that is not to say there is nothing Catholic Christians can learn by way of positive lessons from Jung's writing and career.

One valuable notion highlighted by McLynn, for example, concerns Jung's attitude to culture.

> One of Jung's tenets was that the fragmented culture of the twentieth century was to society what schizophrenia was to the individual. The neurotic could not really be blamed for confusion about life's tasks, for the collapse of the old nineteenth century certainties and the "organic" moral code left him uncertain what those tasks really were. So the real reason for neurosis was not lack of sexual satisfaction but failure to recognize the individual's cultural task.[66]

That is surely a just and worthwhile observation, and one that thoroughly merits the attention of Catholic theologians in some renewed version of that Cinderella of the theological sciences, pastoral theology. Jung's work deserves continued attention—not least via the criticism of its strengths and weaknesses delivered by Fr. Victor White.

---

66. McLynn, *Carl Gustav Jung*, 214.

seven

Richard Sorabji

EMOTIONS AND THE PSYCHOTHERAPY
OF THE ANCIENTS

This chapter is about psychotherapy in the ancient philosophers. Ancient philosophy lasted at least eleven hundred years, from 500 B.C. to 600 A.D., but I am going focus most of all on a particular school, the Stoic school, which was founded in Athens shortly after Plato and Aristotle. Plato taught Aristotle. Aristotle died in 322 B.C. Just twenty-two years later the Stoic school was founded in the same city of Athens, 300 B.C. Thus Stoicism, like Aristotelianism and like Platonism, started in Athens. But in 86 B.C., the Roman general Sulla sacked Athens, and then there was a dispersal of philosophy, a lot of it to Rome, some of it to Alexandria, which was the sort of Washington or New York of those times, some of it to islands such as Rhodes. Athens never had total hegemony after that, although it did revive from time to time. I am going to take Stoicism from 300 B.C., when it was founded, up to the first century A.D. in Rome with Seneca and Epictetus.

The Stoics were the people who really invented cognitive therapy. They thought that there were four basic emotions and that all other emotions could be brought under the heading of those four. The four emotions were: appetite, fear, pleasure, and distress. In order to apply cognitive therapy to the emotions you have to define them. According to the rather rationalistic Stoics, the emotions are judgments. Every emotion involves, and indeed is, two judgments: the judgment that there is harm or benefit at hand for you and your friends, and the judgment that it is appropriate to react accordingly. Emotions are intellectual judgments of value. When they say judgments they mean judgments in a rather special sense, because they distinguish mere appearance from judgment. You cannot help the appearance that things are bad or that things are good. That is quite involuntary, but what the Stoics said is that we can always step back and say to ourselves: "Look that is how it appears, but is this appearance right? Ought we to give our assent to this appearance?" Most people do not do that. Most people no sooner have an appearance that things are good or bad than they immediately assent without even realizing that they had any opportunity to withhold assent, but we are all of us free. We could always withhold assent, and Stoicism trains you to withhold assent. It trains you to say to yourself: "Well, it appears bad, but is it really bad? Does it really matter?" And when they say that an emotion is a judgment that things are good or bad for you or your friends and that it is appropriate to react accordingly, they mean not merely that it is an appearance to that effect, which you may however question, but that it is an appearance to which you have given your assent, probably unthinkingly. If you are a Stoic, you will think very carefully before you give assent, because very often the things we think really bad or really good, on reflection turn out not to be so.

Admittedly, there is something else associated with emotions, but it's not really part of the emotions. It is the physical or mental shock that we experience, but that is an accompaniment of the emotion. It happens like this: when you first have the appearance that things are bad or good, the appearance is enough to give you a shock. It might be that you go pale. It might be that your knees knock, your teeth chatter, your hair stands on end. It might be a mental shock: you have a sinking feeling, or you have an expansive feeling, which is a mere sensation. That is not the emotion itself. It is an accompaniment, which you cannot avoid, but which does not really matter. So an emotion is not the initial appearance that things are good or bad and that it is appropriate to react. It is not that plus the resulting mental or physical shock. The emotion is the assent that you give when you think to yourself, "yes, that appearance is right," which most people do unthinkingly. That is the Stoic analysis of emotions. And so the Stoics conclude that emotions are something that we can cure cognitively if we do not want them, because we can withhold assent if our attitude, our evaluative attitude, is wrong.

Stoicism, then, is not a matter or gritting your teeth; it has absolutely nothing to do with gritting your teeth. It is an intellectual process in which, with any luck, you will find you can change your attitude by intellectual effort, not by will power. And philosophy is a great help, because it tells you what two thoughts you have got to attack if you want to get rid of an emotion. You either attack the thought that things are really bad for you or good for you, or, if you cannot attack that one, you can always attack the other one, or try to, that it is appropriate to react accordingly. Philosophy tells you which of the two thoughts to target. And there is something else very useful that philosophy does; philosophy or Stoic philosophy tells you that all these shocks—the hair standing on end, and trembling, and so on—these aren't the emotion and they do not matter. And that is important because of the William James effect. William James famously said, "We don't cry because we are sad. We are sad because we cry." There is some truth in that. So often people think, "Look I'm crying. I must have been maltreated." But of course that does not follow at all. You are crying, so you are crying. Right. But the important question is: Have you actually been maltreated? Are you in a bad situation? Or is this just an illusion due to false pride, or something else? That is the question. Your crying shows only that you are crying. We all suffer shocks; that is neither here nor there. So it is a cure to the William James effect that philosophy is offering, and the Stoics help you. They help you to attack these two propositions: all right, you think you are in a bad situation, well, here are some helps to see if you couldn't rethink that.

They like to borrow a story from an earlier philosopher. This philosopher was actually even before Aristotle, and even before Plato, and even before Socrates. He was a pre-Socratic philosopher. He was Democritus, and the story about him is that the king of Persia asked him to come over to Persia and advise him because his wife had died. "Please bring her back to life," he said to the greatest of the Greek philosophers. "Certainly, sir," said Democritus. "I have only one small favor to ask of you first. Would you please get three citizens in this great empire of yours to swear on her tomb that they have never suffered anything like you have?" The king of Persia could not find three citizens in his whole empire who were able to say that they had never suffered any such thing. In other words, it can be very helpful to realize you are not the only one. Sometimes the impression that things are really bad can be cured by realizing you are not the only one.

Here is another technique: relabeling. One Stoic says, "look, if you're caught in a traffic jam, think of it as a festival." Try that next time. Another contribution was made by the erotic poet Ovid, in the first centuries B.C. to A.D. He got into a great deal of trouble for the poems he wrote and was exiled. He wrote a takeoff of the philosophical technique of relabeling. He wrote one poem about how to seduce somebody—and by the way this was intersex, it was how men can seduce women, and women, men. And his advice was: relabel. If she has rather mousy hair, call it honey-colored. If she is a bit fat, call her rounded, and so on. And then he also wrote a poem about how to fall out of love, terribly useful advice actually, at any rate, for young people who have not yet made their final choice. How to fall out of love: just reverse the labels. Actually your beloved is beautifully rounded, but think of her as a bit fat. And she has got beautiful honey-colored hair, but think of it as mousy. This is the way to fall out of love, relabeling.

And here is another technique for attacking the thought that things are really good or things are really bad. Are you sure that things are bad, or are they merely unexpected? Not so long ago, somebody in England thought he had won the national lottery; then he found he had made a mistake and he had not, so he committed suicide. Why? He didn't win the national lottery the week before either, or the week before that, but he didn't commit suicide. What was wrong? Was this any worse than any other week? It really wasn't worse. The only new element was that it was unexpected. Always ask yourself: is it really bad or is it just unexpected? This is actually very helpful advice.

So here is a lot of good advice about how to attack the first thought, that things are really bad. But there is also advice on how to attack the second thought, that it is appropriate to react accordingly. Seneca in the first century A.D. writes to an imperial lady who has lost her son: "Yes, look, this is all very well, but you lost him three years ago, and you are neglecting your grandchildren." Seneca is not denying it is a bad thing, because she wouldn't take that in. He is saying it is not appropriate to spend your time with all this sinking feeling in you because it makes you neglect the grandchildren. Or, to an angry person it is said, "See how ugly it makes you look. Look in the mirror." The only problem with this advice is that a few people look very beautiful when they are angry. Or another thing to think about anger is, "ah, but look, I've done the same thing myself." So the Stoics don't leave you without help. They actually advise you how you can attack one or the other of the two thoughts, which occur in every emotion.

I had a little debate, which we put in print, with Bernard Williams, who thought that philosophy cannot do this sort of thing.[1] But I am

---

1. Richard Sorabji, "Is Stoic Philosophy Helpful as Psychotherapy?" and Bernard Williams, "Stoic Philosophy and the Emotions: Reply to Richard Sorabji," in *Aristotle*

arguing that the Stoics are absolutely right. Philosophy can help you with calming unwanted emotions, and I very much recommend these cognitive techniques. They are extremely useful and very cheap, and they are very fast. You don't pay anybody for this therapy. You don't waste any time. You can get on with your work, which is important. You just get into the habit of asking yourself: "Yes, but look, what is it that really matters?" I disagree with the Stoics because I think sometimes things happen that really do matter, and they think that is very, very rare. I believe that sometimes things really do matter, but very often, it will turn out, if you ask yourself questions, that it isn't what matters that has happened. It takes almost no time at all to keep asking yourself this question by way of habit, and this is Stoic therapy.

I have talked to modern cognitive therapists in England such as David Clark and to others in the USA, to try and see how this relates to modern cognitive therapy. It's not really a difference that sometimes modern cognitive therapists make use of behavior, not just of thought processes, because that is true of the ancients too. An example from modern cognitive therapy concerns a man who was convinced he was going to have a heart attack even though all the medical tests showed that his heart was absolutely fine. So the cognitive therapy eventually took the form, when they knew it was safe, of telling him that when he felt this fear coming on, he should start doing star jumps very energetically. And this piece of behavior, star jumping energetically, helped to convince him that there was nothing wrong with his heart. But that is not so different from the ancient cognitive therapists, the Stoics, recommending that you look in the mirror—that is a piece of behavior—to see how ugly anger makes you look. They have nothing against using behavior to help you to appreciate some cognitive point.

You might think that there is another big difference, and to some extent that is true, in that the Stoics want you to change your evaluative judgments: Something good has happened. Something bad

and After, ed. Richard Sorabji, Supplement 68 to Bulletin of the Institute of Classical Studies (1997): 197–213.

has happened. It is appropriate to react. All of those are value judgments. Whereas quite often the modern cognitive therapists are attacking factual misjudgments: I am fat; nobody is interested in what I say; I am going to have a heart attack. But this is not a clear distinction. After all, all those issues—like I am fat; no one is interested in what I say; I am going to have a heart attack—are being raised only because of their connection with evaluation: things are very bad for me. And also, the Stoics themselves sometimes deal with factual questions. Seneca wrote wonderful letters about everyday life. He really reaches out and talks to you about the problems in your life in these letters. Seneca says, "Look, we all get worried about our health, but why don't you just assume it is going to be all right?" He is dealing with a factual question there; he admits that that is not a very Stoic attitude on his part, but for beginners at the beginning of the letters, he can use non-Stoic techniques. Or again, he says to the imperial lady who has lost her son, "Your son's soul is probably living on." The Stoics did not believe in immortality, but they thought that certain very virtuous people might live on a little bit after death, so he says to her, "Your son's soul is still living on." So factual questions are tackled. Conversely, modern cognitive therapy does deal with evaluative questions. People say, "Well, I'm frightened about this, because if this happens, then that would happen." And the cognitive therapist, the modern one, may say, "But would it be insupportable if it did happen?" The "insupportable" question is an evaluative question. There isn't a sharp, clear distinction that the ancients are interested more in the evaluative and the moderns more in the factual. Actually, in the end, both parties are basically interested in the evaluative, because that is what causes the unwanted emotion.

The modern cognitive therapists make quite a lot of use of imagination. There was a person who thought he was going to have a heart attack; he kept imagining himself dead on the floor. So they got him to imagine himself sitting very comfortably in an armchair, just imagining himself dead on the floor. This exercise of the imagination was part of the cognitive cure. The ancients too appealed to imagination. After all, relabeling is a form of imagination, isn't it? Think of "her hair is mousy." Or saying, "Think of your health as okay. It's going to be okay," involves an exercise of imagination. It was not based on evidence at all.

I have been concealing one enormous difference in Stoicism, but it does not matter. I have been concealing that there is what is to me an unacceptable side of Stoicism. I feel that with the Stoics and with philosophy generally, you can often learn a tremendous amount from great philosophers, even while disbelieving part or even a large part of what they say. You read them because you can learn from some of what they say, and I feel that about the Stoics. The Stoics had a view I reject, that nothing matters except your character. They tried to train that into their own pupils who signed up wanting to become Stoics, but they did not try to impose it on other people. Rather, they said, "Our cognitive therapy will work whatever you believe, whatever ethical system you have. We can apply it to everybody and we are not going to insist on this point. In fact," they said, "it is much better in cognitive therapy not to insist on this point that only character matters, because, except for convinced Stoics, nobody else is going to believe it anyhow, so it will be ineffective therapy." So although there is this huge difference in Stoicism, it was not brought to play in their cognitive therapy. Of course, the therapy may help you to see that some particular thing you thought was terrible—the traffic jam, for example—really doesn't matter; it may help you with that. But they are not going to try to convince you of their general theory that nothing matters except character. And so this huge difference does not actually impinge on their cognitive therapy.

I will just mention some other exercises that they tell us they perform. Seneca says that when he went to bed—this tells you something about his domestic life—his wife turned the light out, and he stayed awake on purpose, interrogating himself about everything he had done that day and whether he could not have done it better, whether he was not a little bit too hasty and irascible with somebody who was not getting the point, and so on and so on and so on. You might think that that would prevent him sleeping, but actually he said it made him feel very tranquil and put him to sleep, and you can see that actually he is a little bit lenient with himself, because he says, "No, no, Seneca, you really should not have been quite so hasty. Remember next time not to be so hasty." He is not very cruel with himself, but he does go over his conduct in order to improve it for the future.

I was taught by my grandmother—I don't know whether she had read any Stoicism—that when you are handed a glass of water, at lunch or at dinner, you should never take it straight to your lips. Always put it down on the table first and let it rest, as if there was plenty of time. This is a little exercise that the Stoics tell you to help you remember to think: "It doesn't matter." A little bit of thirst doesn't matter. Another test: when your favorite dish is coming round a big table—the strawberries, is it? or the oysters, or whatever it may be—don't say to yourself, "My goodness, he's taking four. Will there be enough left for me?" No, wait, don't think anything until the plate has arrived. With all these little exercises you see how rich the Stoic's daily mental life is. He or she is doing all these little exercises all the time.

Another exercise they performed sometimes after walking into dinner. The dinner was probably, I am afraid, prepared by the slaves, although the Stoics were unusual in thinking that slavery was a wrong thing. They would sometimes go into dinner and then turn on their heels and say, "No, no dinner tonight," just to help themselves practice thinking, "It doesn't matter if I get dinner or not." And they always recommend something that you will find in Islam as well: whenever you want something, want it with the reservation: "God willing." That is a little bit of reservation.

I really got the feeling of Stoicism thanks to a great American, who has only very recently died. Admiral Stockdale was the vice presidential candidate three or four elections ago, and when I read that he had survived four years of torture in Vietnam and four years of solitary

confinement by practicing the precepts of one of the Stoics, I invited him to London to explain to us what Stoicism was like in practice,
and I think I learned more from that than from all the reading I have
done. What Stockdale found was this: he was the senior officer among
the U.S. forces who were in captivity in Vietnam. He was tortured like
many of the other captives, and under torture, he and the other captives all gave away more than their name and number. Military rules
in America as in England say that you should give away only your
name and number. They all gave away more. And the result of that
was they were so deeply ashamed that they had become completely
malleable, so deeply ashamed that they could not face each other, and
therefore the Vietnamese captors could get what they wanted, which
wasn't the information at all. What the Vietnamese captors wanted
was that the Americans should go on television to denounce the war
against Vietnam. Stockdale had something in common with the Stoic
whom he was following. He was following Epictetus, the great Stoic
writer who had been a slave and who had had his leg broken when
he was a slave. Stockdale had had his leg broken when he parachuted
out of his crashing plane and they fired at his parachute so that he fell
very heavily. Under torture they deliberately made use of the pain in
his leg. So he had something in common with Epictetus. But he had
more in common than that. He said to his men: "The Stoics tell us we
have got to distinguish between what is in our power and what is not
in our power. It is not in your power or mine to withhold information under torture. We all give away more than our name and number. That is not in your power, and so it does not matter. That is the
rule of the Stoic. The only things that matter are the things that are in
your power, and the only thing in your power is your character. Now
it is not in your power to avoid giving more things away, but there
is something that is in your power that you have overlooked. It is in
your power deliberately to disobey your captors on some small issues
and thereby to get tortured again. That is in your power." He persuaded some of the Americans deliberately to disobey the captors as he

himself did and to get tortured again, and of course again they gave away more than their name and number, but it did not matter. This information was irrelevant anyhow. What they recovered was their pride. Their shame was lost. Their pride was regained. Not one single one of those soldiers, sailors, and airmen, not one single one of them, agreed to go on television, because they had regained their pride. So the Vietnamese could no longer get, at least from them, the only thing they actually wanted.

I was very impressed by Stockdale's account, and so I turned to Mrs. Stockdale in the audience and I said to her, "Presumably Stoicism was no good to you, Mrs. Stockdale, a philosophy that tells you that it does not matter whether your husband returns alive or not." And at the time she agreed that Stoicism had been no use to her, but when I read their book, which they wrote jointly, called *In Love and War,* I realized that Mrs. Stockdale too in her own way had been following Stoicism.[2] Negotiations had not progressed with the Vietnamese about the status of these prisoners. These prisoners were not prisoners of war, because the government of Richard Nixon had refused to agree that there was a war, and had not declared war. And so under international law, the Vietnamese did not have to give these prisoners the normal rights. They could not write letters home, for example. Mrs. Stockdale never knew how her husband was faring or that he was even alive. Mrs. Stockdale wanted President Nixon to acknowledge that there was a war and there were prisoners. After four years, she took offices within a mile of the White House, and within a month she had, with the help of the wives of other prisoners, got Nixon to acknowledge that there were American prisoners and to start negotiations about their conditions. She must have had a very good idea of what is up to us. Many people would just assume, "Well, how can it be in my power to persuade the president of the United States?" But she did. She also did something that, to me, was shocking when I first

2. James Stockdale and Sybil Stockdale, *In Love and War: The Story of a Family's Ordeal and Sacrifice during the Vietnam Years* (Annapolis, Md.: Naval Institute Press, 1990).

read it, and then I realized it was utterly Stoic. She took advice from a psychiatrist as to whether she should assume her husband would come back or not. The psychiatrist said, "Assume he will not," and encouraged her to go on a singles' holiday. She had not the slightest desire to do this. In fact, it was against everything she wanted. They were an absolutely devoted couple. She wasn't looking for somebody else in any way whatsoever. She forced herself to go on a cruise intended for singles. I then realized that that was actually Stoic advice. The Stoics say: "Expect what is conventionally called bad fortune. Don't think of it as bad; that would be un-Stoic. Only bad character is really bad. But expect what is conventionally called bad fortune." The Stoics say that because, if you remember what I said about expectation, part of people's feeling that they have suffered something bad is so often due to their having expected better. So that was Stoic advice. And when Admiral Stockdale came back to the USA as a war hero and was offered anything he liked—headship of a military academy, a research grant for life—he found much in civilian life rather trivial. But I came to realize that Stoicism has advice for good fortune as well as bad. It is a philosophy not just for the prison camp; it is a philosophy for good times as well.

But because there are certain limitations to Stoic philosophy, I want to leave time to talk about other people too. I will just say, before I move to the limitations, that in the third century A.D. this philosophy was passed over to the Christians, who totally transformed it 180 degrees by turning it into advice, not about how to avoid emotional agitation, but advice about how to avoid temptation, and Christianity is impregnated with this altered Stoicism, with all the advice being transformed into advice about how to avoid temptation. Now there are limitations to the Stoic advice. One thing is they are only advising you about the ordinary ups and downs of life. They are not in competition with psychoanalysis. Psychoanalysis is dealing with something deeper than the ordinary ups and downs and life. Stoicism is not making any claims about that. It might say, "Go to the doctor or go to the magician if you want to ask me about something mysterious. There's nothing mysterious about what we are telling you. We are just giving you good sense." Incidentally, I think psychoanalysis would have been very unwelcome to the whole of the ancient world, because people would never say, "It is because of what my parents did that I am in such a mess." I think they would have thought that was an impious thing to say about your parents.

There is another thing that Stoicism cannot deal with: it cannot deal with bad moods, because it tells you how to deal with particular situations, whereas a mood is not addressed to a particular situation. A mood is seeing everything black. It is no good saying to somebody who is in a bad mood, and who starts telling you how awful the breakfast is, "Oh, well, lunch is going to be wonderful." No: if lunch is wonderful, there will be something else that is wrong. So this does not address bad moods. It is also not well-adapted to children, or not to young children anyhow, because it is very intellectual. So there are gaps in this therapy. It also does not at all address your emotional effect on other people. It is a very self-directed therapy about how to correct yourself, but it says nothing about what has been called, rather helpfully I think, emotional intelligence: your effect on your employers, your colleagues, your wife, your doctor, and so on. I think that for a layperson a book like *Emotional Intelligence* is extraordinarily helpful;[3] the Stoics don't contribute to that.

And actually one of the Stoics himself made a complaint about orthodox Stoicism. There was a Stoic about the time when philosophers were dispersing from Athens who taught on the island of Rhodes, a great philosopher, though his name isn't very generally known, Posidonius, who said: We Stoics have got it all wrong. We are too intellectual. If we are to understand the emotions, we have got to remember Plato telling us that there's not just a rational part of our soul; there are also emotional parts of the soul, one to do with domination, aggression, indignation, and so on and another to do with the appe-

---

3. Daniel Goleman, *Emotional Intelligence* (New York: Bantam Books, 1995).

tites, for food, drink, sex, money, and so on. Plato emphasized this in a book called the *Republic;* we are forgetting it at our peril. By all means, educate people to make correct judgments, educate their reason, but that on its own is not going to cure their emotions. You have got to educate the emotional parts of the soul, which Plato compared to horses. Plato said that reason was like the charioteer and the emotional parts of the soul were like horses. Well, Posidonius says, these horses make irrational movements and we have got to cope with them too, and Plato taught us how to do so. I will be coming to Plato in a little while.

For all these reasons, Stoicism does not help us calm our emotions in all cases, so I just want to look, but very much more briefly, at half a dozen other Greek schools or Greek individuals who had advice on therapy. The first one I will take is a person called Galen, the greatest doctor of all time up until the Renaissance. Galen lived a bit before 200 A.D., partly in Rome. He said that the qualities in our bodies are hot, cold, fluid, and dry, and the soul is just the ratio of hot, cold, wet, and dry in our bodies. That is what the soul is. Plato had talked about an immortal soul. Galen says that he does not know about that. He is not denying it, but that is not his province. The soul that he knows of is just the blend of hot, cold, fluid, and dry. He did write a treatise about how to cure or control emotions by thought in the Stoic style. He did believe in that, but first you have got to get your body right. First, he says, come to me as a doctor and I will tell you in what climate to live and what food to eat, because you have got to get the balance of hot, cold, fluid, and dry right in your body first or you'll get nowhere with your emotions. It has been found in England in Aylesbury prison that the prisoners became very much better behaved when they were given a better diet. The British Home Office does not want to know this because they are afraid it would increase the food budget, but of course, if it is true, it will greatly decrease the overall budget because it would reduce recidivism. A debate like the ancient one is going on nowadays: How should we treat emotions that have gone wrong? Should we treat them by cognitive therapy? Or should we treat them by physical means? More often people think of the physical means as drugs rather than diet.

At first, I could not think what to say about this debate. But I was very influenced by reading a particular book about the brain. The book, by Joseph Ledoux, is called *The Emotional Brain*.[4] What Ledoux found out, but only for frogs admittedly, and only for the emotion of fear admittedly, was that there are two pathways into the brain. One goes to the higher cortex and brings messages to the thought processes, but the other goes straight by a much shorter route, half the length, to a little part of the brain called the amygdala, literally "the almond," and that immediately creates the physical effects of emotion. And—this is the important point—it can create the physical effects of the emotion without your ever getting the thoughts at all. This happens when things have gone wrong in a certain way. For example, imagine somebody has been injured in a traffic accident. At the time of the accident, the horn was jammed on. He did not notice that at the time. There were so many other things to notice. Years later he hears a similar horn sound and suddenly he is all jangled in fear, but he has no idea what is wrong. He has no idea of any danger. He does not even know that the horn was jammed on at the time of the earlier accident. What has happened is that the amygdala has been triggered, but there are no danger signals to alert the higher cortex. Here you have got the physical agitation without the thoughts. The same happens in some cases of post-traumatic stress, which in the First World War was called shell shock. It was suffered by people who had undergone too much bombardment in the trenches, though they were very brave people. There is a wonderful movie about it based on a book called *Resurrection*. The story involves some of the finest war poets, who were hospitalized. They were just trembling. They could not physically function in the trenches. What would happen to

4. Joseph Ledoux, *The Emotional Brain: The Mysterious Underpinnings of Emotional Life* (New York: Simon and Schuster, 1998).

them was that a door would slam in the hospital and they would say to themselves, "Oh, it's all right; it's just a door slamming." But that had no effect whatsoever. The connections between the higher cortex and the amygdala had been so damaged by the bombardments that the amygdala would not quiet itself on the basis of messages from the higher cortex. These people dived under their beds; they were absolutely white and trembling; nothing would induce them to come out, even though they might be saying, "I know it's only a door slamming." These abnormal cases show you that in the normal cases there is communication between the amygdala, which controls the physical agitations of fear, and the higher cortex, which is involved in the thought functions. So understanding emotion cannot confine itself to one or the other—the thoughts or the physiology, the Stoics or Galen. In normal cases, both are involved. Calming the amygdala can help the thoughts; calming the thoughts can calm the amygdala. There seems to be a connection. So a full definition of emotion would not be quite so intellectual as the Stoics' or quite so physical as Galen's. It would combine the two. I mentioned Plato. Plato does deal with moods; Plato does deal with children. Plato says that emotional therapy must start for the child even in the womb. The mother must take stately walks to temples. She must not go prancing around, because the baby even in the womb must be accustomed to the right rhythms, because that affects the emotional parts of the soul. Of course, it does nothing to the reason; it does nothing to a baby's thoughts. But you have got to get the emotional parts of the soul rightly structured. These are the horses, while reason is the charioteer. Freud, by the way, when he talked of the rider and gave his three-fold division of the soul, had surely been influenced by his reading of Plato's *Republic* or other works. The Stoic who said we must remember Plato explains that we must follow Plato's advice not only about the baby in the womb—we should follow that—but also about the baby when it is born. It must be given the right music and the right gymnastic exercises and surrounded by the right furnishings, because all these things affect the emotional parts of the soul even though they say nothing to the reason, and do not involve any thoughts. Posidonius, the Stoic who said, "Let us go back to Plato," explains how, for the child who is dull-spirited, you will have high-pitched rhythms in the music you expose them to; for children who are over-spirited, you would have low-pitched rhythms, much gentler ones.

Let me move to Plato's great mentor, Socrates. Socrates, we are told, when he was afraid he might get angry, used to put a smile on his face and slow down his walk. That is the phenomenon that has been studied very much by Paul Eckman in modern times; it is the only case of it I have found in Greek philosophy. According to Ledoux, what is happening in such a case is that by altering the facial and walking behavior, you produce feedback on the amygdala so that the amygdala calms down a bit, and then the amygdala sends messages to the higher cortex and you start thinking, "Oh, it is not so bad; I have not been so maltreated," and so on. There is another little story about Socrates. It is about the practice of physiognomy. A physiognomist came up to Socrates and said, "Ah, yes I can see from your features that you are a womanizer." All Socrates's colleagues burst out laughing, because he was very ascetic, and preferred the company of young men anyhow. But Socrates said, "No, no, he is absolutely right. My nature was to be a womanizer. The only thing that stopped me being a womanizer was the power of philosophy." Philosophers like to tell this story, of course.

I have got just three more schools I am going to mention. Plutarch of Chaeronea was a philosopher of the first century A.D. and a Platonist. He said, Each of us has got to tell a narrative about his life or her life in order to be tranquil. Some people just let their lives go by and forget what has happened. They do not tell a story about themselves. They are like the picture of the man in hell, who has been set as punishment to weave a rope, and as he plaits the rope he throws it over his shoulder. What he does not notice is that, as he throws it over his shoulder, a donkey is eating up the rope behind him. That is what you are doing to your life if you just forget what has happened and do not tell the story of your life to yourself. No, you must deliberately weave a story of your life. You must think of your whole life. This is a very Greek and Roman view, that in morals and in psychology you must think about the whole of your life. And you must weave not only the good parts into the story, but the bad parts; a good picture needs black parts to create contrast. Do not wallow in the bad parts of your life, like beetles in the place called "death to beetles," which must have been some tarry puddle where beetles fell and wiggled their little legs and never got out. No, do not wallow, he says, in the bad parts of your life, but do not forget them either. Weave them into the tapestry; that is the route to tranquility. There is a Platonist giving you some fresh advice; nobody else, I think, says exactly that.

Now for the last two groups: the Epicureans were represented partly by Epicurus, who set up his school in Athens in 307 B.C., again just after Aristotle's death, but just before the Stoics. He is represented in beautiful Latin verse in the first century B.C. by the Latin poet Lucretius. He is a philosopher of the unconscious. He says that actually we are motivated by the fear of death. That is why we go around trying to get terribly rich, terribly famous, traveling hither and thither, because we think that if we are energetic enough and famous enough, somehow it will counteract death, although we do not articulate that stupid thought, because if we articulated it, it would be obvious how silly it was. What you need to learn from Epicurus is that death does not actually matter. The chief way in which it does not matter is that you need not fear punishment after death because, according to Epicurus, we are a bunch of atoms and we will be dispersed, and so will not be there to punish. But he also does, on one interpretation, probably a wrong interpretation, address one of the other fears about death, for people who do not like the thought of future nonexistence. This is an interpretation only. I do not happen even to agree with it, but there is an argument knocking around in Greek thought, and something a bit like it is in the Epicureans. The argument is this. Almost nobody feels horror at the thought of their past nonexistence before they were born. Well, what is the difference between the past nonexistence and future nonexistence? They are mirror images of each other. It surely is irrational if you feel horror—and not everybody does—at the idea of possible future nonexistence, if you do not feel horror at the idea of definite past nonexistence. There is some irrationality about it. That argument was put to Boswell by Hume, the philosopher, when Hume was dying, but it did not console Boswell.

I recommend looking at Nabokov's autobiography, *Speak, Memory,* because he is the only person I know who felt a certain sort of horror about his past nonexistence.[5] He saw a film of his parents waving out of the window just before he was born; they had already bought the baby carriage, but the baby carriage was empty because he had not yet been born, and his parents were waving happily, happily, although he did not yet exist. This absolutely horrified him, and the empty baby carriage looked like nothing so much as a coffin. Well, that is unusual. Most people do not feel horror at their past nonexistence, and so they are irrational if they feel horror at their future nonexistence. Pointing out the irrationality is a philosophical way of trying to calm you. I do not think it works, because I think the truth is that natural selection has programmed us to treat the future differently from the past. If there were any little babies born who did not treat the future differently from the past, I expect natural selection will have wiped those little babies out. Just consider the matter of taking precautions. Such babies would not take proper precautions. So natural selection has made it rather inevitable that Boswell was going to go on feeling horror at his future nonexistence, as a possibility. Nonetheless, I think this argument does something, because it prevents you thinking: "Ah, yes, how rational it is to fear my future nonexistence as a possibility." It is not rational; it is just programmed in by natural selection. It is not rational, and that it is not rational is shown by this argument, that you are irrational in not treating earlier nonexistence equally.

5. Vladimir Nabokov, *Speak, Memory: An Autobiography Revisited* (New York: Vintage, 1989).

The other thing that the Epicureans recommend is this: switch your attention from the bad. But the great statesman Cicero, at the end of the Roman Republic in the first century B.C., said he tried and it didn't work. He was kicked out of office because Julius Caesar won the civil war. From being the most admired statesman in Rome, he was out of a job. His daughter simultaneously died. He looked at all these philosophical schools to see what the best philosophical advice was. He could not stop crying, he says. And Epicurus's idea of switching your attention did not help him. The Stoics were more useful in saying, switch your beliefs.

The last school is Aristotle's school. Aristotle was the pupil of Plato. His most important contribution to therapy of the emotions was his idea that in society theater performs an indispensable role. Plato, who so much loved the theater, and so much loved poetry, was wrong to say that the ideal city would have no theater on the grounds that tragedy stirs up the emotions and makes us all into crybabies. No, said Aristotle, stirring up emotions such as grief and fear and pity in moderation actually reduces the emotions; it gives you catharsis of emotions. And I am agreeing with the controversial view that this means it reduces those emotions. There was a lot of discussion of whether that was true. Some people warned: do not try it on anger; do not stir up a little bit of anger in the theater and think that that will reduce the anger. It will not work on all the emotions, and Aristotle was careful to say it would not.

There is a nice question with which I will leave you. Aristotle tells us that comedy also gives you catharsis, or reduction of the emotions. By stirring emotion up moderately it reduces the emotion. What emotion would comedy reduce, I wonder? Readers may have their own suggestions. I believe Aristotle thought that comedy stirs up disdain for the characters who are mocked. Stirring it up moderately in the theater will then reduce disdain.

I have tried to give you a quick survey of all the schools. Stoicism was only one school, but I dwelt on it because I think it was the most helpful one for our purposes.

eight

⬎

Daniel N. Robinson

REASON AND PASSION . . . AGAIN

A persistent theme in philosophy, both ancient and modern, with authorities extending as far back as the Old Testament and Homer, finds human nature to be a house divided, emotions living on the lower floors and creating such havoc that the rationality living on the upper levels is often fitful and beside itself. Indeed, the ancient Greek ἔκστασις (ekstasis) is quite literally being "beside oneself." The very first word in *Iliad* is anger (Mῆνιν) and the entire epic charts the wages of passion's decisive victories over our better judgment. Plato's dialogues are somewhat mixed in their message here, for in them we discover that ἔρος (eros) is at once destructive and an aspect of the divine. Three of the dialogues, *Symposium, Republic,* and *Phaedrus* explore this in some detail, often in graphic terms.

Brief reflections on the *Phaedrus* will be useful. In it, we meet again the metaphor of the charioteer pulled by a pair of winged horses (246a6–7) as different as black and white—for they are black and white. The white one has the most honorable impulses, whereas the black horse is wild and inferior in all the noble elements. Only when reason brings the latter under control—which is to say when rationality rules animality—can a worthy destination be reached. Under the sway of the black horse's impulses, we are drawn to all varieties of excess: gluttony, wantonness, eroticism (238b).[1]

An informing term, used recently by Bennett and Hacker in their critical appraisal of contemporary neuroscience, is the *mereological fallacy*.[2] It is the fallacy committed when a complex process or function is divided into constituent parts and taken to be merely a sum of the individual processes and functions. In yet another form, it is the fallacy of assuming that a phenomenon can itself be reduced to such parts while surviving somehow as the phenomenon itself. To examine each note of a sonata separately is to know nothing of the sonata as sonata. With this in mind, we might well ask whether the partitioning of mental life into rational and emotional components can be achieved while preserving the very character of mental life itself. An inquiry of this sort properly begins with a definition or at least clarification of terms, itself no easy assignment.

If the alleged fundamental tension between what are called "reason" and "passion," or the "rational" and the "emotional," we must be sure that the entities in conflict are real and are of a nature that admits of conflict and tension. What is to count as an emotion? How many are there? Do they occur in isolation or generally in mixtures? Does it matter that they vary in intensity and frequency? Are they always "contextual"? Are they subject to evaluation for aptness or adequacy? Are they by nature *irrational?* And just what are *reasons?* Are reasons always rational? Are reasons devoid of affective elements or any

1. On eroticism, the Socrates of Plato's *Phaedrus* is different from the one featured in Xenophon's *Symposium*. An interesting reflection on this difference is provided by John Cooper, *Reason and Emotion* (Princeton, N.J.: Princeton University Press, 1999), 20–28.

2. M. R. Bennett and P. M. S. Hacker, *Philosophical Foundations of Neuroscience* (Oxford: Blackwell, 2003).

kind? Are reasons "disinterested," as it were, or "dispassionate"? How are good reasons distinguished from those that are not so good or are even "bad"? If justifications are said to be reasonable, is it by way of reasons that emotions are "justified"? Is it the case that an emotion stands as something of a "justification" for having a good or bad reason for acting?

A fair amount of serious psychological and philosophical speculation on the putative conflict between rationality and emotionality has proceeded without much attention paid to these questions. Where, for example, is the locus of the rational? It is trivially true that rationality is a feature or attribute inextricably bound up with the utterances, endeavors, and achievements of actual persons and, to that extent, is located wherever they are. Nonetheless, it is also the case that ascriptions of rationality are not reserved solely or even primarily to the self-reports of the persons thus uttering, endeavoring, and achieving. There are both logical canons and broad, pragmatic criteria routinely invoked to establish whether persons are "rational" in their activities. One who affirms the truth of two contradictory propositions is said to be irrational in the circumstance, "rational" here being synonymous with "logical." In matters of this sort, therefore, it would be more apt to say that the locus of "rationality" is not spatial but conceptual, and found wherever one finds entities capable of framing and comprehending propositions. The Law of Contradiction is not confined to one jurisdiction or another but applies universally across all assertions claiming truth-value. To ask, then, if the locus of Smith's rationality is wherever Smith's *body* happens to be would, on this account, be like asking whether the Law of Contradiction moves more quickly when Smith is cycling than when standing still.

Nonetheless, conceptual truths and logical canons do not begin to exhaust the domain of rationality, at least as the term connotes "reasonableness." Implicit in a rational course of action are judgments not readily subject to purely logical analysis. There is a wide gulf between the strictures of logic and the broad, open-textured realm of what is "reasonable" in a given case. The contrast is vivid and suggestive between the universal reach of propositional logic and that utterly contingent and contextual nature of the "reasonable" in actual practice. Where life is actually lived, only shifting probabilities reign, and the use of Bayes's Theorem takes more time than one typically has, even if one knows anything about it.

The history of the social sciences has not been indifferent to all of this. In a foundational essay published in 1738, Daniel Bernoulli left no doubt but that the *psychological* must be regarded as central among the factors to be considered in any quantitative, scientific approach to decision making.[3] It is in the actor's subjective estimations of gain, rather than the objective mathematical probabilities, that decisions are grounded. Persons averse to risk choose smaller gains with a higher likelihood over less probable but greater gains. However, whether one eschews risk or actually seeks it will depend on many factors, among them whether the cost of risk is significant in the life of the specific actor. One for whom a loss of $100 is negligible does not judge risk with that sense of urgency likely to beset the impoverished. Clearly, there is an "affective" dimension to this seemingly rational calculus, but also a rational moderating of the emotional investment in the various options. One begins to see that the problem here might not be one of teasing apart two distinct "processes," but coming to grips with the artificiality of the very concept of a "process."

So far, I've drawn attention to the somewhat strained version of what we take to be the "Reason" side of the alleged "Reasons-Passions Conflict." A few words are in order regarding the "passion" side. To begin, I note the difference in what is connoted by the related but different terms "emotion," "passion," and "mood." The first of these tends to be used as a class-term under which are subsumed particular feelings such as anger, love, grief, joy. Under the usual conditions, one is able to give some sort of reason for the felt emotion. "Passion" tends

3. Daniel Bernoulli, "Exposition of a New Theory on the Measurement of Risk," *Econometrica* 22 (1954): 23–36. (Original work published 1738.)

to be used to refer to a controlling state, less readily explained, even resisting the cognitive resources of the one whose passion it is. To have a "passionate" attachment to another, or to opera or to vintage cars, is to be drawn irresistibly and abidingly, whereas the namable emotions tend to come and go and will often surrender to little more than a deep breath or two. Moods, too, have this transient character and often overcome one who cannot explain either the source of the mood or its evanescence. The point that should be clear from this is that the realm of "feelings" as such is occupied by contents differing not merely in quality and intensity but in their intelligibility and their contextuality. One may be in a sad mood without apparent cause, but not so in a state of indignation or love.

It would seem to be a general feature of the named emotions that there are specific conditions so reliably associated with them as to count as their "causes," but in the sense of being the *reason* for the feeling. I would submit that a useful way of distinguishing between mere feelings—including non-contextual moods and otherwise blind passions—and authentic emotions is that the latter are inextricably bound up with cognitive, rational, interpretive activities. Thus understood, there is not a tension between reason and emotion, but a complementarity such that the actual rational dimensions of life invariably include feelings that qualify as "emotional," as distinct from moods and passions. If a single word might apply equally to the rational and the affective in such a way as to reveal the nature of the complementarity, I would offer *interest* as the term of choice. Let me illustrate this in the context of decision making, picking up the thread from where it was left by Bernoulli.

Over the past two centuries, what Bernoulli offered as a new theory has developed into a significant chapter in the history of the social sciences.[4] Considered broadly, research in this area has established not simply the so-called subjectivity of decision making, but also the

4. See, e.g., D. Kahnemann and A. Tversky, "Choices, Values and Frames," *American Psychologist* 39 (1984): 341–50.

highly *personalized* character of the subjectivity itself. Just how a decision is likely to affect the specific actor—how it figures in that specific life under those specific circumstances—is decisive in any attempt either to predict or to plausibly explain the decision to choose a given course of action. What matters centrally are not gains and losses neutrally or statistically considered, but *interests,* as these bear on actual persons. And where such significant interests are at stake, there inevitably will be found *emotions.* To take an interest, to take a great interest, is to invest a situation with what is personal, meaningful, and *felt.* To the extent, then, that the subject of so-called rational decision making must incorporate this personal equation, which itself includes the actor's appraisal of the situation and its bearing on significant personal interests, it is clear that what is called *rational decision-making* has already been shaped and colored by affective contents. Let me put this in axiomatic form:

(a) a decision is rational when it bears reasonably on the interests of the actor;

(b) the interests of the actor include those conditions, possibilities, and aspirations about which the actor has non-negligible feelings;

(c) the interests of the actor are actually and authentically the actor's own and known directly;

(d) actions performed by the actor that are clearly at variance with the protection or advancement of just those interests for which the actor has such feelings are, in the circumstance, non-rational, perhaps irrational.

In this more axiomatic form, one truism incorporates yet another: To the extent that a decision's rational standing depends on the coherent relationship between the felt interest and the decided course of action, the element of rational deliberation is an essential feature of the overall situation. The point is worth repeating and illustrating. To wit: It is not sufficient that there be reasonable conduct and also a realistically and keenly felt interest. Mary is keenly interested in getting to the bank, which is ten miles away, before it closes. To reach the bank in time requires driving up to the legally maximum speed. But school is letting out, there are children running hither and thither, and safety would call for a speed less than the lawful maximum. Nonetheless, Mary drives at the lawful maximum. Here we have a realistic interest, keenly felt, which, *ceteris paribus,* makes driving with dispatch reasonable. But it is *unreasonable* to be merely "lawful" in the circumstance. The combination of having a good reason and having a keenly felt interest is insufficient, for what is lacking are the moderating influences of still other reasons, reached through deliberation and with the aid of such signal interests as the desire not to harm.

The point, of course, is that, in actual life, not only is the emotional an integral feature of the rational, but the rational is omnipresent in all attempts to preserve and promote one's significant interests. Interests may be and often are in conflict. It is not inevitable that the greater will prevail in setting a course of action, nor is it invariably the case that one has full comprehension of one's interests. Indeed, if action were no more than a response to feelings, there would be little need for rational deliberation at all. Part of the whole point of such deliberation is weighing the merits of those feelings that incline one to act.

Further refinements of these terms and concepts are required, beginning with an attempt to clarify the very meaning of the word "emotion" as it has come to be used in psychology and philosophy. Use has been profligate, and it is necessary to impose some order. Just what is an "emotion," in what sense is it "felt," and how is it related to the one's "interests"? How has philosophy come to understand and approach these questions, and what guidance has been forthcoming from science?

Just what an emotion is remains arguable, but research and theory have combined to set down seven basic emotions found in a large number and variety of cultures. The authoritative work in this area is that of Paul Ekman.[5] His evolutionary theory of emotion is indebted to

5. Paul Ekman, *Emotions Revealed* (New York: Henry Holt, 2003).

Darwin's foundational work on the same subject.[6] Ekman's study of facial expressions and his detailed examination of the pattern of activation of the facial musculature have led him to identify as the seven basic emotions those of anger, sadness, fear, surprise, disgust, contempt, and happiness. The speed with which arousing conditions result in the characteristic expressions is often in the range of microseconds, indicating that an undeliberated and presumably non-cognitive adaptive mechanism is at work. Nonetheless, it is obvious that what excites anger or contempt or happiness will depend on factors having nothing to do with biological functions, even if the expression of these sentiments is stereotypical at the level of the facial muscles. Beyond this, there is the difference between such basic emotions and what are commonly called moods in that the latter are not readily or reliably associated with specific and causally effective conditions. Typically, one is angered by the utterances or actions of another, surprised by the appearance of an unexpected stimulus, saddened by the loss of a loved one, etc. But there are also broad, more or less atmospheric states of mind; a general sense of well-being or of impending trouble or of deep disappointment. Those reporting such states often cannot point to a specific cause or condition and surely would not maintain a fixed facial expression throughout the duration of the mood, which might be a fraction of a lifetime.

Jaak Panksepp's *The Foundations of Human and Animals Emotions,*[7] which appears in a Series in Affective Science, defends the evolutionary and neuroscience model of emotion rigorously but with a sensible respect for the complexity of the subject, not to mention the ethical implications arising from the very assumptions on which such research is based.[8] What the new "affective science" is able to add to

6. Charles Darwin, *The Expression of the Emotions in Man and Animals* (London: John Murray, 1872).

7. New York: Oxford University Press, 1998.

8. It is to Panksepp's credit that, having argued for human and animal emotions falling along a continuum—and thus giving credibility to the view that many species are surely endowed with feelings—he acknowledges the ethical burdens borne by those

the Darwinian account is a wealth of information drawn from neurochemical, physiological, and anatomical studies of the nervous system. Panksepp draws upon these studies and concludes that a rich and varied emotional life arises from the functions of the nervous system and serves the purposes of the individual organism and the species as a whole.

Throughout his book Panksepp has chapter titles and major sections in which the brain (somehow) creates joy, rage, loneliness, grief. In this, he writes in a contemporary genre that has been adopted even by the popular press. Most of what was once attributed to persons is now routinely attributed to brains, as if the attribution itself settled the most fundamental questions. It should be clear, however, that if sentiments and feelings and moods are features of conscious life that are unlike anything in the domain of physics, little is gained by moving the problem of explanation from the person to the person's brain. Similarly, so-called functionalist explanations, as old as ancient Greek philosophy and fully canonized by Darwin and his disciples in the nineteenth century, say nothing whatever about the phenomenology of emotional life. To learn (as if it were at all surprising) that fear and rage have survival value is not to account for the emotional feelings. It is instead to locate them within the larger framework of such self-preservative functions as digestion and respiration, neither of which requires consciousness. There is no obvious reason why a creature, confronted by a dangerous set of conditions, could not be designed to take flight without having any feelings whatever. Nor is it obvious that such activities as mating or gathering in numbers or sheltering a litter require an emotional component or are even more effective as a result of emotion.

Consider again Paul Ekman's influential research and theory. Extensive studies of different cultures turn up not only stereotypical facial and postural signs of emotions but words for these that appear to

who expose such animals to conditions of captivity, distress, pain, and isolation. At the end of the day, however, the mission of science seems to overtake such scruples.

translate readily from one culture to another. What counts as "happiness" in one culture is expressed pretty much as it is in another and is referred to by words and phrases more or less alike. It would not stretch credulity to assume that the same is the case with human cognitive resources and with the biological basis of motives and desires. Taking all this into account, there is an undeniable fact that sits uncomfortably amidst this sameness: the immense, qualitatively distinct, historically enduring differences among the world's identifiable cultures. Creatures possessing the same fundamental cognitive, motivational, and emotional "structures" nonetheless create and maintain widely differing systems of law, approaches to life, attitudes toward each other, religious and political allegiances, aesthetic preferences. Compared with any other species, human intra-specific variations are simply orders of magnitude greater than what is found in the larger animal economy. The variations are sometimes greater between neighboring tribes (with virtually identical environmental conditions and resources) than between geographically dispersed nations.

A finding of this sort, were it at the level of musculo-skeletal formations or metabolic physiology, would suggest nothing less than epidemic transformations in the basic physiological functions of entire human collectives. Evolutionary theory could survive such findings only by explaining them in terms of mutation and pathology. With a figurative shrug, we are inclined to say simply that there is "cultural diversity," as if the adjective somehow removed the difficulty. The difficulty, however, arises from the very power of culture qua culture to moderate, modify, and transform the manner in which affective and cognitive resources are deployed to such an extent as to render specious any theory casting biology as determinative. When Hamlet asks of Gertrude, "Oh shame! Where is thy blush?" the question is not about facial expression and coloration, but about what Hamlet takes to be his mother's moral blindness. Were she to attempt to explain her actions in the language of brain chemistry and evolutionary theory, the audience would assume that this was Shakespeare being ever so cleverly droll. If, on the other hand, she were to claim that, all in all, the cultural values then prevailing permitted and even encouraged a widowed queen to marry her brother-in-law, the murderer of her husband, and now the new king, all within a month's time, Hamlet would surely have condemned the custom and the queen who honored it. The point, of course, is that even the powerful forces of culture are themselves subject to enervation by one person's passionate grief or powers of moral discernment or even mere quirkiness.

Such considerations were at the center of ancient thought, particularly when Stoic philosophy examined the relationship between emotion and reason. Two excellent treatments of the subject have appeared recently, making clear that one who has the feelings that qualify as emotional must be satisfied that these are the right feelings for the prevailing conditions.[9] It is not uncommon for someone to complain of feelings that "don't seem right" or are "far too intense" or "persist beyond all reasonable bounds." Stoic commentators were not inclined to regard any feeling as an emotion unless accompanied by the requisite rational judgment of the object or event to which the feelings were responsive. The relationship between feeling and fact or feeling and judgment is, on this understanding, subject to appraisal. If Gertrude had said to Hamlet, "Your uncle, Claudius, killed your father and I condemn him for that. Therefore I am really deeply proud soon to be his wife," there would be a clear violation of the very logic of emotion: an object of contempt causally yielding pride through association. It wouldn't matter if, in the circumstance, the brain functioned normally, its happiness and contempt "centers" each displaying heightened activation. Indeed, whatever the neurophysiological facts might be, Gertrude's two sentences in the circumstance would be unintelligible to Hamlet and even to herself.

9. See pp. 464–77 in John Cooper, *Reason and Emotion* (Princeton, N.J.: Princeton University Press, 1999); and chapters 1 and 11 in Richard Sorabji, *Emotion and Peace of Mind: From Stoic Agitation to Christian Temptation* (Oxford: Oxford University Press, 2000).

Rehearsed here is not the trite fact that human emotions are complex, contextual, individuated, and so on. Rather, a sober question arises from these truisms as to just how much progress in the matter of human emotion can be gained by way of neurobiology and evolutionary theory. Progress takes different forms, of course. Further research will certainly add to the existing fund of correlations between rather stereotypic expressions of emotion and specific regions of the brain and chemical pathways within it. But progress toward ever more complete and convincing explanation is a different matter. It is as if one wished to explain the appearance between 1150 and 1300 A.D. of more than one hundred Gothic cathedrals in Europe and Great Britain, only to be told that evolutionary neurobiological processes are the grounding of an instinctual need for shelter. If this is the right sort of explanation, then it would be reasonable to place along the same continuum nests, heaps, mounds, holes, shells, leaves, townhouses, and Chartres. This is not convincing.

Philosophers reading this will recognize the position I'm advocating as cognitivist and may all too quickly think that it is vulnerable to versions of cognitivism advocated by the Stoics of old and by such of our contemporaries as Tony Kenny, Robert Solomon, Justin Oakley, and others.[10] For a state to qualify as emotional it must be accompanied by one or another "propositional attitude," such as a belief. For one to be angry with Sue one must believe that Sue has wronged one, and so on. To feel love for Hermione, one must desire to be in Hermione's company, believe her to be worthy, and the like. And, just in case desires and beliefs of this nature are required of emotions, the counterintuitive consequence that seems to follow is that non-human animals and pre-verbal children are devoid of emotion. Interesting though it

10. Anthony Kenny, *Action, Emotion and Will* (London: Routledge and Kegan Paul; New York: Humanities Press, 1963); Justin Oakley, *Morality and the Emotions* (London: Routledge and Kegan Paul, 1992); Robert Solomon, "The Philosophy of Emotions," in *Handbook of Emotions*, ed. Mark Lewis and Jeannette Haviland-Jones, 3–15 (New York: Guilford Press, 1999).

is, the debate between cognitivist and non-cognitivist is finally beside the point under consideration. The point under consideration pertains not to the fundamental character of "an emotion," which may be little more than a word, but to a sound psychological and scientific approach to actual life and its competent interpretation. The question, then, of whether an infant or a dog or cat should be an object of emotional ascriptions would be provisionally settled by examining the extent to which behavior suggests some sort of deliberation prompted by some recognizable or plausibly inferred interest. Having long enjoyed the company of dogs and cats—a benefit apparently not conferred on Descartes—I am quite comfortable with the judgment that they do make decisions and that at least some of their decisions are best understood as proceeding from expectations that qualify as beliefs. That, in addition to all this, they would somehow have to frame propositions in order to be joyful in seeing the stick in the air or the ball of wool rolling on the carpet seems to me something of a merely academic scruple designed to please journal editors.

Is my position finally "Aristotelian"? This can be misleading. Aristotle's treatment of the emotions ranges over many of his works and differs somewhat among them. What I share with Aristotle is his realism regarding the facts of nature, including human nature, and his commitment to understand complex phenomena in terms of the ends they realize or represent or suggest. He was not given to the mereological fallacy and would, I suspect, not be won over to accounts of emotion reduced to events in any organ, including the brain. It is safe to say that he would still insist that biological processes are not actual accounts of lived life, for they are not accounts of anyone's life at all. Put another way, every life is someone's, and so too is every feeling and every reason for acting. Accordingly it is mistaken to assume that the combination of evolutionary biology and neuroscience offers a preferred path to a richer understanding of emotion. To the extent that evolutionary biology and neuroscience provide no more than generalizations regarding the appearance and functioning of processes and systems more or less universally distributed within a gene pool, then to that extent they can offer no distinguishing explanation or account of a given person, a given life, a given emotion. The reason is obvious: persons find themselves in unanticipated circumstances, left with choices often fewer and less appealing than desired, uncertain as to the consequence of selecting one over another, and then surprised by the turn of events loosely determined by the choice itself. The circumstances themselves are only trivially physical; what counts is how they are perceived and understood, for it is in these judgments that one concludes that this or that interest hangs in the balance.

Does all this again rule out infants and furry or feathered beings? There are, to be sure, "feelings" without reasons for them, some so intense as to warrant therapy or medication for full-fledged human beings. Consider "free-floating anxiety" or the sense of impending doom or an overwhelming but seemingly unoccasioned depression. Are such conditions to be regarded as authentic emotions, and if so, do they not raise doubts about cognitivism itself? Let me repeat my resistance to this challenge: questions of this sort threaten to hold thought hostage to a word, but there can be little clarity of thought where there is ambiguity of expression. At issue is whether one or another feeling, emotional in tone and quality, is one for which a reasonable account can be given by the experient, for it is finally what our fellow human beings are moved by that creates our need for understanding and for proper responses. Where the feeling is strong and abiding, and where it is endured by one who has no explanation for it, it seems right to assume that it is caused, and caused as other sensations are, such as pain and tickle. Reduced to a maxim, the thesis advanced to cover the human cases is "No emotion without a reason." The direct implication is that the right sort of account of emotions is that first-person narrative: that slice of autobiography in which feelings are intelligibly tied to context, belief, judgment, and perception. With infants and non-verbal animals of every stripe, the account must be "first person" in only the figurative sense, and here we must be willing to don the simple and ill-fitting garb of the behaviorist. Thus sheltered from naked vanity, we will grant to the balance of the animal kingdom states and feelings by which the pursuit of interests becomes intelligible. If this seems to disconnect us from the rest of nature, not to worry: it is only a theory that is threatened by the gambit. If Jack is angered by what Jill finds merely silly, and if France takes umbrage with what Japan calls "champagne," surely it is possible for us to be thrilled by what bores a fish or causes the wren to find another branch. The uniformities of nature, such as they are, are to be found, not legislated. Meanwhile, it will be a great gain to psychology to begin to take ever more seriously the busy world of persons, striving to realize in fact what is desired in thought and urged upon them by their stronger sentiments. It will be a great gain when this more realistic inquiry begins with reasonable assumptions about just what goes into a good reason for action, and just what goes into a truly warranted set of beliefs, desires, and sentiments. Unless the discipline of psychology is prepared to take a stand on the sorts of life—personal, social, and civic—likely to preserve and refine both the rational and the emotional, the study of each and either is likely to be merely actuarial and arid.

CONTRIBUTORS

Benedict M. Ashley, O.P., has doctorates in philosophy (University of Chicago) and political science (University of Notre Dame), and the post-doctoral decree of master of sacred theology conferred by the Order of Preachers. He is emeritus professor of moral theology at Aquinas Institute of Theology, St. Louis, and senior fellow of the National Catholic Bioethics Center. Among other honors, he has been awarded the medal *Pro Ecclesia et Pontifice,* conferred by John Paul II. Among his publications are (with Kevin O'Rourke, O.P.) the widely used textbook *Health Care Ethics,* 5th ed. (Georgetown University Press, 2007), *Living the Truth in Love* (Alba House, 1996), *Theologies of the Body: Humanist and Christian,* 2nd ed. (National Catholic Bioethics Center, 1997), *Choosing a World-View and Value-System* (Alba House, 2000), *The Ashley Reader* (Sapientia Press of Ave Maria University, 2006), and *The Way toward Wisdom: An Interdisciplinary and Intercultural Introduction to Metaphysics* (University of Notre Dame Press, 2006), as well as many articles on medical ethics.

Ceslas Bernard Bourdin, O.P., is professor at the Université Paul Verlaine (Metz) and lecturer at the Institut Catholique (Paris). He has numerous articles and books, which include *La genese theologico-politique de l'Etat moderne* (Presses Universitaires de France, 2004), *La Vraie loi des libres monarchies de Jacques VI d'Écosse* (Presses Universitaires de Montpellier, 2008), and *La Médiation chrétienne en question: Les jeux de Léviathan* (Cerf, 2009 in press). He is co-editor (and author of the introduction) of Erik Peterson, *Le monothéisme: un problème politique et autres traités* (Bayard, 2007).

Kevin L. Flannery, S.J., is professor of the history of ancient philosophy at the Pontifical Gregorian University in Rome. He was dean of the Faculty of Philosophy (1999–2005). In 2002 John Paul II appointed him a consultor of the Congregation for the Doctrine of the Faith; in 2005, he was named ordinary professor of the Pontifical Academy of St. Thomas Aquinas. His publications include *Ways into the Logic of Alexander of Aphrodisias* (Brill, 1995) and *Acts Amid Precepts: The Aristotelian Logical Structure of Thomas Aquinas's Moral Theory* (The Catholic University of America Press, 2001), and *Aristotle's Philosophical Psychology of Action* (The Catholic University of America Press, forthcoming), and articles on ancient philosophy, Thomas Aquinas, and various ethical themes.

John Aidan Nichols, O.P., recently served as the John Paul II Memorial Visiting Lecturer in Roman Catholic Theology at the University of Oxford, 2006–2008. He has authored some thirty books dealing with different aspects of historical and dogmatic theology, as well as the relation of faith and culture. Of special note are *Scattering the Seed: A Guide through Balthasar's Early Writings on Philosophy and the Arts* (Continuum, 2006), and *Divine Fruitfulness: Balthasar's Theology beyond the Trilogy* (Continuum, 2007). His other works include *The Thought of Benedict XVI: An Introduction to the Theology of Joseph Ratzinger* (Continuum, 2007), *The Panther and the Hind: A Theological History of Anglicanism* (Continuum, 1993), and *Christendom Awake: On Re-energizing the Church in Culture* (Eerdmans, 1999).

Daniel N. Robinson is a member of the philosophy faculty at Oxford University and Distinguished Professor, Emeritus, at Georgetown University, and serves as visiting professor at the Institute for the Psychological Sciences. He served as president of two divisions of the American Psychological Association, the divisions of the history of psychology and of theoretical and philosophical psychology. He holds awards for Lifetime Achievement and Distinguished Contributions from the American Psychological Association. His sixteen books, more than thirty edited and published volumes, and numerous articles and lectures, have addressed topics in the philosophy of sciences, intellectual history, philosophy of law, ethics, and the basic sciences. His most recent books are *Praise and Blame: Moral Realism and its Applications* (Princeton University Press, 2002) and *Consciousness and Mental Life* (Columbia University Press, 2008).

Roger Scruton is research professor at the Institute for the Psychological Sciences and member of the philosophy faculty at Oxford University. In 2008, he was named fellow of the British Academy. He is an academic philosopher, writer, editor, and publisher who has served as professor of aesthetics at Birbeck College, London, and as professor of philosophy and University Professor at Boston University. Besides philosophical publications, he writes fiction and political and cultural commentary. His most recent books are *Culture Counts: Faith and Feeling in a World Besieged* (Encounter Books, 2007), *Gentle Regrets—Thoughts from a Life* (Continuum, 2005), *Death Devoted Heart: Sex and the Sacred in Wagner's Tristan and Isolde* (Oxford University Press, 2004), and *The West and the Rest* (ISI Books, 2003).

Richard Sorabji, CBE, FBA, is fellow of Wolfson College, Oxford, and emeritus professor of philosophy, King's College, London. In 2007, he became Cyprus Global Distinguished Professor at New York University. He has received many honors and titles, including Fellow of the British Academy, Hon. Foreign Member of the American Academy of Arts and Sciences, and Foreign Member of the Royal Flemish Academy of Belgium for Sciences and the Arts. His numerous books include *Aristotle on Memory* (Duckworth and Brown University Press, 1972), *Necessity, Cause, and Blame* (Duckworth and Cornell University Press, 1980), *Time, Creation, and the Continuum* (Duckworth and Cornell University Press, 1983), *Matter, Space and Motion* (Duckworth and Cornell University Press, 1988), *Animal Minds and Human Morals: The Origins of the Western Debate* (Duckworth and Cornell University Press, 1993), *Emotion and Peace of Mind: From Stoic Agitation to Christian Temptation* (Oxford University Press, 2000), and most recently, *Self: Ancient and Modern Insights about Individuality, Life, and Death* (University of Chicago Press, 2006). Moreover, he has ninety edited volumes to his credit, including *Ethics of War: Shared Problems in Different Traditions* (Ashgate Publishing, 2005), and eighty volumes of translation from the period of transition between ancient and medieval philosophy.

Craig Steven Titus is research professor at the Institute for the Psychological Sciences. He has written *Resilience and the Virtue of Fortitude: Aquinas in Dialogue with the Psychological Sciences* (The Catholic University of America Press, 2006); has edited *The Person and the Polis: Faith and Values within the Secular State* (2006), *On Wings of Faith and Reason*

(2008), *Christianity and the West* (2009), and *The Psychology of Character and Virtue* (2009), all for the Institute for the Psychological Sciences Press; and coedited *The Pinckaers Reader: Renewing Thomistic Moral Theology* (The Catholic University of America Press, 2005), *Sujet moral et communauté* (Academic Press Fribourg, 2007), and *Renouveler toutes choses en Christ: vers un renouveau thomiste de la théologie morale* (Academic Press Fribourg, forthcoming).

INDEX OF SUBJECTS

INDEX OF NAMES

The John Henry Cardinal Newman Lectures
EDITED BY CRAIG STEVEN TITUS

1. *The Person and the Polis: Faith and Values within the Secular State* (2007)

2. *On Wings of Faith and Reason: The Christian Difference in Culture and Science* (2008)

3. *Christianity and the West: Interaction and Impact in Art and Culture* (2009)

4. *The Psychology of Character and Virtue* (2009)

Monograph Series

Fergus Kerr, *"Work on Oneself": Wittgenstein's Philosophical Psychology* (2008)

Kenneth L. Schmitz, *Person and Psyche* (2009)

Philosophical Psychology: Psychology, Emotions, and Freedom was designed and typeset in Minion by Kachergis Book Design of Pittsboro, North Carolina. It was printed on 55-pound Colonial White and bound by Lightning Source of La Vergne, Tennessee.

Breinigsville, PA USA
04 October 2009
225218BV00002B/2/P